POPE BENEDICT XVI

POPE BENEDICT XVI

The Significance of His Theological Vision

THOMAS P. RAUSCH, SJ

Paulist Press
New York / Mahwah, NJ

Cover photo Pope Benedict XVI during a general audience at the Vatican, January 16, 2013. Courtesy of the U.S. Department of Defense.
Cover design by Sharyn Banks
Book design by Lynn Else

Library of Congress Cataloging-in-Publication Data
Names: Rausch, Thomas P., author.
Title: Pope Benedict XVI : The Significance of His Theological Vision / Thomas P. Rausch, SJ.
Description: New York/Mahwah : Paulist Press, 2022. | Includes index. | Summary: "This important book is a respectful yet critical examination of the thought of Pope Benedict XVI"—Provided by publisher.
Identifiers: LCCN 2022005811 (print) | LCCN 2022005812 (ebook) | ISBN 9780809156313 (paperback) | ISBN 9780809187607 (ebook)
Subjects: LCSH: Benedict XVI, Pope, 1927– | Catholic Church—Doctrines.
Classification: LCC BX1378.6 .R39 2022 (print) | LCC BX1378.6 (ebook) | DDC 282.092 [B]—bendc23/eng/20220603
LC record available at https://lccn.loc.gov/2022005811
LC ebook record available at https://lccn.loc.gov/2022005812

ISBN 978-0-8091-5631-3 (paperback)
ISBN 978-0-8091-8760-7 (e-book)

Published by Paulist Press
997 Macarthur Boulevard
Mahwah, New Jersey 07430
www.paulistpress.com

Printed and bound in the United States of America

For Herbert J. Ryan, SJ
Mentor and Friend

CONTENTS

CONTENTS

Contents

ABBREVIATIONS

Documents of Vatican II

AG   *Ad Gentes:* Decree on the Church's Missionary Activity

DH   *Dignitatis Humanae:* Declaration on Religious Freedom

DV   *Dei Verbum:* Dogmatic Constitution on Divine Revelation

GS   *Gaudium et Spes:* Pastoral Constitution on the Church in the Modern World

LG   *Lumen Gentium:* Dogmatic Constitution on the Church

NA   *Nostra Aetate:* Declaration on the Relationship of the Church to Non-Christian Religions

SC   *Sacrosanctum Concilium:* Constitution on the Sacred Liturgy

UR   *Unitatis Redintegratio:* Decree on Ecumenism

Other

CA   Augsburg Confession

CDF   Congregation of the Doctrine of the Faith

DI   *Dominus Iesus*

DS   H. Denzinger, A. Schönmetzer. *Enchiridion Symbolorum, definitionum et declarationum de rebus fidei et morum.* 33rd ed. Freiburg: Herder, 1965.

ITC   International Theological Commission

PG   *Patrologia Cursus Completus: Series Graeca.* Edited by J.-P. Migne. 162 vols. Paris, 1857–86.

PL   *Patrologia Cursus Completus: Series Latina.* Edited by J.-P. Migne. 217 vols. Paris, 1844–64.

WCC   World Council of Churches

ACKNOWLEDGMENTS

As a scholar, Joseph Ratzinger, now Pope Benedict XVI, has been amazingly prolific. One of his latest bibliographies lists 99 books and 409 articles and reference works, and it runs only to 2004.[1] But not all lists agree. Wikipedia lists sixty-six. But Benedict has no magnum opus, no comprehensive development of his thought. D. Vincent Twomey, one of his former students, says that he "is acutely conscious of the fragmentary nature of all he has written, but he makes a virtue out of this weakness, which is caused by the simple fact that he was called to sacrifice his preferred life as an academic to serve the Church, first as Archbishop of Munich, then as prefect for the CDF, and then, of course, as Pope Benedict XVI."[2] I have listed in the bibliography the works used for this present volume. In referring to Pope Benedict, I will follow the convention of using his given name, Joseph Ratzinger, when talking about his life or works written before he became pope and using the name he chose after his election when referring to him after his election to the papacy.

For the chapter "From Professor to Pope" in the present volume, I want to acknowledge my indebtedness to John Allen's biography, *Cardinal Ratzinger: The Vatican's Enforcer of the Faith*, for the basic story of the pope's life. As a journalist who covers the Vatican, Allen has followed Benedict's career for years. The book was reissued in 2005 under the title *Pope Benedict XVI*.[3] A third book, *The Rise of Benedict XVI*, speaks much more positively of Benedict. In Allen's revised judgment, Benedict is not a transitional pope but a humble man who, as an original thinker, is uniquely qualified for his office.[4] I have also found Aidan Nichols's fine introduction, *The Thought of Pope Benedict XVI*, helpful.

I have long been interested in Ratzinger's thought but began a more serious study of his work after he was elected pope. I am grateful to a number of people who made this work possible. Diane

Winston, Knight Chair in Media and Religion at the University of Southern California (USC), invited me to take part in a symposium on Pope Benedict at USC. Robert Hurteau at Loyola Marymount University (LMU) encouraged me to develop a course on Benedict for LMU. Seattle University invited me to teach in the William F. LeRoux Chair, giving me the time to do much of the writing, and the Jesuits there welcomed me into their community. Michael Downey and Christopher Ruddy reviewed the original manuscript and made helpful suggestions. Richard Garcia, our graduate assistant, contributed greatly with his careful proofreading. The responsibility for the interpretation rests with me alone.

The first edition of this book, published in 2009, was written during the early years of Benedict's pontificate. This revised edition has been updated to reflect its final years and his surprising resignation. I am grateful to Mark-David Janus, CSP, for suggesting a revised edition and to Paul McMahon for his encouragement and always careful editorial work.

INTRODUCTION

With the election of Cardinal Joseph Ratzinger as Bishop of Rome on April 19, 2005, the Catholic Church for the first time in centuries had a professional theologian as pope. Educated at Munich's Ludwig-Maximilian Universität, Ratzinger completed his doctorate in 1953. He first came to prominence as the theological *peritus*, or expert, for Cardinal Josef Frings of Cologne at the Second Vatican Council. I remember reading Ratzinger when I was beginning my own theological studies in 1969. I was particularly impressed by a little monograph he coauthored with Karl Rahner entitled *The Episcopate and the Primacy*.[1] While Ratzinger was more conservative than many German theologians of his day, he was always worth reading, with his deep roots in the Catholic tradition.

Since those days, of course, Ratzinger had emerged as a world-class figure, both as a theologian and as a churchman. His almost twenty-four years as prefect of the Sacred Congregation for the Doctrine of the Faith (CDF), the Vatican congregation charged with defending Catholic doctrine, did much to keep him in the public eye. It was not that he had sought this office; his real love was scholarship. Three times he had asked to be relieved of his responsibilities; three times Pope John Paul asked him to stay on. Few, however, suspected that he would succeed the pope he had served so well.

Pope John Paul II

Pope John Paul II dominated his age as few others have done. The third longest-reigning pope in history and the first Slav on the Throne of Peter, he presided over the Roman Catholic Church for almost twenty-seven years. He will long be remembered for his remarkable ministry.

Among his many accomplishments, Pope John Paul had been particularly creative in showing the papacy's potential for religious leadership on a global level. History will credit him with having played a major role in the collapse of the Communist system across Europe, even using the term *solidarity* as a theological concept in his first social encyclical, *Laborem Exercens* (1981), to show his support for Lech Walesa's Solidarity union. In a dramatic move, he called for a celebration of the new millennium with a great Jubilee Year, inviting the church to an examination of conscience and a "purification of memory." Repeatedly he requested forgiveness for the sins of the church's members, sins often done in the church's name in its efforts to defend the truth, sins against Christian unity and against the Jewish people. He asked for forgiveness for violations of the rights of immigrants and ethnic groups, including the use of forms of evangelization that did not respect other cultures and the conscience of individuals, forgiveness for sins against the dignity of women and sins against the poor and defenseless, including the unborn.[2] His example was followed by other religious leaders. On January 23, 2002, in response to the terrorist attacks of September 11, 2001, he hosted a meeting of hundreds of leaders of the world's religions at Assisi for prayer and a renunciation of violence in the name of God; this was not the first time that he had called such leaders together for common witness.

The picture of him sitting quietly in conversation with his unsuccessful assassin, Mehmet Ali Agca, has become an icon of forgiveness. He did much to bring about a new understanding between Catholics and Jews, and Muslims prayed for him in his final illness. Young people in particular resonated with this pope; they appreciated his humanity and his uncompromising vision, even if they did not always follow his teachings. His intense, single-minded commitment to his ministry taught many the meaning of being a disciple of Jesus, in his living as much as in his dying.

Among John Paul's personal disappointments could be mentioned his inability, despite his best efforts, to bring about reconciliation with the Orthodox churches, especially the Russians, who tend to identify being Russian with being Orthodox. Also disappointing to him was the alienation or loss of faith of so many in Western Europe as well as the rising materialism in Eastern Europe, the failure of the new European Constitution to mention Europe's religious heritage, and his inability to prevent the 2003 war against Iraq, despite his insistent preaching of peace.

His legacy for the internal life of his own church is less impressive. Many feel that the promise of the Second Vatican Council was compromised, if not diminished, under his tenure. He recentralized power and decision-making in Rome, in many ways failing to honor the collegial understanding of episcopal authority so central to the council. In the last few years, an increasing number of bishops and even cardinals spoke out against the way that authority was being exercised by Rome, something almost unprecedented in the history of the church.[3]

Even many who greatly admired John Paul were unhappy with his neglect of church governance. Feeling confined by Rome, he was happiest on the road, when the actor in him had the stage to himself. He left the day-to-day business of the church's government in the hands of the Roman Curia, the church's bureaucracy. He was also not the best judge of people; Catholics across the ideological spectrum would agree that one of the greatest failings of his papacy was the mediocre quality of many of his episcopal appointments.

His successor would be challenged by many problems that remained in the church's internal life, among them, revitalizing the practice of the faith in Europe; countering the idea that the views of ordinary Catholics counted for little; addressing the lack of truly collegial government; providing for greater accountability of church leaders, a need made obvious by the sexual abuse of young people by members of the clergy; addressing the shortage of priests and the concerns of women; renewing the church's teaching in the area of sexuality; and reconciling to the church the many who have been alienated—academics, gays, and women among them.

Then on April 2, 2005, after a long and debilitating illness borne with remarkable courage, this once strong and vital man passed quietly to the Lord while much of the world watched and prayed.

The Succession

As the cardinals gathered in Rome, there was considerable speculation about who would be the next pope but little agreement about who the leading candidates were. The conclave began on April 18. I was in Germany at the time, teaching in our study abroad program. A little after six o'clock in the evening of the second day, I turned on the TV in my apartment for some news. Smoke was issuing from the stovepipe over the Sistine Chapel, and a vigorous debate was going on about whether it was black, the sign of an inconclusive ballot, or white, meaning that someone had been elected. At 6:04 the bells of the basilica began pealing, indicating that it was white. So soon?

I sat glued to my chair, until about 6:40, when Cardinal Jorge Medina Estevez stepped to the balcony, greeted the crowd with great drama in several languages, and after the traditional Latin formulas, pronounced the name, "*Iosephum….*" My heart sank, and then I heard Medina slowly finish his sentence with "*Sanctae Romanae Ecclesiae Cardinalem Ratzinger.*" Cardinal Joseph Ratzinger of the holy Roman Catholic Church.

While Ratzinger's name was always listed among the *papabile*, few thought him electable, given the controversy generated by his twenty-four years as prefect of the Vatican's Congregation for the Doctrine of the Faith. Both Jesuit Father Tom Reese, editor of *America* magazine, and John Allen, Vatican correspondent for the *National Catholic Reporter*, two of the most astute Vaticanologists, had said he wouldn't be elected. He was too controversial, too identified with Pope John Paul.[4] But they were wrong. After just four ballots, Cardinal Joseph Ratzinger had been elected to the Chair of Peter.

When he stepped to the balcony a few moments later, now as Benedict XVI, dressed for the first time in the white cassock of the pope, he looked nervous, hands clenched above his head, his smile rather strained. Perhaps he sensed that many would not welcome his election. As David Gibson wrote in his 2006 biography, *The Rule of Benedict*:

> As head of the Congregation for the Doctrine of the Faith, the former Holy Office of the Inquisition, Ratzinger held the second-most powerful job in the Vatican and was responsible for maintaining discipline and excluding dissent. By nature and job description, he was the "bad cop" to John Paul's "good cop." He had silenced theologians, censured books, and offended women, homosexuals, and

4

other Christian churches with his unvarnished description of what he saw as their inherent shortcomings. As a reward for all his hard work, Ratzinger was labeled everything from God's Rottweiler to Cardinal No to *Der Panzerkardinal* and, of course, the Grand Inquisitor.[5]

In their initial statements, the North American cardinals seemed quite aware of their peoples' discomfort and tried to address it. New York's Cardinal Edward Egan said the next day at a news conference, "He's a very loving, lovely person, very unassuming, and shortly you will see this. You need to be slow in making judgments. Sometimes it's good to watch for a while and see if what you've heard is true." Toronto's then Cardinal Aloysius Ambrozic suggested that because of his job people were not able to see other dimensions of his personality: "There's a real difference between the image and the reality." Cardinal Roger Mahony of Los Angeles added, "His job was preserving the doctrine of the church against dilution or errors. That was his job; that is what Pope John Paul II asked him to do, but that is not his job now. I think you will see emerge his far more spiritual and pastoral sides. I have seen him in those roles, and I think people will be very, very surprised in a good sense."[6]

At a general audience a few days later, Pope Benedict explained the name he had chosen, recalling both his predecessor Pope Benedict XV, who had worked so hard for peace during the First World War, and Benedict of Nursia, the great founder of the Benedictine Order, who he said represented "a fundamental reference point for European unity and a powerful reminder of the indispensable Christian roots of its culture and civilization."[7]

Joseph Ratzinger

Who is this man, Joseph Ratzinger, newly elected Pope Benedict XVI? I have probably voiced complaints about Cardinal Ratzinger in his position as prefect of the Congregation for the Doctrine of the Faith as often as any of my theological colleagues. Still I must admit that I feel a certain kinship with him. When I read about his reaction to the wave of student protest that swept across Tübingen in 1968 and 1969, with its heavy overtones of Marxist ideology, I remember my own experience in those years as a young Jesuit scholastic preparing to go on to theology and the priesthood. Despite the difference in our ages, in a certain sense we are contemporaries.

Both years were terrible to live through, marked by civil disobedience, ideological turmoil, and cultural change with occasional outbursts of rage and violence. It seemed as though the thin veneer of civility that kept baser emotions in check was being peeled away. The Flower Power Revolution of the mid-sixties had morphed into an increasingly violent drug culture. The United States was in the middle of an exhausting war in Vietnam, and the country was rife with protest. The students I taught, many of them facing the draft, were angry at authority—whether governmental, parental, academic, or ecclesiastical. The nonviolence of Martin Luther King Jr.'s civil rights movement and the various peace movements had been overshadowed by the Black Panthers and the Students for a Democratic Society (SDS). The year 1968 saw the assassination of Dr. King in April and Robert Kennedy in June; it was the summer of Alexander Dubček's Prague Spring, the riots at the Democratic National Convention in Chicago in August, and the Tlatelolco Massacre of hundreds of students, possibly many more, in Mexico City in October. In Europe, hundreds of thousands affiliated with the so-called New Left, led by Marxist intellectuals and dissenting Communist groups, staged massive protests in London, Paris, Berlin, and Rome.

Joseph Ratzinger had moved from a professorship at Münster to Tübingen in 1966. But Tübingen was soon caught up in the student uprising that swept like a flood tide across Europe. With Ernst Bloch, a Marxist philosopher teaching there, the reigning paradigm based on Bultmann's theology and Heidegger's philosophy gave way to new ones based on Marxist thought. According to Ratzinger, Bloch dismissed Heidegger for being "petit bourgeois."[8] Two other Tübingen faculty members contributed to its increasingly engaged and, in his view, politicized theology. Jürgen Moltmann's "theology of hope" was influenced by Bloch's Marxist analysis, and the famous Ernst Käsemann, Tübingen's professor of New Testament exegesis, argued that theology had been used to support oppressive systems and that the church itself was often complicit in the exploitation of the poor.

Ratzinger was horrified by this atmosphere. He felt that the integrity of both the academy and the faith was at stake. In one of his clearest statements, he writes, "The destruction of theology that was now occurring (through its politicization as conceived by Marxist messianism) was incomparably more radical precisely because it took biblical hope as its basis but inverted it by keeping the religious ardor but eliminating God and replacing him with the political activity of man." Even the cross was dismissed as a sign of sadomasochism.[9]

In 1968 I was teaching philosophy in Los Angeles, preparing to move on to the priesthood, and while the Marxist thought that so troubled Ratzinger in Tübingen was not much in evidence in the United States, much of what I was reading in popular Catholic sources, reflective of the postconciliar ferment in theology, suggested that the institutional church would wither away like the capitalist state in a new, more personalist future. I remember reading in a liberal Catholic paper that a poor mother who breaks bread for her children at home does the same thing sacramentally that a priest does in celebrating the Eucharist in church. Others were suggesting that there was no need for an institutional priesthood in the coming church, that the rule of celibacy would soon be changed, or that the vow of chastity meant not continence but simply celibacy, the giving up of marriage. It was the time of the "Great Exodus," with thousands leaving the priesthood or their communities, including several bishops. Two young Jesuits ordained in my province in 1969 left within six months of their ordination; one of them celebrated Mass only twice.

Granted I was young and impressionable in those years, but I was also facing a decision about continuing on in a church that to many seemed to be coming apart before our eyes. I moved to the Graduate Theological Union (GTU) in 1969, literally helping transport our theologate from the redwoods and vineyards of the Santa Cruz Mountains to the tear gas–filled streets of Berkeley. It was a theological community in turmoil. Many of the seminarians in the nine divinity schools constituting the GTU were there to gain a 4-D exemption from the draft, more activist than academic or pastoral in their interests. When President Richard Nixon sent U.S. troops into Cambodia in 1970, the whole GTU went on strike. Many of the students wanted to shut the institution down until the war was over. Although I had planned to do further studies in philosophy, I decided at that time that the questions I had were really drawing me toward graduate work in theology.

I first came across the name of Joseph Ratzinger during those troubled days in Berkeley. We read, among others, Karl Rahner, Edward Schillebeeckx, Harvey Cox, Hans Küng, Rudolph Bultmann, John A. T. Robinson, Charles Davis, and Joseph Ratzinger. I learned that Ratzinger, who had been a *peritus*, or expert, at Vatican II, was known as centrist, somewhat conservative, but a brilliant scholar in the areas of Catholic dogma and ecclesiology. I read more of him when I went on to do my doctoral work at Duke, as my topic was ecclesiology. Always I learned from him.

I met Ratzinger briefly after finishing my PhD in 1976. I had gone to Germany in the spring, partly to meet him, and he graciously received me in his home in Regensburg. I had made use of a work on ecumenism done by one of his students, and I had many questions that I wanted to ask him, and did, in our rather straightforward American fashion. I remember at one point he said to me gently, "Your questions are very direct," and I made the appropriate apologies.

I remember two other things from that conversation now so many years ago. As our visit drew to a close he said that he had to excuse himself as he was taking part in a *Mai Andacht*. My German not being that good, I asked him what an *Andacht* was. He explained that it was a special devotion to Mary in the month of May, and I remember thinking that for a professor he was quite pious. The other thing I remember is that when I was leaving, he walked me to the street, showing me where to catch the bus so that I could get home without difficulty. That kind of graciousness was typical of him. A few months after I met him, he was appointed archbishop of Munich-Freising, and in 1981 he moved to Rome.

As a theologian, Joseph Ratzinger played a key role at the Second Vatican Council and in the years that followed. As prefect for the Congregation for the Doctrine of the Faith, he watched zealously over Catholic theology in the name of the church. As pope he became the public face of the church, articulating its faith and defining the parameters of its theology. Yet he has remained a theologian as well as pope and on at least one occasion has invited criticism of his nonmagisterial writing.[10]

This revised edition seeks to give a retrospective on his final years as pope and his resignation, perhaps one of the most significant moves in his long career. I hope it will stand as a respectful exploration of the theology and impact of the man that history will remember as Pope Benedict XVI.

Chapter 1

FROM PROFESSOR
TO POPE

Joseph Aloysius Ratzinger was born on Holy Saturday, April 16, 1927, and baptized that same day in the parish church of the Bavarian village of Marktl am Inn, on the border with Austria. Because it was a very cold, wintry morning, his older sister Maria (b. 1921) and his brother Georg (b. 1924) were not able to attend. His family, middle class but of slender means, was deeply Catholic. His father, Joseph, was a rural policeman, and his mother, Maria, occasionally cooked for a small hotel to help supplement her husband's income. Two influences seem to stand out as formative from his earliest years. One was the traditional Catholic life of the Bavarian villages in which he grew up. The other was his fascination with the rich splendor of the Catholic liturgy.

Bavarian Roots

Ratzinger's roots lie in Bavaria, then and now the most conservative region in Germany. Even today it is largely rural. His family moved three times by the time young Joseph turned ten, to Tittmoning on the border with Austria in 1929, to a small village called Aschau-am-Inn in 1932 because of his father's criticism of the Nazis, and to Traunstein, a larger town of about eleven thousand, in 1937. Unlike most of Germany, which was only about 30 percent Catholic, Catholics were the majority in Bavaria, about 70 percent, with most of the Protestants living in the northern area of Franconia.

Bavarian culture was deeply Catholic, from its roadside shrines to its Baroque and onion-domed churches, and its impact on the young Ratzinger was profound. Who but a Bavarian could write, "We experience a Baroque church as a unique kind of *fortissimo* of joy, an Alleluia in visual form."[1] Even today Bavarians greet each other with *Grüss Gott*, literally "God greet you," or, more accurately, "God bless you," rather than a secular "Good morning." If life in Bavaria was explicitly religious, it was also highly regulated; as John Allen writes, "One could not hunt in the forests or fish in the stream owned by the village without permission; one could not slaughter one's own livestock without registering the deed; one could not plant new crops without authorization; one could not do even minor work on one's own house without sanction from the village authorities. The system ensured stability and kept the peace among neighbors."[2]

Ratzinger's family was pious, perhaps exceptionally so. They went to church as a family three times on Sundays and prayed the rosary at home. Catholic faith was the bedrock of their lives. Looking back, Ratzinger writes, "I shall never forget the devotion and heartfelt care with which my father and mother made the sign of the Cross on the forehead, mouth, and breast of us children when we went away from home, especially when the parting was a long one."[3] Next to his family, perhaps the most formative influence in the shaping of his faith was the liturgy. In his memoirs he describes his love for the rhythm of the liturgical year, the light that transformed the darkness at the Easter Mass, and the different prayer books and missals in Latin and German he had as a child.[4]

During the years the family lived in Traunstein, Ratzinger studied Latin and Greek, which were at the center of the local *gymnasium*'s classical curriculum. Pictures of the young Joseph show a sensitive boy; he was small for his age and not at all athletic. In 1939, at the age of twelve, he entered the minor seminary at Traunstein to begin his long journey to the priesthood. He also began to play the piano, developing a love for Mozart that would last all his life. Thus, the culture of his formative years was both traditional and homogeneously Catholic.

The Nazi Period

The German National Socialist Workers (Nazi) Party had its origins in Bavaria, though not all Bavarians were Nazis, and Traunstein was one of the few areas in Germany where the Nazis did not receive a majority in the 1933 election. Fiercely anti-Communist, many Bavarians initially welcomed Hitler after the Reichstag elections of March 1933, but their enthusiasm quickly cooled. They felt threatened by the Nazi Party's economic policies and, after 1934, by its struggle with the church (*Kirchenkampf*), which many saw as a new expression of the earlier *Kulturkampf* of Bismarck, who was both Prussian and Protestant. Ratzinger's father was never a Nazi Party member, and though he did not keep his opinions to himself, his opposition was generally not public. Active resistance was dangerous but not unknown.

Allen offers a number of examples of people from Traunstein who actively resisted the Nazis, first of all the Communists and the Social Democrats. Others included Christoph Probst, a young man from a nearby village who was involved in the so-called White Rose group, a nonviolent resistance group of students at the University of Munich led by Hans and Sophie Scholl, who were executed in 1943, Probst with them, for distributing anti-Nazi leaflets. Also actively resisting were about forty Jehovah's Witnesses living in Traunstein, who protested publicly, and the town's pastor, Father Josef Stelzle, who preached against the Nazis and died shortly after the end of the war.[5]

In 1941 Ratzinger became an unwilling member of the Hitler Youth; membership became compulsory for boys in Germany at that time, and he would have had no choice in the matter. Along with his whole seminary class, he was assigned to an antiaircraft "Flak" battery in 1943. A year later he was drafted into regular service in a labor battalion. While Ratzinger was able to continue his studies privately, he was not isolated from the effects of the war. One boy in his Flak unit was killed and several were wounded. He saw slave laborers from Dachau working at the BMW plant his unit was guarding and later witnessed Hungarian Jews being rounded up for shipment to the East. Never in combat, he simply left for home after Hitler's suicide, a dangerous thing to do, as deserters were usually shot by SS fanatics in those final days of the war. Captured by the Americans at his family home in Traunstein, he was forced to put on his uniform again and join an endless procession of German prisoners marching along the empty autobahn to a POW camp near Ulm. After a brief time as a prisoner of war, he returned home in June and resumed his seminary studies that fall along with his brother Georg.

Ratzinger's written reflections of what Germans call *die Nazizeit* tend to be more philosophical than personal. John Allen has observed, "One gets the impression that the Third Reich has meaning for Ratzinger today primarily as an object lesson about church and culture, and only the details consistent with that argument have passed through the filter of his memory."[6] He sees the Nazis' crimes as the result of their atheism and their primary target Christianity, especially Catholicism. For example, when he visited Auschwitz in May 2006, a year after his election as pope, he asserted at the nearby Birkenau extermination camp that the rulers of the Third Reich "wanted to crush the entire Jewish people, to cancel it from the register of the peoples of the earth," and "by destroying Israel, by the Shoah, they ultimately wanted to tear up the taproot of the Christian faith and to replace it with a faith of their own invention: faith in the rule of man, the rule of the powerful."[7] A number of Jews were upset that he neglected to condemn anti-Semitism or to acknowledge the church's share of responsibility for its long history. In David Gibson's words, "What the Nazi experience seems to have bred in Joseph Ratzinger, or the preexisting trait it reinforced in him, was a kind of distancing, a pattern of removing himself from unpleasantness, isolating the pure ideal—of the faith, the church, the family, the nation—from the inevitable corruptions of the world."[8]

It is interesting to contrast the careers of Ratzinger and another German theologian, Johann Baptist Metz. They were contemporaries, both Bavarians, born scarcely a year apart. Both grew up during the Nazi period and came of age during the Second World War. Both were POWs after the war, were later ordained, and became theologians. But Metz's work, unlike Ratzinger's, was to be profoundly influenced by his experience of living through the terrible period of the Third Reich, both personally as a soldier in the German army during the final days of the war and as one of the German people who seemed in some way complicit by their lack of resistance. He raises troubling questions about the kind of religion that "allowed us Christians to continue our untroubled believing and praying with our backs to Auschwitz."[9]

A student of Karl Rahner, Metz later broke with him because he found Rahner's transcendental anthropology too abstract. Influenced by Marxist-inspired ideology critiques, by his own efforts to address the inability of both German Enlightenment thinking and Catholic theology to resist National Socialism, and by the emergence of new third-world theologies, particularly after the Medellín Conference of 1968, Metz sought to rethink Christian theology and faith as praxis based on messianic discipleship of Jesus.[10] Thus, his work turned toward a critique of what he called "bourgeois," or middle-class religion. He characterized his work as a postidealist, political theology. He did not transform Christian faith into a social ideology but stressed the need for Christians to deprivatize their faith, to take seriously the world in all its pain, "to work against just these dangers of an extreme interiorization of Christian salvation and its attendant danger of Christianity's uncritical reconciliation with prevailing political powers."[11]

While Metz's work is credited as being a major influence in the development of liberation theology, Ratzinger has waged a relentless campaign against both political and liberation theology. He sees them as based on a mistaken notion of eschatology that ends up historicizing it, politicizing Christianity, and emptying theology of its transcendental dimension. But Ratzinger and Metz are not the only German theologians to draw different lessons from the Nazi period about the social and political implications of Christianity and especially ecclesiology. In a book on Catholic theologians who lived through that period, Robert Krieg suggests that how a churchman responds to social issues is influenced by his ecclesiology: "Bishops and theologians who operate—whether consciously or unwittingly—out of *societas-perfecta* ecclesiology may succeed in preserving ecclesiastical structures and practices but may ignore injustice in the church and the abuse of human rights in society."[12]

Theology and Priesthood

In 1945 Ratzinger resumed his seminary studies, this time in Freising, and in 1947 he was accepted at the Herzogliches Georgianum, a more advanced theological institute affiliated with the university in Munich. As the university was still largely rubble after the war, the theological faculty and students of the Georgianum took up temporary residence at Fürstenried, a former royal hunting lodge just south of Munich. From the beginning, Ratzinger's interest was academic theology. He began reading de Lubac, Heidegger, Jaspers, Nietzsche, Bergson, and the Jewish philosopher Martin Buber, whose work impressed him deeply.

One of his professors was Friedrich Wilhelm Maier, whose scholarly work on the "two-source" theory, Mark and "Q" as the sources behind the Synoptic tradition, had resulted in his removal from his academic position thirty-five years earlier, a victim of Rome's crusade against Modernism. Thus, from early in his academic career, Ratzinger was aware of those who had suffered from Roman authority. In an early book on Vatican II he refers to "men such as Henri de Lubac (who had suffered so much in connection with repressive measures against the so-called new theology) and John Courtney Murray (the chief architect of the council's schema on religious liberty)."[13] Allen refers to this as a recurring motif in Ratzinger's thought. "He experiences an injustice at the hands of church authorities, directed either at himself or others, and expresses regret for the bitterness and hurt it caused. He avoids, however, any structural conclusions about the proper use of such authority."[14]

The priesthood was to pose its own challenges to Ratzinger. In 1996 he told journalist Peter Seewald that although he felt called to academic work, his vocation to the priesthood presented him with a crisis. If he said yes to it, it might mean that his whole life would be spent in the normal tasks of pastoral, priestly ministry; "I couldn't study theology in order to become a professor, although this was my secret wish. But the Yes to the priesthood meant that I had to say Yes to the whole task, even in its simplest forms."[15] Yet he went ahead and, on June 29, 1951, he was ordained in Freising together with his brother Georg in an ordination class of more than forty. The brothers Ratzinger celebrated their *Primiz*, or first Masses, in their village outside Traunstein on July 8. Joseph was assigned to a parish for a year, his only full-time experience of priestly pastoral ministry.

A year later he completed his doctorate, working under Gottlieb Söhngen, a professor of fundamental theology at Munich who was his teacher and mentor. Söhngen suggested that he turn to Bonaventure for his *Habilitationsschrift*, a second dissertation or book-length manuscript necessary in Germany for obtaining a university position. Interestingly, his second reader, Michael Schmaus, an expert medievalist, originally rejected his work, claiming it did not meet scholarly standards. Ratzinger suggests that Schmaus might have been put out because he had not chosen him as his director.[16] After he revised the manuscript, dropping the part that Schmaus most objected to, it was accepted.

The Professor

In 1959 Ratzinger was called to the chair in fundamental theology at the university at Bonn. In his early days there, he included among his lectures topics such as "Church, Sacrament and Faith in the *Confessio Augustana*" and "Melanchthon's *Tractatus de Potestate Papae*," most unusual for a Catholic theologian in those days. While he was at Bonn, in the Archdiocese of Cologne, a seminary classmate introduced him to Cardinal Joseph Frings, the archbishop. Frings was impressed with the young theologian and brought him to the Second Vatican Council as his *peritus*. In 1963 Ratzinger moved to the university at Münster.

The Second Vatican Council

Vatican II was to transform the still relatively unknown theologian, only thirty-five years old when it opened, into a major figure. It is difficult to underestimate the significance of the role Ratzinger played at the council. In his memoirs, written almost twenty-five years after the council concluded, he denies having found grounds to reject what was being proposed by the Roman preparatory commission, meaning the schema on the church and that on divine revelation. But he did have some serious reservations; he found that in spite of their solid foundation, the drafts might have drawn more on the results of the recent renewal in biblical and patristic studies and "gave an impression of rigidity and narrowness through their excessive dependency on scholastic theology."[17] Ratzinger himself was to help shape several of the council documents.

His greatest contribution was in the development of the Dogmatic Constitution on Divine Revelation, *Dei Verbum*. He spoke to the German bishops shortly before the council opened, suggesting a new approach to the draft, or "schema," for the constitution. Admitting that his schema was too brief and composed in haste, he then worked with Karl Rahner on developing a new draft, though he says that the work was much more Rahner's than his own. In the process, it became obvious to him that "Rahner and I lived on two different theological planets."[18] Finally, he served on the commission that drafted what became the final text of *Dei Verbum*, a document that incorporated many of the principles outlined in the Rahner-Ratzinger draft. After the council, he wrote the commentary on *Dei Verbum* for the semiofficial *Commentary on the Documents of Vatican II*, edited by Herbert Vorgrimler.[19]

Ratzinger also played a significant role in shaping the Dogmatic Constitution on the Church, *Lumen Gentium*, perhaps the council's most significant document. With its collegial understanding of the episcopal office, acknowledging the bishops' share in the government of the church, the document went a considerable way toward reinterpreting the one-sided emphasis on papal authority that had come from Vatican I. Ratzinger is credited with helping shape articles 22 and 23, both crucial to *Lumen Gentium*'s teaching on collegiality. During the third session, he worked on an editorial committee, along with Yves Congar, redrafting the Decree on the Missionary Activity of the Church (*Ad Gentes*). Clearly Ratzinger was among those theologians who played a significant role in shaping the teaching of the council.

The Postconciliar Years

Even before the council had ended, Ratzinger had begun showing a growing uneasiness with the way the council was being understood. In his memoirs he speaks of finding on his return to Rome in the council's final years a growing impression that everything was open to revision, as well as a growing resentment against Rome and the Curia. As theologians began seeing themselves rather than the bishops as those most expert in the faith, the popular perception grew that the church and even its Creed were subject to change, while the emphasis on the church as the "people of God" seemed to suggest a new idea of a "church from below" or a "church of the people."[20] Although it might be objected that these memoirs, written long after the council, were shaped by later controversies, Ratzinger had already warned in 1966 about mistaking renewal to mean the cheapening of religion, overzealousness in the reform of the liturgy, a tendency to seek modernity rather than truth, and, most of all, a tendency to picture everything in black and white.[21]

In 1966 Ratzinger accepted a position at Tübingen, perhaps the premier center for theology in Germany with its distinguished Catholic and Protestant faculties. Hans Küng, the dean at the time, apparently overrode the usual procedures to gain Ratzinger the appointment. In no small part, Ratzinger's move reflected a desire to move closer to his native Bavaria. When he began teaching at Tübingen, riding to class on his bicycle, his lectures were packed with more than four hundred students. His seminars were so popular that, according to Helmut Moll, later a staffer at the CDF,

> to join a seminar on Mariology you had to take a pre-examination on Greek and Latin Marian texts from the early centuries. But there was no comparison between Ratzinger and the others. The lectures that I had heard in Bonn from professors of neo-scholastic bent appeared arid and cold, a list of precise doctrinal definitions and that was it. When I listened in Tübingen to Ratzinger speaking about Jesus or of the Holy Spirit, it seemed at times that his words had the accent of prayer.[22]

While at Tübingen, Ratzinger published his *Introduction to Christianity*, largely a transcription of his Tübingen lectures. His most successful book, it has been translated into at least nineteen languages, including Arabic and Chinese. Respected by his colleagues, he was elected dean. But Tübingen was soon caught up in the student uprising that swept like a flood tide across Europe in 1968, as we have seen. Traditional theology was being recast in Marxist terms, while the activism of students and the "non-professorial staff," in other words, the adjunct professors and some graduate students, made teaching difficult. He describes a flier distributed by the Union of Protestant

Theology Students that "accused the Church of sharing in the guilt of capitalist exploitation of the poor, and it ascribed to traditional theology the function of propping up the system."[23] Ratzinger felt that his integrity was at stake. While he has denied a famous story that students once snatched the microphone from his hand during a lecture, he was profoundly troubled. Even Hans Küng canceled his lectures at the end of 1968 because he was tired of having them "invaded."[24] In 1969 Ratzinger moved to a new and more conservative university just opening at Regensburg on the Danube in his native Bavaria. By now his parents had died, and his brother Georg had been appointed choir director for the Regensburg cathedral and its famous choir. Thus, Regensburg became Ratzinger's home.

Shortly after arriving at Regensburg, he was appointed to the International Theological Commission (ITC), set up by Pope Paul VI to bring together some of the best theologians as theological advisers to the church and the Holy See. Many saw it as an effort to balance the more conservative Congregation for the Doctrine of the Faith (CDF), the new name given to the old Holy Office by Paul VI in December 1965, a congregation that itself became the successor to the Roman Inquisition in 1908. Two members of the ITC became good friends of Ratzinger. One was Henri de Lubac, a French Jesuit famous even before the council as part of a theological movement known as *ressourcement* that posed an alternative to the old neoscholastic approach by returning to the sources: scripture, the liturgy, and the fathers of the church. The other was Hans Urs von Balthasar, a former Jesuit born in Switzerland, whose theological aesthetics offered a challenge to secular modernity. Like Ratzinger, von Balthasar, and de Lubac, other theologians such as Jean Daniélou and Joseph Jungmann had become disillusioned with many of the postconciliar changes that they saw as reflecting the spirit of modernity rather than the deepest instincts of the tradition. In 1972 Ratzinger joined de Lubac and von Balthasar, along with Walter Kasper and Karl Lehmann, to launch *Communio*, an international journal of theology and culture now published in about sixteen languages, to balance the increasingly liberal, or in their view partisan, journal *Concilium*. While Ratzinger had growing concerns about the liturgy, particularly with the prohibition of the use of the old missal of Pius V once Pope Paul VI promulgated the new *Missale Romanum* in its first edition in 1969, the Regensburg years were generally happy and productive.

Bishop and Cardinal

After the death of Cardinal Julius Döpfner in July 1976, the apostolic nuncio to West Germany came to visit Ratzinger with a letter appointing him archbishop of Munich and Freising. Though he claims he was shocked and surprised by the appointment, after consulting his confessor, he accepted, writing his answer on the stationery of the nuncio's hotel. He was just forty-nine years old.

Ratzinger was ordained archbishop on the Vigil of Pentecost, 1977. In his memoirs he explains the symbols he chose for his office. His episcopal motto, "Co-workers of the Truth," reflects his long concern for truth, both as a theologian and now as a bishop. The shell recalls Augustine's story of the child he encountered on the beach, trying to put the ocean into the little hole he had dug in the sand, and his remark that the hole could no more contain the ocean than his intellect could understand the mystery of the Trinity. And the bear with packs strapped to his back harks back to the legend about Corbinian, the founding bishop of Freising, who according to the legend forced a bear to carry his belongings to Rome after it had killed his horse.

Ratzinger's time as archbishop in Munich was short, little more than four years. Pope Paul VI made him a cardinal in June 1977. Thus he was able to participate in the two papal conclaves of 1978, the first that elected Albino Luciani of Venice as John Paul I in August and the second that quickly followed in October, which elected Karol Wojtyla of Krakow as John Paul II. Several journalists credit Ratzinger with helping Wojtyla gain the support of the Germans. After first offering Ratzinger the position as prefect of the Congregation for Catholic Education, John Paul appointed him prefect of the Congregation for the Doctrine of the Faith in 1981 and he moved to Rome.

The Prefect

How Ratzinger would conduct himself as prefect of the CDF should have come as no surprise; he had already given some clear signals. In 1977 he had exercised his right as archbishop according to the 1924 concordat between Bavaria and the Holy See to deny

Johann Baptist Metz the chair in theology at Munich's Ludwig-Maximilians Universität. Though he had once recommended Metz for a chair in fundamental theology at Münster, Metz's thought had subsequently moved in the direction of the political theology so problematic for Ratzinger. Karl Rahner, in one of his strongest statements of protest, publicly rebuked Ratzinger for making "a farce out of your responsibility to protect academic freedom in the university."[25] Also in 1977, the German bishops began an investigation of Hans Küng for his two books *Infallible: An Inquiry* (1970) and *On Being a Christian* (1974). Though Ratzinger and Küng had been good friends during Ratzinger's days at Tübingen and frequently dined together, Ratzinger had written scathing criticisms of both books. Now as a bishop, he became involved in the process against Küng. On December 18, 1979, the German bishops declared that Küng was no longer qualified to be a Catholic theologian or, as Ratzinger had said in an interview with the German Catholic news service, no longer deserving of a *missio canonica*, or license to teach Catholic theology.

Liberation Theology

As he settled into his new role in Rome, the CDF began to exhibit a new energy that reflected his strong views. It is important to note that Ratzinger's theological objections are not confined to a theologian's writings. They extend to the principles underlying his or her thought, to what he sees as its trajectory or ultimate consequences.

The first to find themselves the objects of his scrutiny were the liberation theologians of Latin America, especially the Brazilian Franciscan Leonardo Boff, but also his brother Clodovis; Juan Luís Segundo of Uruguay and Jon Sobrino of El Salvador, both Jesuits; Segundo Galilea from Chile; Hugo Assman from Brazil; and Gustavo Gutiérrez of Peru, generally acknowledged to be the father of liberation theology. Ratzinger has never been comfortable with a theology that looked for eschatological fulfillment within history, something he learned from his earlier study of Bonaventure and his struggle with the Spiritual Franciscans. But it was liberation theology's use of Marxism as a tool of social analysis that particularly alarmed him, just as it had Pope John Paul II.

To be fair, Ratzinger did not initiate the CDF action against the liberation theologians. The Congregation had begun a file on Boff as early as 1975 and in 1980 opened one on Sobrino. But Ratzinger had already warned about Marxism and the advocacy of social revolution during a trip to Ecuador in 1978. At a news conference in Munich on his return to Germany, he stated, "Where evangelization is neglected and social aid is robbed of its Christian basis, where the much-discussed theology of liberation is blended with Marxist presuppositions, the door is opened to ideological means of struggle," suggesting that the growth of the Mormons and Jehovah's Witnesses in Latin America showed that the liberationist agenda was not really meeting the spiritual needs of the people.[26]

The growing influence of the liberation theologians and the new energy of the CDF under Ratzinger's direction meant that a collision was inevitable. In 1971 Boff sketched a new church emerging from the Latin American base communities, "a concretization of church, without the presence of consecrated ministers and without the eucharistic celebration." While he saw this situation as painful, it did not mean that the church would disappear: "The church abides in the people of God as they continue to come together, convoked by the word and discipleship of Jesus Christ. Something *is* new under the sun: a new church of Christ."[27] In 1981 Boff published his most controversial book, *Church: Charism and Power*, analyzing the church's hierarchical structure in Marxist terms:

> Throughout its history, the Church has defined itself at times with the ruling classes. The unequal social structure, revolving around the ownership of the means of production, slowly came to predominate within the Church itself. An unbalanced structure in the means of "religious" production was created; in socioanalytical language (so as not to give a moral connotation), there has also been a gradual expropriation of the means of religious production from the Christian people by the clergy. In the early years, the Christian people as a whole shared in the power of the Church, in decisions, in the choosing of ministers; later they were simply consulted; finally, in terms of power, they were totally marginalized, dispossessed of their power.[28]

Such an approach to ecclesiology, using Marxist terms such as *power*, *class structure*, *means of production*, and *division of labor*, and representing a church from the base without ordained ministers or Eucharist, was sure to raise red flags for Ratzinger.

The next five or six years would see a number of CDF interventions against liberation theology. In 1983 Ratzinger asked the bishops of Peru to begin an investigation of Gutiérrez, and Pope John Paul II made his famous visit to Nicaragua, publicly shaking a reproving finger before the media of the world at Father Ernesto Cardenal, then serving as the minister of culture in the Sandinista government. In August 1984 the CDF issued its "Instruction on Certain Aspects of the 'Theology of Liberation,'" warning about deviating from the faith by borrowing from various currents of Marxist thought in "an insufficiently critical manner." The instruction objected to the use of the concept of the class struggle in liberation theology, warned against identifying the kingdom of God with the movement for human liberation, and rejected its challenging the sacramental and hierarchical structure of the church.[29]

Shortly after the instruction was released, Boff was summoned to Rome to discuss his book. He came, accompanied by three supportive members of the Brazilian hierarchy. A meeting of bishops from Peru in Rome had failed to result in a condemnation of Gutiérrez. The CDF issued a formal notice on Boff's *Church: Charism and Power* in March 1985, and in April Ratzinger ordered that he was not to publish, teach, or speak publicly until further notice; Boff was effectively silenced.

In April 1986 the CDF published a second instruction on liberation theology; at first glance it seemed more positive, but it remained seriously critical, a point Ratzinger clarified in a 1988 commentary.[30] The appointment by the Vatican of more conservative Latin American bishops, a number from Opus Dei, ultimately began to turn the tide against the liberation theologians, leaving them without the episcopal protection they had earlier enjoyed. Though the silencing of Boff was lifted in 1986, he was frustrated by repeated requests to clarify his views and finally left the priesthood in 1992 after another restriction on his teaching. Allen sees two events in 1989 and 1990 as marking the close of the era of liberation theology in Latin America. One was the fall of the Berlin Wall and, thus, of Communism across Eastern Europe; the other was the electoral defeat of the Sandinistas in Nicaragua.[31] Ratzinger had won his first great battle. But that did not mean that his campaign against the proponents of liberation theology was over. On March 14, 2007, the CDF published a warning of certain "dangerous or erroneous propositions" in two works of Jon Sobrino, particularly in regard to his Christology, though no penalties were imposed.

Relativism

In a talk given in Guadalajara, Mexico, in May 1996, Ratzinger identified the theology of liberation in its radical forms as the most urgent challenge for the faith of the church. But with the collapse of the Communist governments of Europe at the end of the 1980s, "a kind of twilight of the gods for that theology" as he described it, he began to single out relativism as the central problem for the faith. He also pointed to the pluralist theology of religion as in some ways taking the place that the theology of liberation occupied in the previous decade. Ratzinger describes relativism "as a position defined positively by the concepts of tolerance and knowledge through dialogue and freedom, concepts which would be limited if the existence of one valid truth for all were affirmed." He pointed out that relativism appeared to be the philosophical foundation of democracy, for it espouses the view that no one can presume to know the truth and all roads are fragments toward that which is better. Thus, a liberal society would be a relativist society. Ratzinger is not against democracy. But he cautions that without the affirmation of truth there are no correct political opinions but only a coexistence of positions negotiated on the basis of dialogue and tolerance.[32] He believes firmly in a truth accessible to reason that can be found and embraced in the teachings of the Catholic Church. Here emerges again what remains a consistent theme in Ratzinger's writings, the threat posed by a secular, postmodernist culture. Using the example of a Swedish preacher who received a prison sentence for presenting the biblical teaching on homosexuality, he calls relativism a kind of "new denomination" that places restrictions on religious convictions.[33]

Thus, faced with societies moving rapidly in directions contrary to the magisterium's understanding of Christian truth, especially on questions involving gender, sexuality, and the family, his office became caught up in what have often been called the "culture wars," the ongoing battles over women's issues, inclusive language, gay rights, bioethical issues, and before all else, the church's right to identify the truth and teach with authority. When the 1985 Extraordinary Synod of Bishops, called by Pope John Paul II to mark the twentieth anniversary of the Second Vatican Council, recommended the preparation of a new universal catechism for the church, Ratzinger received the responsibility to oversee the project. He has also identified what he calls the "canon of issues": women's ordination, contraception, celibacy, and the remarriage of divorced persons.[34] Here we can mention only a few of these issues.

Women

In 1991 Ratzinger met with a delegation from the Catholic bishops of the United States in the midst of drafting a pastoral letter on women (though what many women really wanted was a letter on sexism). After several interventions from Rome, each of which further weakened the letter, the bishops decided in November 1992 to drop the whole project.

The question of the ordination of women also engaged the CDF. On May 22, 1994, Pope John Paul II issued *Ordinatio Sacerdotalis*, an apostolic letter on the restriction of priestly ordination to men. The letter declared "that the Church has no authority whatsoever to confer priestly ordination on women and that this judgment is to be definitively held by all the Church's faithful" (no. 4). Some wondered what kind of authority was claimed for this teaching, since it was not recognized as something either revealed or infallibly defined.

There were rumors that Ratzinger had dissuaded the pope from making his statement an infallible declaration. Because the letter did not end the debate, a year later his office issued a brief *Responsum ad Dubium* (October 28, 1995), which argued that, while *Ordinatio Sacerdotalis* was not itself an infallible statement, it required "definitive assent" as something that "has been set forth infallibly by the ordinary and universal Magisterium." Yet it was not clear to many theologians that the church's criteria for judging that a teaching of the ordinary and universal magisterium was infallibly taught had been fulfilled.[35] Others spoke of "creeping infallibilism." Another apostolic letter from the pope, *Ad Tuendam Fidem*, released on May 18, 1998, added new penalties to canon law for dissenting from truths proposed in a definitive way by the magisterium, even if not revealed, because they are necessarily connected with revelation. In an accompanying commentary, Ratzinger listed a number of examples of truths to be definitively held, among them the reserving of priestly ordination to men; the immorality of euthanasia, prostitution, and fornication; the legitimacy of a papal election or ecumenical council; the canonization of the saints; and the invalidity of Anglican orders.[36]

Homosexuality

Several CDF documents and actions dealt with changing attitudes toward homosexuality. In October 1987 *Homosexualitatis Problema* (apparently directed toward the United States, as it was released in English) stated, "Although the particular inclination of the homosexual person is not a sin, it is a more or less strong tendency ordered toward an intrinsic moral evil; and thus the inclination itself must be seen as an objective disorder" (no. 3). The letter warned bishops to resist pressure groups and to withdraw support from any group challenging church teaching. Many found the language of this document lacking in compassion. In July 1990 Ratzinger wrote the bishops, instructing them to oppose efforts to legally recognize domestic partnership or to allow gays to adopt children, arguing that it was not unjust to take sexual orientation into account in areas like foster care, the employment of teachers or coaches, or military recruitment and that rights for homosexuals were based on the general human rights, not on special rights for homosexuals, since the church must promote the good of the entire civil society.

On May 31, 1999, the long efforts to restrict New Ways Ministry, an outreach to gays and lesbians by Father Robert Nugent and Sister Jeannine Gramick, came to an end when Ratzinger ordered them to cease all ministry to homosexuals for not clearly conveying the authentic teaching of the church on homosexuality. Nugent returned to parish ministry and died in 2014. Gramick, who was asked by her congregation to refrain from speaking publicly about homosexuality, transferred to the Sisters of Loretto to continue her ministry. In December 2021, she received a handwritten note from Pope Francis commending her for her compassionate work.

One document from the CDF that was especially offensive to homosexuals, released in 2003, stated that allowing the adoption of children by those living in homosexual unions "would actually mean doing violence to these children, in the sense that their condition of dependency would be used to place them in an environment that is not conducive to their full human development."[37] Another issued in 2005 said that those with "deep-rooted homosexual tendencies" could not be admitted to seminaries or Holy Orders."[38]

Theologians and Churches

Other scholars who have been disciplined by the CDF under Ratzinger's tenure include moral theologian Charles Curran, finally dismissed from his position at the Catholic University of America after a long investigation for dissenting on certain noninfallible teachings of the magisterium (1987); Ivone Gebara, a Brazilian nun silenced for two years for her writings on liberation theology, feminism, and ecology (1995); Tissa Balasuriya, a Sri Lankan theologian briefly excommunicated for his little-known book *Mary and Human Liberation* (1997); controversial theologian Matthew Fox, silenced for his work on "creation spirituality" (1998); and Jesuit Tom Reese, editor of *America* magazine, long under pressure from Ratzinger's office, who was forced to resign shortly after the latter became pope (2005).

Interventions in different churches included restricting the authority of Seattle archbishop Raymond Hunthausen in certain areas (1986), overruling the efforts of the U.S. bishops to move toward a moderate use of inclusive language in biblical and liturgical texts (1994), and overriding the efforts of the German bishops to work out an acceptable compromise in regard to a new law requiring women seeking an abortion to first accept counseling (2000).

Religious Pluralism

Late in his tenure as prefect, Ratzinger began to focus increasingly on the theology of religious pluralism. The first to feel his scrutiny was Belgian Jesuit Jacques Dupuis, a professor at the Gregorian

University who had previously spent thirty-six years in India. Widely respected in both the East and the West, Dupuis sought to walk a fine line in his book *Towards a Christian Theology of Religious Pluralism*, recognizing that the mystery of Christ is constitutive of salvation for all men and women, without denying that other religions may contain incomplete manifestations of the divine mystery.[39] Thus, his position is *inclusivist*, rather than *exclusivist* (salvation only through explicit faith in Christ) or *pluralist* (many valid ways to salvation). He also taught that Christian missionaries should be concerned not primarily with making converts but with building up the kingdom of God.

In 1998 the CDF began an investigation of Dupuis's work, instructing him that he was to keep silent about the details of the investigation and not spread the ideas the Congregation considered controversial in his teaching, writing, or lectures. On January 24, 2001, the CDF released a "Notification" concerning his book, stating that it "contained notable ambiguities and difficulties on important doctrinal points, which could lead a reader to erroneous or harmful opinions." Father Dupuis, deeply hurt by the investigation, died at the age of eighty-one on December 28, 2004.

Perhaps the most controversial document to come out of the Congregation for the Doctrine of the Faith under Ratzinger's prefecture was the 2000 declaration *Dominus Iesus*, the result of tensions between the Asian churches and Rome over how best to proclaim the gospel in an Asian context.[40] Many felt that the declaration was directed at Father Dupuis. Among other things, it stressed the following:

- Revelation in Christ is complete (no. 5) and is not complemented by other religions (no. 6).
- Christ is unique and has an absolute and universal significance (no. 15).
- Members of other religions, objectively speaking, are in a gravely deficient situation in comparison to those in the Church (no. 22).
- In interreligious dialogue, the mission *ad gentes* retains its full force. The church must be committed to announcing the necessity of conversion to Christ (no. 22).

At the news conference announcing the release of the declaration, Ratzinger said it had been prompted in part by the "worrisome influence" of the "negative theology" of Asia on the West.[41] While acknowledging that the church teaches that good things can exist in other religions, he said that "one cannot close one's eyes to the errors and illusions that are also present" in them.

The declaration also stated, "Just as there is one Christ, so there exists a single body of Christ, a single Bride of Christ: 'a single Catholic and apostolic Church'" (no. 16) and that "the ecclesial communities which have not preserved the valid episcopate and the genuine and integral substance of the eucharistic mystery, are not churches in the proper sense" (no. 17). This goes beyond what Vatican II said explicitly about their ecclesial status, though its logic may have moved in that direction.

Many of the church's dialogue partners, both Christian and non-Christian, found *Dominus Iesus* offensive. Some Catholic–Buddhist dialogues almost came to grief over its negative tone, as the Buddhist participants threatened to withdraw. Various members of the hierarchy, including Pope John Paul II, found themselves doing damage control. The pope assured the World Alliance of Reformed Churches (WARC) that the Catholic Church's commitment to ecumenical dialogue was "irrevocable."[42] Cardinal Edward Cassidy, president of the Pontifical Council for Promoting Christian Unity, said in an exchange with faculty and students at the Catholic University of America that *Dominus Iesus* "has had a very negative impact" on ecumenical relations around the world.[43] Ratzinger had to explain in an article in the Vatican newspaper that *Dominus Iesus* was not a critique of other religions but an invitation to Christians to strengthen their own faith.[44]

The Transition

In the final years of Pope John Paul II's long pontificate, there was plenty of speculation about who would succeed him. And though Cardinal Ratzinger's name was usually mentioned among the *papabile*, few Vatican observers gave him much of a chance. He was too controversial, had made too many enemies in his days at the CDF, and was too old (seventy-eight years old when the conclave began). His 1985 book *The Ratzinger Report* left no doubts about his gloomy assessment of contemporary Catholicism.[45] On the other hand, he was a known entity, uncompromising on doctrine, concerned to defend the church from the encroachments of modern culture, particularly from the secular culture of Europe. If mild in personality, his public persona, with his intellectual gifts, international reputation, obvious spirituality, and personal graciousness, made him tower over the other candidates. He certainly had the gifts of intellect and personality to be pope. Few others had the stature to succeed Pope John Paul II.

Pope John Paul died on April 2, 2005, at 9:37 p.m. Almost immediately Ratzinger's star began to ascend. As the cardinals gathered on April 4 for the general congregations preceding the conclave, they began a time together that would give them the opportunity to discuss the state of the church and to get to know one another. Journalists summarized the issues they would face in the conclave itself. Chief among them, a new and aggressive secularization, particularly in Europe; the competition between Catholicism and Islam; and the new problems brought on by advances in biotechnology, with its accompanying moral dilemmas. As dean of the College of Cardinals, Cardinal Ratzinger presided over the congregations, giving the cardinals the opportunity to observe him at close range.

On April 8 he presided with remarkable dignity and grace over the pope's funeral Mass, with 164 of the church's 183 cardinals and some 500 bishops concelebrating. His homily, invoking the spirit of the departed pope, was deeply moving to those in the congregation. From then on, as David Gibson wrote, "Joseph Ratzinger would increasingly emerge on the radar screens of the cardinals, first as a viable candidate, then as a likely candidate, and finally as an inevitable candidate."[46] Already he had behind him a solid block of votes. Finally, on April 18, after the congregations had ended, he presided at the Mass "For Electing the Roman Pontiff." Though he spoke warmly about friendship with the Lord, his homily shocked some of the cardinals, with its somber tones and warnings about a church tossed on the waves, flung from one extreme to another, from Marxism to liberalism, even to libertinism, from collectivism to radical individualism, from atheism to a vague religious mysticism, from agnosticism to syncretism:

Today, having a clear faith based on the Creed of the Church is often labeled as fundamentalism. Whereas relativism, that is, letting oneself be "tossed here and there, carried about by every wind of doctrine," seems the only attitude that can cope with modern times. We are building a dictatorship of relativism that does not recognize anything as definitive and whose ultimate goal consists solely of one's own ego and desires.[47]

Cardinal Ratzinger could not have made his platform clearer.

That evening the cardinal electors processed into the Sistine Chapel for the conclave, took an oath of secrecy, and then with an *Extra omnes* from the papal master of ceremonies, all others were ordered out. In just twenty-four hours the conclave was over. On the first ballot that evening, Ratzinger received forty-seven votes. By the fourth ballot the next afternoon, he had been elected with just seven votes to spare. The professor had become the pope.

The Pope

History will be the judge of how Pope Benedict exercised the heavy burden of his office. Initial reactions were generally positive. From the beginning he took care to emphasize the positive, observing that Catholicism is not a collection of prohibitions but a positive option. He also sought to diminish the cult of personality that had surrounded the office under Pope John Paul. He traveled less and wanted the bishops to take greater responsibility for their churches. His initial episcopal appointments were characterized by intelligence and pastoral skills rather than ideology. He repeatedly called attention to the special needs of Africa, responding to the concerns of the African cardinals voiced at the general congregations that preceded the conclave.

Deus Caritas Est

His first encyclical, *Deus Caritas Est* (December 25, 2005), was for many a pleasant surprise. He begins by emphasizing that being a Christian "is not the result of an ethical choice or a lofty idea but the encounter with an event, a person, which gives life a new horizon and a decisive direction" (no. 1). What is primary for our lives is God's love (no. 2), which he speaks of as both *eros* (ascending love) and *agape* (descending love) (no. 3). He rejects Nietzsche's claim that Christianity had poisoned *eros*. Instead, he reclaims *eros*, arguing that, when purified by faith, *eros* draws us toward the divine. *Eros* and *agape* can never be completely separated, for God's *eros* for human beings is also totally *agape*; that is, it is a love of desire that is at once gratuitous and forgiving. Benedict goes so far as to speak in language reminiscent of Andrew Greeley of God's passionate love for us (no. 10). Similarly, love of God and love of neighbor are inseparable, as we read in 1 John; "both live from the love of God who has loved us first." If we fail to love our neighbor out of a desire to be devout or to perform our "religious duties," our love for God will grow arid (no. 18).

In the second part of the encyclical, the pope speaks of the practice of love by the church animated by the outpouring of the Spirit:

> The entire activity of the Church is an expression of a love that seeks the integral good of man: it seeks his evangelization through Word and Sacrament, an undertaking that is often heroic in the way it is acted out in history; and it seeks to promote man in the various arenas of life and human activity. Love is therefore the service that the Church carries out in order to attend constantly to man's sufferings and his needs, including material needs. (no. 19)

The church's "service of charity," its *diakonia*, is directed toward the integral human good. "The Church's deepest nature is expressed in her three-fold responsibility: of proclaiming the word of God (*kerygma-martyria*), celebrating the sacraments (*leitourgia*), and exercising the ministry of charity (*diakonia*)" (no. 25).

As the pope repeatedly emphasizes, the just ordering of society is the fundamental responsibility of the state, for justice is both the aim and the criterion of all politics. Politics and faith meet, not because the church exercises power over the state but because it forms consciences and, through its encounter with the living God, can help others see what the requirements of justice are. Some felt that the encyclical did not sufficiently emphasize the complementarity of charity and justice. Thomas Massaro applauds the pope's separation of the spheres of church and state but adds that "there is a risk in sending this message so forcefully that believers lose energy for participating in political and economic life precisely as believers, and thus shrink from bringing their Gospel-based values to temporal affairs."[48] Benedict argues that even in a just society love will remain necessary (no. 28) and that working for such a just ordering of society is the work of the lay faithful (no. 29). Unlike John Paul's encyclicals, which frequently cited his own works, Benedict's references are biblical and philosophical, with references to the fathers of the church as well as to church documents.

Spe Salvi

After love, Benedict turned to the theological virtue of hope in his 2007 *Spe Salvi*, an encyclical that shows his virtuosity as a theologian. Whether parsing Latin and Greek terms, illustrating his arguments with images from early Christian art, or weighing with sympathy contemporary objections to faith, he brings into his text philosophers such as Francis Bacon, Immanuel Kant, Karl Marx, and representatives of the Frankfurt School; recent saints like the former African slave Josephine Bakhita (d. 1947) or Vietnamese martyr Paul Le-Bao-Tinh (d. 1857); and spiritual writers and theologians such as Dostoevsky, Henri de Lubac, and the late Cardinal Nguyen Van Thuan. Thus, the encyclical is a beautifully written dialogue with modern culture.

His basic argument is that a world without God is a world without hope, the hope of eternal life that is "performative," shaping our lives in a new way (no. 10). A collateral theme, reflecting the pope's Augustinianism, is that faith in progress is not enough; science cannot restore the lost "Paradise" (no. 17). He quotes the Jewish philosopher Theodor Adorno (1903–69), that progress, "seen accurately, is progress from the sling to the atom bomb" (no. 22). The search for truth is costly; while we must always struggle against suffering (no. 36), we cannot insulate ourselves from it by withdrawing from anything that might involve hurt without drifting into a life of emptiness and meaninglessness (no. 37). When "my own well-being and safety are ultimately more important than truth and justice, then the power of the stronger prevails, then violence and untruth reign supreme" (no. 38). But God does not abandon us; if God cannot suffer, he can *suffer with*, and does in Jesus (no. 39).

As he has argued before, Benedict maintains that God alone can create justice (no. 44). "Anyone who promises the better world that is guaranteed to last forever is making a false promise; he is overlooking human freedom," freedom that must be constantly won over for the cause of good (no. 24). In the end, God's justice is grace, but not a grace that simply cancels out justice or makes wrong into right. In other words, justice will ultimately prevail, which is itself a message of hope. As Dostoevsky says, in the end evildoers "do not sit at table at the eternal banquet beside their victims without distinction, as though nothing happened" (no. 44). Still, it is a justice realized only in the world to come.

In his commentary on *Spe Salvi*, N. T. Wright argues that a positive exposition of God's kingdom could offer a vision for the renewal of life within this world as well as beyond it.[49] Benedict's dialogue partners are many, both secular and religious. But his encyclicals remain Eurocentric, with no one from the global South and no women, excluding the saints he introduces as examples. Pneumatology remains underdeveloped—a comment raised in regard to his other works.

In one of the more creative sections of the encyclical, Benedict retrieves the Catholic concept of purgatory, showing how it is rooted in the early Jewish idea of an intermediary state or Paul's writing that a person whose work is lost will be saved "but only as through fire" (nos. 44–47; 1 Cor 3:15). In the style of his predecessor Pope John Paul II, the encyclical ends with a personal address to Mary, the mother of God.

Benedict had begun to draft an encyclical on faith to complete his trilogy on the theological virtues but resigned before he was able to complete it. It was issued as *Lumen Fidei* under the name of his successor, Pope Francis, who acknowledged, "I have taken up his fine work and added a few contributions of my own" (no. 7). Still, the voice seems most often that of Benedict.[50] The encyclical shows how love is the source of knowledge and truth, reflecting Benedict's Augustinian epistemology.

Benedict's Style

Behind the gentle Bavarian smile, Benedict remains the theologian that for so long he was. His tendency is to speak the way a university professor does, isolating difficulties with a particular clarity and force. He does not sugarcoat his opinions but presents his unvarnished vision of the truth. Popes generally speak in a different idiom. Since they are pastors of the universal church, everything they say is public and will be reduced to "sound bites," scrutinized, and weighed. The least nuance will be lifted up. They must invite and persuade, in spite of the power that goes with the office.

There are numerous examples of occasions, both before and after his elevation to the Chair of Peter, where Ratzinger or Pope Benedict has spoken with an alarming directness and has had subsequently to explain himself, if not apologize. Here are some examples. Concerned about the Western attraction to Buddhism, in a March 20, 1997, *L'Express* interview, he spoke of the "narcissism" (*l'autoerotisme*) of Buddhism or of some Western appropriations of Buddhist spiritual practice.[51] Buddhists around the world were greatly offended. The CDF declaration *Dominus Iesus* (2000), the result of tensions, also caused considerable offense, as we have seen.

After his election as pope, Pope Benedict visited the Nazi death camp at Auschwitz during a trip to Poland in 2006. In his address he argued that the causes for the Holocaust were to be found in a "spurious and godless reason" and in "the cynicism which refuses to acknowledge God and ridicules faith in him." Some Jews were offended by his failure to condemn anti-Semitism or to acknowledge the church's share of responsibility for the history of anti-Semitism or its role under Nazism. On his return to Rome, Benedict condemned anti-Semitism explicitly. A month later the Vatican published a book detailing the pope's views on anti-Semitism and the Holocaust.[52]

Perhaps the greatest crisis of Benedict's young pontificate came as a result of an address he gave at the University of Regensburg on September 12, 2006, in which his unvarnished words, while directed primarily toward the secular West, managed to inflame almost the entire Muslim world. He stressed in his address that human violence could never be attributed to God's will, insisting that faith could not be separated from reason without undermining Western civilization's most profound convictions. Nevertheless, he was also raising the question of the relation between religion and violence. Unfortunately, he quoted a fourteenth-century Byzantine emperor, Manuel II Paleologus, who had raised the same question: "Show me just what Mohammed brought that was new, and there you will find things only evil and inhuman, such as his command to spread by the sword the faith he preached." The question, if not necessarily the citation, was entirely appropriate for a university lecture. As James Schall notes, "No single idea is more dangerous to our kind than the idea that God approves violence in His Name."[53] And Benedict was not afraid to raise it. But it was his quoting Manuel II that was picked up by the media. Muslims, many of whom had not read the entire address, were enraged.

As a result, the pope had to return to his address on at least four separate occasions in the effort to explain himself, expressing his regret that his words had been misunderstood, disassociating himself from the Byzantine emperor's comments, and finally adding a clarifying footnote to the original text. He had not meant to criticize Islam, he said, but he acknowledged that his speech was open to misinterpretation. He also held a special meeting with representatives of the Muslim community in the Vatican. Passions cooled considerably after his very successful visit to Turkey. When he was being guided through Istanbul's famous Blue Mosque, the grand mufti paused abruptly and said, "I am going to pray." Facing Mecca, Benedict bowed his head, and silently, his lips moving, prayed beside him for about a minute, a gesture widely seen as one of respect for Islam.

Conclusion

Clearly Pope Benedict, despite the age at which he began his papacy, had no intention of being a caretaker pope. Indeed, he brought his own unique gifts to the office and found his own voice as the church's chief pastor. According to John Allen, Benedict "has a deeper theological and cultural preparation, a greater grasp of the dynamics of ecclesiastical governance, and an immediate international stature that it took John Paul II years to cultivate."[54] From his long years as a professor, he was well read in the history of theology and referred to it constantly in his work. His homilies are often reflections on the fathers of the church. His first two encyclicals are beautifully written meditations on two of the three theological virtues that also engage contemporary culture.

The meeting of the Synod of Bishops on the Eucharist in October 2005 offered a suggestive example of his leadership. The discussion was much more open than previous synods, with an additional hour at the end of the day when the bishops could comment on other interventions, rather than simply deliver preprepared speeches as in the past. Several bishops, commenting on the shortage of priests, suggested the possibility of ordaining *viri probati*, married men of tested virtue. Others raised the issue of intercommunion or eucharistic hospitality. The final *propositiones*, or recommendations, reaffirmed that shared communion with non-Catholic Christians "is generally not possible" and said an "ecumenical concelebration" of the Eucharist would be even more objectionable.

The negative criticism occasioned by *Dominus Iesus* should not prejudge the question of Pope Benedict's approach to interreligious dialogue. Francis X. Clooney, SJ, Parkman Professor of Divinity at Harvard, is helpful on this question. After a careful review of then Cardinal Ratzinger's writings on interreligious encounter, he notes that the pope has little to say about proselytizing and conversion. Clooney notes two key points in the works. First, Benedict insists that those entering dialogue do so as committed believers; in Clooney's words, "We do no good for others or ourselves if we fall silent about Jesus, or mention him merely in passing, as if he were optional, not the center of our lives. Directness of speech will serve us well."[55] Second, dialogue must always be a search for the truth, not simply a *modus vivendi*. The pope's target, here, was not other religions but secular modernity, which seems to value tolerance over truth, particularly those Western scholars who seem to have forgotten that truth actually exists and can be discovered.[56] In light of the hegemony of the postmodernist ethos so present in the academy today, this is a point that needs to be made.

Benedict wanted a dialogue with Islam, but, unlike his predecessor, he also called for reciprocity in relationships, that is, religious freedom for Christians in Muslim countries (a mosque in Rome but not a church in Riyadh), not as a quid pro quo but as the honoring of a basic human right. In an address to the Roman Curia in December 2006, he said that the Muslim world is faced with the same task that the Enlightenment imposed on the Catholic Church and that it addressed fruitfully at the Second Vatican Council, namely, that it must welcome what he called "the true conquests of the Enlightenment, human rights and especially the freedom of faith and its practice, and recognize these also as being essential elements for the authenticity of religion."[57]

Thus, Benedict was a realist. His style was blunt, with a professorial instinct to isolate real issues and address them directly. While this cost him, it was not a bad thing. Even his controversial address at Regensburg in 2006 managed to lift up these questions of reason and faith, and thus of human rights and religious authority in Islam, as well as Islam's attitude toward violence done in its name. In a moment in history when most Muslims perceive Europe as completely secular, if not irreligious, Pope Benedict was perhaps the one world leader who could command their respect, raising these issues, precisely because he spoke as a leader who was also a believer. While his style as pope was far more pastoral and positive, he had no intention of compromising what he understood as the truth of the faith. As George Weigel said, he "is a man thoroughly convinced that ideas have real-world consequences and that decent human societies cannot be built on a foundation of falsehoods."[58]

As pope, Benedict continued his own scholarly work, just as he did by special dispensation as prefect of the CDF. In the preface to his 2007 work on Christology, *Jesus of Nazareth*, he wrote that this work "is in no way an exercise of the magisterium, but…solely an expression of my personal search for the 'face of the Lord' (cf. Ps 27:8). Everyone is free, then, to contradict me."[59] So the professor still speaks in the person of the pope.

Chapter 2

THEOLOGICAL VISION

As a theologian, Pope Benedict XVI was enormously competent. At home discussing biblical texts and their languages, the fathers of the church, or the writings of contemporary theologians and philosophers, he was a man of culture as well as of learning. A member of the Académie Française, the Rhineland-Westphalia Academy of Sciences, and the European Academy of Sciences and Arts, he is best known for his works on episcopacy, ecclesiology, tradition, and eschatology. Wikipedia puts the number of his books at sixty-six; other sources list more. One cannot read him without being amazed at the breadth of his scholarship. While clearly an intellectual, his pastoral concern has always been to safeguard from harmful speculation the faith of those whom he calls the "simple faithful."

While unfailingly gracious in person, Pope Benedict was reserved, diffident, even shy in his manner. But as Joseph Ratzinger he was also something of a polemicist. He often responded to critics directly and was not above using sarcasm in dismissing arguments he deemed frivolous. He has expressed his distaste for abstract theological texts, and though he can be as abstract as any philosopher, there is a passion in his writing, a concern to present the truth of the faith as he sees it against the wisdom of the world, which without the gospel is no wisdom at all. Even as cardinal prefect of the CDF, he was not afraid of controversy, responding at times to his critics by name. If he knows the church's theological tradition intimately and can articulate it with grace, his own theological wisdom flows from certain distinctive fonts.

Ratzinger was never comfortable with the neo-Scholasticism so dominant at the time he did his studies. He found it abstract, dry, and lifeless. This included Aquinas. In his memoirs, he writes, "I had difficulties penetrating the thought of Thomas Aquinas, whose crystal-clear logic seems to me to be too closed in on itself, too impersonal and ready-made."[1] His own theology has always been rooted, first in scripture, then in the liturgy and the fathers of the church, the "return to the sources," or *ressourcement*, that was to bear enormous fruit at the Second Vatican Council. If he was also concerned with *aggiornamento*, that bringing up-to-date and renewal of structures and life sought by the more progressive members of the council, his deepest instincts have been for *ressourcement*.

In a second polarity, the traditional tension between Catholicism's two greatest doctors, Augustine and Aquinas, a tension evident at the council and in its aftermath, Pope Benedict has always been on the side of Augustine. Augustine was not dry; he wrote with passion. In commenting on the 1985 Extraordinary Synod of Bishops, Avery Dulles noted the presence of two major schools, the first of which, "led by figures such as the German cardinals Ratzinger and Hoeffner, had a markedly supernaturalistic point of view, tending to depict the church as an island of grace in a world given over to sin. This outlook I call neo-Augustinian."[2] Ratzinger is not reluctant to acknowledge his debt to Augustine. In an address to seminarians at Rome's major seminary in February 2007, he reminisced about his own seminary studies: "I was fascinated from the beginning especially by the figure of St. Augustine and then also the school of St. Augustine in medieval times, St. Bonaventure, the great Franciscans, the figure of St. Francis."[3] But just as Augustine's thought owes much to the Platonic tradition, particularly to the Neoplatonism that was so strong in his own time, so Ratzinger owes a considerable debt to the heritage of Plato. Plato, Augustine, and Bonaventure have all left their marks on his thinking.

First, from Plato he learned to understand and privilege truth as the intelligible. Second, his anthropology or view of the human is deeply Augustinian. Finally, his epistemology and understanding of eschatology are profoundly stamped by his study of Bonaventure. In attempting to give an overview of Ratzinger's theology, we will consider the formative influence of these three thinkers and examine how they have affected his approach to modernity.

The Platonic Heritage

Ratzinger's episcopal coat of arms bears the motto *Cooperatores Veritatis*, "Co-workers of the Truth" (3 John 8). He has always seen his vocation, as a scholar, bishop, and pope, to be in the service of truth. He sees truth as illumining the world of the sensible and the experiential from beyond, finding its ultimate embodiment in the Logos, the person of Christ who is the way, the truth, and the life (John 14:6). Indeed, much of the criticism he has received over the years can be attributed to his professorial way of boldly speaking the truth as he sees it. His understanding of truth very much reflects the Platonic heritage that has so nourished his thought. First, like Plato, Ratzinger locates the true and the good beyond the world of experience, in the spiritual. Second, his notion of wisdom, though illumined by his faith, is very much formed by Plato.

Truth as the Intelligible

Plato and the Neoplatonism that so influenced Augustine located the true and the good in the spiritual realm, reflective of Plato's world of the forms or ideas. Though this tradition saw an epistemic connection between these forms and human knowledge, the material world that we experience every day was only a poor reflection of the ultimately real. The true was the intelligible, not the merely sensible. Knowledge comes from recollection. Or as Ratzinger once told Peter Seewald, "To a certain extent I am a Platonist. I think that a kind of memory, of recollection of God, is, as it were, etched in man, though it needs to be awakened."[4]

While Aquinas also emphasized the intelligible as the object of human understanding, he was formed in the tradition of Aristotle, who was considerably more empirical or experimental in his approach to human understanding. With his esteem for the physical sciences, Aristotle prized what humans could learn by careful observation and achieve through the application of critical reason. Ratzinger's epistemology is much more Platonic than Aristotelian; in a remark that cleverly reverses the popular view of the seventeenth-century controversy with Galileo, he once argued that Galileo's opponents were Aristotelian empiricists, while Galileo himself was a Platonist who placed more emphasis on understanding than on what appeared to the senses.[5]

Ratzinger sees Plato as doing battle against the radical enlightenment of his day that denied that truth was in any way accessible to human beings. Of course, he sees parallels here with contemporary, post-Enlightenment Western civilization with its skepticism, limiting knowledge and truth to what can be empirically demonstrated. For modern thought, ultimate reality remains unknowable, while the postmodernist ethos reduces all knowledge and "meta-narratives" to systems of meaning, "socially constructed" on the basis of one's social location, meaning that all knowledge is relative to issues of gender, race, ethnicity, and sexual identity, which filter how we perceive the world. Ratzinger's objection to the "dictatorship of relativism" is rooted here, in the modern reduction of knowledge to what is constructed on the basis of social location and thus is relative. Against this contemporary relativism, Ratzinger juxtaposes wisdom.

Wisdom

In his discussion of the gift of wisdom, Ratzinger goes back to Plato, who so shaped the development of wisdom in the Christian tradition. Plato taught that truth is an attribute of God. If humans cannot actually possess it, they can love it and search for it, drawn by *Eros*, which moves them to search for the Good and the Beautiful, in this way moving them beyond the limits of the merely intelligible toward the eternal. Ratzinger does not, however, rule out experience; even in the human sphere there is no knowledge without experience, and only the experience of God can yield knowledge of God.[6] Wisdom can learn much from science, particularly to be sober, exact, and methodological. But knowledge cannot be limited to what is rational from a scientific point of view; in language familiar to us today, he says that in a totally rationalized world, which limits rationality to the exact sciences, there evolves "a frightening dictatorship of uncontrolled irrationality." Instead, he argues that when *Eros* is ordered, not just to the intellectual but to the eternal, then "the rational receives fecundity and warmth from the depths of the Spirit in whom truth and love are one."[7]

This theme of *Eros* drawing humans to God reappears in

Benedict's first encyclical, *Deus Caritas Est.* He finds in Plato an ally against the skepticism of our own day. But, finally, he privileges Augustine over Plato, for while Plato's philosophy remained elite and in the last analysis hypothetical, Augustine was able to discover true wisdom in Jesus, the self-subsistent wisdom of God.[8]

The Primacy of the Idea

Nevertheless, there remains a Platonic or Neoplatonic cast to Ratzinger's thought, privileging the idea over the concrete and the empirical, which others have noted. Walter Kasper has several times called attention to the Platonic character of Ratzinger's thought. In the late 1960s, shortly after Ratzinger's *Introduction to Christianity* was published, Kasper wrote a critical review that led to several exchanges.[9] Calling attention to the "latent idealism" in Ratzinger's book, he noted that Ratzinger's starting point was the Platonic dialectic between the visible and the invisible. What was real was the invisible, the ground for the real. Kasper suggested an alternative starting point for a systematic theology, the embodied situation of humans in nature, society, culture, and history. His point was that only in this way could theology take seriously the concrete problems of real people in a world where injustice, hunger, and violence rule.[10] In his responses, Ratzinger denied the accuracy of Kasper's charges.

More than thirty years later, Kasper, now a cardinal himself, raised the same issue in regard to Ratzinger's ecclesiology. Ratzinger has long maintained the ontological and temporal priority of the universal church over local churches. In a disagreement on this point, Kasper observed that the debate was not about any point of Catholic doctrine but a "conflict between theological opinions and underlying philosophical assumptions." Ratzinger's argument, Kasper maintained, is essentially Platonic, starting from the primacy of the idea, while his own position is more Aristotelian, seeing the universal as existing in the concrete reality.[11]

Another example of the primacy of the idea in Ratzinger's thought is what we might call a "principle of reception," with the emphasis always on what is received in its givenness, rather than on what develops or changes in the world of time and experience. Again this suggests a certain conceptual, even a priori, character to his approach to theology and to the problems it must address. Jim

Corkery calls this the priority of *Logos* over *ethos*, of receiving over making, of being over doing, and sees it as lying at the heart and center of Ratzinger's theological synthesis.[12] It shows how Ratzinger thinks, but it also has concrete implications as to how theology addresses challenges in the church and its life.

Thus, from an anthropological perspective, Ratzinger typically argues that the human person is oriented not to some interior depth but to the God who comes from without.[13] In the rite of baptism, for instance, the exorcism implies that the catechumenate is more than instruction and decision; only the Lord can effect our conversion, breaking our resistance to the powers that enslave us and enabling us to believe (37–38). Faith comes not from reaching deep into ourselves but from outside us; it is based on our meeting something (or someone) for which our experience is inadequate.

Ecclesiologically, the church lives from the faith it receives as a gift and from the sacraments that it cannot institute but only receive. It does not resemble a club, creating its own rules and statutes. While there is a certain truth here, Ratzinger's approach seems to leave little room for the church to respond to new challenges in the light of its faith, to renew and reform its structures or sacramental forms. A more historically oriented ecclesiology would show how the church's structures developed in time, often borrowing from political and cultural models.

Liturgically, he argues that the community cannot bestow the Eucharist on itself; it can only receive it. "The Lord does not arise, as it were, from the midst of the communal assembly. He can come to it only from 'without'—as one who bestows himself" in unity with all other communities (293). Similarly, for Ratzinger, a holy day, unlike a holiday, is God's gift to humans; we do not make it, nor is it dependent on our decision; we receive it (82). Ecumenically, the unity of the church cannot come from the base, from a sociological program inspired by neo-Marxism, or from the churches themselves; "it is no longer just a question of institutional ecumenism against 'base' ecumenism but of the ecumenism of a Church man can construct against that of a Church founded and given by the Holy Spirit" (303). Thus Ratzinger's typical impulse is to see meaning as already given and fixed; he does not seem to leave room for development, higher viewpoints, new understandings, and change.

At one point Ratzinger raises the problem of the shortage of priests. But his approach is hardly empirical. He does not look at changing attitudes toward sexuality and the importance of marital intimacy, or at a culture unable to see celibacy as a value, or to families with fewer children reluctant to encourage a priestly vocation. Instead, he questions the efficacy of the Eucharist in the church experiencing the shortage, arguing that "there is a correspondence between the capacity for sacramental marriage in accordance with the gospel and an openness to virginity" (298). While, of course, there may be some truth to what he says, there are certainly other, perhaps more persuasive reasons to be considered.

As far as reform in the church goes, he eliminates the usual arguments, for example, that the church restricts human freedom with its rules, that it has not integrated the rights and freedoms that are the patrimony of the Enlightenment, that we need to move from a paternalistic church to a community church for which we ourselves are responsible. He acknowledges that the church will always need human constructions. But just as Michelangelo sees the image hidden in the block of stone and works by an *ablatio*, the removal of what is not really part of the sculpture, true reform of the church takes place, he argues, by a similar *ablatio*, removing obsolete human constructions, "to allow the *nobilis forma*, the countenance of the bride, and with it the Bridegroom himself, the Living Lord, to appear."[14] Reform is not a matter of tinkering with the structure; it means letting the church's true nature as the embodiment of Christ shine forth.

Regarding the debate over the ordination of women, in a comment on the 1976 CDF instruction concerning the exclusion of women from the priesthood, *Inter Insigniores*, Ratzinger published a commentary that juxtaposed a functionalist conception of law with a sacramental conception of the church. According to Michael Fahey's summary, Ratzinger argued, "The sacramental view recognizes 'pre-existing symbolic structures of creation, which contain an immutable testimony.' The priesthood is not a career at the disposal of the institutional Church but is an independent, pre-existing datum."[15]

Thus, Ratzinger's tendency is to stress the idea over the real and the existential, not unlike Plato's famous allegory of the cave, in which the objective world of ideas lies beyond the world of appearances experienced in the cave. This suggests an a priori dimension to his theology. Others would argue that theology today must always be concerned with the real and the experiential, not just the ideal; praxis is important.

Augustine

The most formative influence on Ratzinger's thought was Augustine (354–430), the great doctor of the church whose ecclesiology was the subject of Ratzinger's doctoral dissertation. In an article about one of his most successful books, his *Introduction to Christianity*, Ratzinger acknowledged his debt to Augustine: "Augustine has kept me company for more than twenty years. I have developed my theology in a dialogue with Augustine, though naturally I have tried to conduct this dialogue as a man of today."[16] Augustine was to shape to a remarkable degree Ratzinger's understanding of the human person and of the world which we inhabit.

Ratzinger's dissertation was on the church as the people and house of God.[17] In it he contrasted the ancient Roman "city of the gods" and its cult with the true City of God now revealed in the church where true worship takes place. True worship means human life lived according to God's will and God's revelation. Specifically, as we shall see, it means the Eucharist. But in a pagan state or secular society, when human activity is no longer governed by a proper relationship with God, the demonic takes over. When God's law is not honored, life is no longer held sacred, materialism and consumerism rule, and the autonomous self emerges with all its self-aggrandizing tendencies. Ratzinger experienced this firsthand in the Germany of his youth, when Nazi neopaganism brought the whole world into conflict. His experience of growing up under the Third Reich only reinforced the Augustinian cast to his theological sensibilities.

Augustinianism and Thomism

The contrast between Augustine and Aquinas can be overemphasized. Aquinas had great respect for Augustine and cited him more than any other author. Augustine was largely responsible for joining the Greek philosophical tradition, particularly that of Plato and the Neoplatonists, to the Christian tradition of the West. He insisted that reason is to govern the other faculties of the soul, thus stressing the superiority of the rational over the merely experiential. Understanding was based on an isomorphism between what is known and what is, that is, between the structure of being and what is known, assisted by God's illumination of the human mind. In this there is little difference between Augustine and Aquinas.

But Augustine's epistemology was far more Platonic than that of Thomas, who depended on Aristotle, as we have seen. For this reason, the Augustinian tradition has sometimes been described as "voluntarist," because it emphasizes the role of the will in knowing, in contrast to Aquinas's emphasis on the intellect.[18] True knowledge is based on a prior choice of the good; we know what we love. Because Augustine regards intelligence as at least damaged by original sin, he esteems wisdom, the gift of God, far more than knowledge. The doctrine of original sin remains one of Augustine's greatest theological achievements, but it colors his view of the goodness of humankind, as would become so clear in the teaching of the Protestant Reformers, particularly as developed in the Calvinist doctrine of total depravity.

This Augustinian emphasis reappears in Ratzinger's thought; he calls attention to the fathers of the church, who saw Jesus's words "Blessed are the pure of heart, for they will see God" (Matt 5:8) as the key to knowledge of God. "The possibility of 'seeing' God, that is, of knowing him at all, depends on one's purity of heart, which means a comprehensive process in which man becomes transparent, in which he does not remain locked in upon himself."[19] Humility plays a key role in Ratzinger's epistemology. He quotes with approval the words of his two mentors: Augustine, who said of his mother, Monica, a woman without the benefit of an education, that because of her simplicity of life, she had reached the pinnacle of philosophy; and Bonaventure, who remarked of an elderly woman of deep faith that she "actually possessed more wisdom than the greatest scholars."[20] As Jim Corkery observes in reference to Ratzinger, "Augustine's extolling of the humble believer over the proud philosopher surfaces repeatedly; and the point is frequently made that it is not proud philosophical insight, but humble, purifying faith that is needed for knowledge of the truth, for knowledge of God."[21] As Pope Benedict would write in his book *Jesus of Nazareth*, "The organ for seeing God is the heart. The intellect alone is not enough."[22]

In contrast, the Thomistic tradition is more intellectualist. While Aquinas, like Augustine, stressed that reason must work with faith, Aquinas tended to be more optimistic on what reason can know on its own. Our intelligence is "nothing more than a participated likeness of the uncreated light, in which are contained the eternal types."[23] In the words of Joseph Komonchak, intelligence "was a created power, resident in each individual and making the human knower the active coagent in understanding and judging rather than the simply passive recipient that the knower appeared to be in the Augustinian view."[24] Thus, Aquinas had far more confidence in what intelligence could know; he taught that the intellect could grasp self-evident truths and had an important role to play in both philosophy and theology.

Ratzinger agrees with Aquinas that all knowledge begins with the senses, that there is a sensory structure to all human knowing, that even our way of thinking about God is dependent on and mediated by the senses, as we have seen. Even faith begins with experience, but it is never limited by experience. There is a self-transcending quality to faith that creates new experiences, allowing us to know something of the always greater God.[25] But without faith, philosophy—that is to say, merely worldly wisdom—remains in darkness. Thus, from Augustine comes the distinction between wisdom (*sapientia*) and knowledge (*scientia*), so important for Ratzinger.

An Augustinian Anthropology

Ratzinger's anthropology remains deeply influenced by the pessimism about the human evident in Augustine. The confidence one finds in Aquinas concerning the integrity of human knowing and willing is absent in Ratzinger. In many ways, Ratzinger's instinctive attitudes toward human intelligence and thus its achievements in "modernity" show him to be much more like Jean Calvin and the Reformers than like Thomas Aquinas and his modern commentators. He frequently quotes Luther, and, like Luther, he emphasizes a *theologia crucis*, a theology of the cross that stresses the priority of grace over human achievement, philosophical reason, or ecclesial power.

Always he accentuates the sinful nature of the human person. In 1985 he told an interviewer that if he were to retire from his position at the Congregation for the Doctrine of the Faith, he would return to the university and devote the remainder of his life to writing about original sin, for "the inability to understand 'original sin' and to make it understandable is really one of the most difficult problems of present day theology and pastoral ministry."[26] His sober, if not pessimistic, Augustinian vision is evident in his lack of enthusiasm for what is for many Vatican II's most optimistic document, the Pastoral Constitution on the Church in the Modern World, *Gaudium et Spes*.

As a *peritus* at Vatican II, Ratzinger was known as one of the progressives. He played an important role in the development of the conciliar texts on the church, divine revelation, and the missions. Yet he found problems with the text on the church in the modern world, precisely for conceding too much to the world. In his reflections on his experience at the council, published a year after it ended, he described a conflict between what he called biblicism and modernity evident among the drafters of the constitution. Those advocating a modern theology, particularly certain French theologians, were legitimately concerned with using a language that contemporary men and women would understand. The text they produced was reasonable and polite, but Ratzinger found it problematic. He contrasted "the very plausible idea of man as a being called to subdue the world and free to decide his own fate" with "the Christological idea that man is saved by Christ alone."[27] Suggesting that the text had opted for dialogue instead of engaging faith's radical claim on human existence, it risked, in his opinion, reducing faith "to a kind of recondite philosophy." In criticizing the schema for "an almost naïve progressivist optimism,"[28] Ratzinger was touching on a theme that would come to dominate his thought when he moved from the university to Rome.

These same themes are present in his reflecting on *Gaudium et Spes* more than fifteen years after the council's close, indicating the consistency in Ratzinger's thought. He acknowledged that the content of *Gaudium et Spes* was entirely in keeping with the tradition. At the same time, he questioned its pretheological concept of world, its emphasis on dialogue, and the "astonishing optimism" it displayed.[29] Here his neo-Augustinianism emerges into focus. Some of the French and Belgian bishops and theologians who drafted the schema saw the "world," with its scientific and technical mentality, as the counterpart to the church, and looked forward to a new cooperation with the world, in order to build it up. The council emphasized the concept of dialogue, seeing the relationship between the church and the world as a "colloquium" or conversation, as though both could enter into dialogue as equals.

Of course, Ratzinger was suspicious of this emphasis. For him and some of the Germans, the world is the realm touched by sin, always in contrast to that of grace. And he found the assumption that nothing would be impossible if both church and humanity could work together simply too optimistic. What seemed to be missing was the "attitude of critical reserve towards the forces that have left their imprint on the modern world."[30] As Joseph Komonchak has observed, "The Augustinian distinction between science and wisdom would have offered a deeper epistemology than that of Aquinas, and greater emphasis on the Cross as the necessary point of contradiction between church and world would have enabled the council to avoid semi-Pelagian language and notions."[31] Ratzinger called *Gaudium et Spes* a "countersyllabus" to the famous Syllabus of Errors of Pius IX (1864), acknowledging that it represented an attempt on the part of the council to reconcile the church to the new era that was inaugurated by the French Revolution;[32] in other words, it was to be a reconciliation with modernity.

Another example of how his own thought is influenced by the heritage of Augustine is evident in his disagreement with his one-time colleague Karl Rahner. Specifically, he objects to Rahner's insistence that what is truly human is truly Christian, as it seems to him to collapse God's special revelation into a more general revelation readily accessible to human reflection. Thus, when Rahner says, "He who…accepts his existence…says…Yes to Christ," Ratzinger argues that this means resolving the particular into the universal, denying the newness or uniqueness of Christianity or of Christian revelation.[33] Furthermore, it seems to ignore the fallen nature of the human person. He writes that both Testaments teach "that man is what he ought to be only by conversion, that is, when he ceases to be what he is….A Christianity that is no more than a reflected universality may be innocuous, but is it not also superfluous?" It means a self-affirmation of the human person rather than the biblical call to conversion.[34]

Here again, Ratzinger's basically Augustinian view of the relationship between the divine and the human emerges; he stresses humanity's fallenness, the discontinuity between nature and grace, and thus the "ultimately paschal" character of God's dealing with us, converting and transforming us, purifying us through grace.[35]

> Ratzinger's anthropological writings embody a distinctive position, a definite "take," on the relationship between nature and grace. This position emphasizes discontinuity over continuity; it indicates that the way of grace is the way of the cross; it puts the stress on grace *healing* and *transforming* nature (*gratia sanans*) more than on grace *elevating* and *perfecting* nature (*gratia elevans*). In itself, this is unsurprising, given Ratzinger's preference for Augustine and Bonaventure over Aquinas.[36]

Thus, Ratzinger's discomfort with Rahner's exaltation of the human is rooted in the Augustinian and Bonaventuran cast to his thought. It also illustrates how different his anthropology is from contemporary Western culture, with its optimistic attitude toward the human and its relativism regarding truth and value. Yet Rahner had his own difficulties with *Gaudium et Spes*. In the summer of 1965, shortly before the text was completed, he criticized it for its inadequate anthropology, its lack of a serious theology of sin, and the optimism that failed to recognize how often our best intentions end in failure. His remarks, while still on the Augustinian side of the debate, remain committed to the Thomistic framework of the text's proponents.[37]

Bonaventure

Ratzinger did his *Habilitation*, the second dissertation required for a university chair in Germany, on the neo-Augustinian thought of St. Bonaventure.[38] As he explains in his memoirs, since his dissertation on Augustine had dealt with ecclesiology, this new effort was to engage him with the theology of revelation.[39] His work on Bonaventure was later to pay dividends at the council. But Ratzinger's own attitude toward secular learning was to be deeply stamped by Bonaventure's epistemology, and even more significantly, his study of Bonaventure's theology of history was to profoundly influence his understanding of eschatology.

At the time that Ratzinger took up the study of Bonaventure, European theology, particularly in Germany, had focused on the concept of salvation history, the idea that God's saving plan for humanity is both worked out and revealed in a special history intermingled with world history.[40] While Catholic scholars had also adopted this concept, Protestant thought tended to divorce a theology of salvation history from the metaphysics so important to Catholic theology. They rejected this joining of faith and metaphysics as a problematic "Hellenization" of the Christian tradition. To address this problem Ratzinger turned to Bonaventure.

Bonaventure's Eschatology

Elected minister general of the Franciscan order in 1257, Bonaventure (1221–74) was caught up in an inner-Franciscan struggle with a group known as the "Spiritual Franciscans," or simply the "Spirituals," disciples of a charismatic Cistercian abbot from Calabria, Joachim of Fiore (1135–1202). According to Joachim's teachings, history is divided into three epochs or ages. The first was the Age of the Father (*ordo conjugatorum*). It embraced the period of the Old Testament when God's people lived under the Mosaic Law. The second was the Age of the Son (*ordo clericorum*), the period beginning with the New Testament, in which God's grace is mediated by the rites and sacraments of the church, administered by clerics or priests. The third was the Age of the Spirit (*ordo monachorum*), which Joachim proclaimed would dawn in the mid-thirteenth century, introduced by St. Francis and his community. The Franciscans were the most spiritual of the traditional orders and would be the new and final order, representing the new people of God, the *ecclesia contemplativa*, arising out of the tribulation of the last days. Ratzinger translates this *novus ordo* as the "new People of God."[41] The Spiritual Franciscans saw themselves as representing the beginning of this new age of the Spirit.

While Bonaventure found much of Joachim's thought problematic, not least for the tensions it had created within the Franciscan order, he also saw Francis as the sign of a new age, recognizing the possibility that this new age had actually begun. As Aidan Nichols says, "Bonaventure, just like Joachim, hopes for a new age of salvation within history. Between Jesus Christ and the final consummation of history he makes space for an 'inner-historical transformation of the Church.'"[42] Bonaventure also taught that

> prior to history's entry into God's eternity there will be a "last age" in which the poverty of the church's Jerusalem beginnings will blossom again in a reign of the poor on earth. Before the name "liberation theology" was ever heard of, Ratzinger had to arrive at some judgment about this uncanny thirteenth-century anticipation of liberationist eschatology.[43]

One can see immediately where Ratzinger would have profound difficulties with Bonaventure's vision. He objects that Bonaventure's eschatology was raising "a new, inner-worldly messianic hope," "a new salvation in history," "an inner-historical transformation of the church"—all of which rejected the view "that with Christ the highest degree of inner-historical fulfillment is already realized so that there is nothing left but an eschatological hope for that which lies beyond all history."[44] It also amounted to making salvation something *in* history, rather than *beyond* it, relativizing if not replacing the unique role of the church by making it primarily contemplative rather than mediational, and anticipating a new mission of the poor against the covetous. What Ratzinger learned from his study of Bonaventure had a profound effect on his thinking, an insight or judgment that would return again in the face of new theologies of liberation with similar tendencies to place eschatology *in* history rather than *beyond* it, or to speak of a church of the poor, or to advocate modern congregationalist ecclesiologies that dispense with hierarchical mediation.

Bonaventure's Epistemology

If Ratzinger was critical of Bonaventure's theology of history, he also learned considerably from Bonaventure's epistemology, which privileged the wisdom of faith over philosophy and the natural sciences. Writing in the mid-thirteenth century, a time in which the recent introduction of the thought of Aristotle was changing the traditional, largely Platonic understanding of theology, Bonaventure saw theology as "nothing other than the understanding of Scripture."[45] Since Christ was the center of all things, philosophy for Bonaventure had to be radically Christian. But under the influence of the Aristotelians, philosophy was becoming increasingly self-sufficient, an autonomous discipline based on natural reason. While Bonaventure did not include Aquinas among the contemporary Aristotelians he was criticizing, he felt that Aquinas showed too much confidence in Aristotle. His own thought moved in another direction. According to Ratzinger, Bonaventure's *Collationes in Hexaemeron* represented "a battle against a self-sufficient philosophy standing over against faith." It was not just anti-Aristotelian but developed "into a general anti-philosophical attitude."[46]

There are, of course, parallels here between Bonaventure's epistemology and Ratzinger's. Ratzinger admires especially Bonaventure's absolute rejection of any philosophy not integrated into Christian wisdom. For both, Christ is the true wisdom. Komonchak refers to Ratzinger's "Bonaventuran" theological vision:

The gospel will save us, not philosophy, not science, and not scientific theology. The great model for this enterprise is the effort to preach the gospel in the alien world of antiquity and to construct the vision of Christian wisdom manifest in the great ages of faith before philosophy, science, and technology separated themselves into autonomous areas of reflection and activity.[47]

Bonaventure, for whom Francis of Assisi was always a model, saw an essential relation between revelation and humility; the relation was such "that anyone who is entirely lacking in *humilitas* is also incapable of receiving any knowledge of revelation."[48] This emphasis, learned from both Augustine and Bonaventure, also becomes characteristic of Ratzinger's thinking.

Attitude toward Modernity

Given the Platonic and Augustinian currents in Benedict's thought as well as his personal history, his evaluation of modernity is ambiguous at best.[49] His Augustinian tendency to contrast the wisdom of the world with that of the church was certainly reinforced by his experience of coming to maturity in Nazi Germany. He looks back on the church and its teaching as the one bulwark against the destructive ideology of the Nazis: "She had stood firm with a force coming to her from eternity. It had been demonstrated: The gates of hell will not overpower her."[50]

While many have argued that his thought moved in a more conservative direction after the student revolts of 1968, much of which he saw as Marxist-inspired, Michael Fahey insists that his thought "shows an amazing consistency."[51] According to Joseph Komonchak, Ratzinger very early aligned himself with a stream of renewal represented by theologians like Henri de Lubac and Jean Daniélou, who advocated a *ressourcement*, or return to the sources of Christian faith and life. "He showed little interest in another stream (represented by figures such as Marie-Dominique Chenu, Bernard Lonergan, Karl Rahner, and Edward Schillebeeckx) which, inspired by Aquinas, proposed and attempted a positive engagement with modern intellectual and cultural movements."[52] Indeed, Ratzinger's attitude becomes evident in his observation that the movement toward renewal in Catholic theology after World War I had been based on *ressourcement*, but since the council, the emphasis has been on *aggiornamento*, so concerned with the present moment that "it regards any recourse to the past as a kind of romanticism."[53]

Benedict wants the church to be distinct from the world and its wisdom. He feels that a tendency to accommodate modern thinking has led to the loss of a sense of identity and mission for the church. Thus, his tendency is to return always to the sources of the faith in the scriptures, the liturgy, and the fathers of the church. But important as this is, it makes him seem less open to advances in learning that could be identified as "secular" rather than "sacred." In the words of one critic, he "sees all traditions and historical experiences outside his own as gray, while the castle of Catholic tradition that he inhabits is suffused with the deep reds and blues of stained

glass and the flame of candles....As the searchlight of orthodoxy
and liturgy drown out the weaker voices of liberal critics...the Pope
and the magisterium—the centralized authority of Roman Catholic
wisdom—have no need to look outside for enlightenment."[54]

For example, like Pope John Paul II, who described contemporary culture as a "culture of death," Pope Benedict, in his instal-
lation homily, used the metaphors of "desert" and "sea of darkness
without light" to describe the contemporary world. While these
metaphors may sometimes be meaningful, they also suggest that
there are no values or advancements in understanding in contemporary culture from which the church might learn, for example,
an emphasis on democratic structures, participation in decision-
making, transparency, the accountability of those in authority, and
the principle of subsidiarity, which honors the right of smaller communities to make decisions appropriate to their life. This makes his
approach seem overly negative.

Still, Benedict continued to stress the integral relationship
between faith and reason. In his *Truth and Tolerance*, he wrote, "Reason needs to listen to the great religious traditions if it does not wish
to become deaf, blind, and mute concerning the most essential elements of human existence."[55] At the same time, faith needs reason if
it is not to fall into a form of fundamentalism. He has long criticized
modern, secular reason, which, in privileging a scientific model of
knowing cut off from its Christian roots, has become pathological
in assuming autonomy without reference to the transcendent. In the
final analysis, only conscience, properly understood, can preserve
people from injustice; no institution can do this by itself. This leads
to questions of ethics.

Ethical Questions

His approach to ethical questions suggests a closed hermeneutical circle. He correctly argues that the scripture does not offer specific moral propositions but rather a structure; it points to reason as
the source of moral norms. Here he sees three agencies at work: the
Christian and human experience of the church at large, the work of
scholars, and the listening and deciding undertaken by the church's
teaching authority.[56] In Nichols's words, the teaching charism of the
pope and bishops "is not meant to substitute for the exercise of the

experiential and learned elements in the Church, but to 'place' the results of the latter within a wider whole: the apostolic Church in its response to the apostolic revelation." While this does not exclude doctrinal development in the area of morals, it does not presuppose it either.[57]

Ratzinger, however, does seem to overload the church's teaching authority with the presumption that it always knows the truth. He does not appeal to extra-ecclesial sources, for example, to advances in knowledge assisted by scientific research, sociological evidence, or psychology. The church today faces many questions that come from such advances, questions that are not answered simply from within the hermeneutical circle of scripture, the tradition, and the magisterium. The question arises concerning what is learned through the sciences—can such historical data also become data for theology? For example, does the church need to rethink its discipline excluding those in second marriages without annulments from receiving holy communion, appealing to the principle of "economy," as do the Orthodox? After the two synods on the family (2014 and 2015), Pope Francis's apostolic exhortation *Amoris Laetitia* (2016) took a step in this direction.

What about the relatively recent discovery of the concept of sexual orientation as given, not chosen, with increasing indications that it is determined very early in a child's life or even before birth? Does this have any implications for the church's understanding of homosexuality?[58] Or the many issues raised by advances in modern medicine, questions in the area of bioethics? Has the church kept pace with a new appreciation of women in society and the implications this might have for the church? Has the church sought to address these issues, drawing on the wisdom of its scholars and bishops and the experience of its faithful, or does it speak simply in the voice of the Roman congregations? Is there some wisdom, born of experience, from which the church might learn?

The apparently closed nature of Ratzinger's hermeneutic circle has led some commentators to argue that he is not really open to what might be learned from other sources. As Komonchak observes, there are in his writings "very few positive references to intellectual developments outside the church; they almost always appear as antithetical to the specifically Christian."[59]

Theological Pluralism

The phenomenon of globalization has brought new challenges to the church and its theology, with the inevitable tensions between the local and the universal. How can a universal, multicultural church embrace theologies that reflect the unique insights, problems, and approaches that make up the diverse cultures of the Catholic Church? Can there be genuinely Asian or African theologies? Will Rome be open to the whole issue of theological inculturation? Or does the theological language that developed in the West become a standard for the newer theologies of Asia, Africa, or Latin America?

Many theologians today argue that effective evangelization depends on regional churches being able to develop their own theologies, reflective of their own contexts.[60] Others are much more cautious, suggesting that local theologies pose a threat to the unity and universality of the church. In an early reflection on the highlights of Vatican II, Ratzinger seemed more open to local theologies. He observed that the implantation of Christianity in Asia had so far failed, in part because it had been unable to move beyond Occidental culture. "To this hour there has arisen no really indigenous Asiatic Christianity reflecting a genuine grasp of the spirit and culture of the Orient."[61]

Yet as prefect of the CDF, Cardinal Ratzinger was reluctant to use the term *inculturation*. In 1993 he told the bishops of Asia that they should avoid the term, using instead *interculturality*. The idea of inculturation seemed for him to imply that "a faith stripped of culture could be transplanted into a religiously indifferent culture whereby two subjects, formally unknown to each other, meet and fuse." Interculturality suggests a meeting of two cultures, such that one does not destroy but can enrich the other.[62] His point here is an important one. As Francis Schüssler Fiorenza points out, Ratzinger does not think it possible to conceive of Christianity independent of culture. He fears that such a transcultural vision of Christianity would entail a loss of its distinctive Christian identity.[63]

But he also seems to presume the normativity of Western culture for Christian theology. In his interview with Vittorio Messori, he said that "there is no way back to the cultural situation which existed before the results of European thought spread to the whole world."[64] His 2006 academic lecture at Regensburg seemed to go even further. He pointed out that the Septuagint, the Greek translation of the Hebrew Scriptures produced in Alexandria between 300 and 200 BCE, was more than a mere translation; it was "an independent textual witness and a distinct and important step in the history of revelation" in which a profound encounter of faith and reason is taking place, evident in the later Wisdom literature.[65] The New Testament also reflects this Greek spirit. Thus, for Ratzinger, the Western rapprochement between faith and the use of human reason is part of biblical revelation; it is "part of the faith itself."[66]

He sees Western thought as having moved beyond this synthesis between Christian faith and Greek reason, the result of the call for a "de-Hellenization of Christianity" that had already begun to emerge with the Reformation's rejection of metaphysics, with its principle of *sola scriptura*. This same rupture of reason and faith was continued by liberal theology in the nineteenth and twentieth centuries and in the contemporary effort to argue that the early church's synthesis of faith and reason under the influence of Hellenism is not binding on other cultures.[67] Indeed, he argues that Christianity has more in common with ancient cultures and, indeed, with other religions, both of which teach that humans must turn toward God and the eternal, than with the relativistic and rationalistic world of today that has cut itself loose from these fundamental insights.[68]

While Benedict's privileging of Western thought, at least in its historic synthesis of faith and reason, makes him less open to non-Western modes of thinking in principle, the point of his address at Regensburg was to insist that the modern, Western self-limitation of reason to the empirical and the demonstrable rules out a genuine dialogue with other cultures and religions, particularly with those that see the exclusion of the divine from the universality of reason as an attack on their deepest convictions. This, of course, was the main point of the address, which was largely lost because of the controversy over his remarks about Islam.

Nevertheless, Benedict's point here was crucial. Without a concept of reason open to the questions of religion and the divine, a critical dialogue with religion that examines the rationality of faith remains for the West impossible. Nor will such a culture be able to enter into a genuine dialogue with a religion such as Islam, which looks upon Western culture as essentially atheistic.

Interreligious Dialogue

Ratzinger's attitude toward dialogue differs considerably from that of his predecessor, John Paul II. In his encyclical *Redemptoris Missio*, John Paul affirmed that the "Spirit's presence and activity affect not only the individuals but also society and history, peoples, cultures and religions" (no. 28). In other words, for John Paul, the Spirit is mysteriously at work in some way in other religions. Though he holds firmly to Jesus as the one mediator between God and humankind, he also recognizes what he calls "participated forms of mediation," which acquire meaning only from his mediation (no. 5).

Ratzinger, however, seems much less willing to recognize the Spirit's work in other religions. While the declaration *Dominus Iesus*, which came from Ratzinger's CDF, quotes John Paul's remarks in *Redemptoris Missio* (no. 55) that God "does not fail to make himself present in many ways, not only to individuals, but also to entire peoples through their spiritual riches, of which their religions are the main and essential expression even when they contain 'gaps, insufficiencies and errors'" (*DI* 8), it also distinguishes between faith as a supernatural virtue and gift of grace found only in Christianity and belief (*DI* 7). James Fredericks asks,

> *Dominus Iesus* concludes that "the sacred books of other religions, which in actual fact direct and nourish the existence of their followers, receive from the mystery of Christ the elements of goodness and grace which they contain." If the grace contained in the Sutras and the Upanishads, the Qur'an, and the Dao-de-jing is from Christ and not merely the product of human wisdom untouched by grace, how then can Christians maintain a stark, un-nuanced distinction between "theological faith," on the one hand, and "belief in the other religions" which is merely "that sum of experience and thought that constitutes the human treasury of wisdom and religious aspiration"?[69]

What emerges in Ratzinger's language here is a characteristic distinction between the natural and the supernatural, reflective of his own Augustinian emphasis on the primacy of grace. *Dominus Iesus* spoke of those in other religions as capable of receiving divine grace but added, "*Objectively speaking* they are in a gravely deficient situation in comparison with those who, in the Church, have the fullness of the means of salvation" (no. 22). In many ways Pope John Paul's approach to other religions was more like Rahner's, more willing to recognize the ubiquity of the Spirit's presence.

Ratzinger's emphasis on evangelization in *Dominus Iesus*, while making an effort to incorporate what Vatican II says positively about other religious traditions, is so focused on the need to evangelize, to recognize the equal dignity of persons but not of doctrinal content, and to announce "the necessity of conversion to Jesus Christ" even in interreligious dialogue (*DI* 22) that it fails to communicate a sense that to enter into dialogue with another religious tradition can itself be a truly religious act. It is not simply a means of evangelizing but a way of approaching the mystery of God's truth, for these religions "often reflect a ray of that truth which enlightens all men and women" (*NA* 2).

Conclusion

Though Joseph Ratzinger was one of the youngest of the *periti* at the Second Vatican Council, his instinctive tendency was much more toward *ressourcement* than *aggiornamento*. Few contemporary theologians were more rooted in tradition, particularly in the biblical and patristic tradition of the church. From his long years as a professor, he was well read in contemporary theology and referred to it constantly in his work.

Yet his particular gift has been to expound the tradition with a remarkable clarity rather than to reinterpret it creatively for new situations and problems. His optic on the human was colored by his love for Augustine. His own thought, often described as neo-Augustinian, has more in common with Augustine and the Reformers, especially with Luther and his *theologia crucis*, than with Aquinas or modern interpreters such as Karl Rahner and Bernard Lonergan. While he contrasted Rahner's theology as speculative and philosophical, conditioned by Suarezian Scholasticism and its new reception in the light of German idealism and Heidegger, he characterized his own intellectual formation as shaped by scripture, the fathers, and "profoundly historical thinking."[70]

Yet it is not clear how much historical consciousness had really shaped his thinking. There is a decidedly Neoplatonic cast to his thought, deepened by his study of Bonaventure, which has left him suspicious of any wisdom that is merely secular. At the same time, his preference for the idea over the real and the existential gives an a priori character to much of his theology and raises the question of how "new data," whether from recent discoveries, from the social sciences, or from practical human experience, are integrated into his theological reflection. His tendency was to stress the supernatural over the merely natural. Still, despite the Augustinian cast to his thought, he has stressed throughout his life the compatibility of faith and reason. In his *Truth and Tolerance*, he wrote, "Reason needs to listen to the great religious traditions if it does not wish to become deaf, blind, and mute concerning the most essential elements of human existence."[71]

His firm conviction of the complete character of the revelation of Jesus Christ (*DI* 4) made him somewhat ambivalent in regard to dialogue with non-Christian traditions. His concern always was to safeguard the absolute truth possessed by the church, not just from the "acids of modernity," but also from the modern tendency to see all religions as equally valid ways to the truth, which is detrimental to the church's mission. This is not entirely wrong. As Francis Clooney emphasizes, "In the West we have forgotten that dialogue is a search for truth, not simply a *modus vivendi*."[72] Benedict argued that if all religions are equal in principle, "then mission can only be a kind of religious imperialism, which must be resisted." The truth of God's revelation in Christ must be offered as a gift, but freely and in love.[73]

Thus, an obvious strength of Ratzinger's theology was his adamant refusal to let secular modernity define the rules of the dialogue. In his view, the West since the Enlightenment has cut itself loose from its Christian roots with its historical synthesis of faith and reason, reducing knowledge to a narrow model based on scientific reason and the criterion of verifiability. Christianity cannot be reduced to an illumination in the depths of the person; its nature is historical because it is based on events.[74]

Even biblical interpretation has been subjected to this same rationalism, as we shall see in the following chapter. Without a place for the transcendent, or for Christian revelation, Western intellectual culture has settled for technical knowledge rather than wisdom. Rather than constructing a society based on shared moral values rooted in God's revelation, modern society relies on social engineering. Religion has been confined to personal interiority, thus to the realm of subjectivity. Each person is left free to construct his or her personal faith.

Of course, Pope Benedict rejects all this. His theology begins from the principle that God has spoken in our history, that the divine self-disclosure takes place in the person of Jesus, the Word made flesh. He has challenged secular rationality not just as a religious leader but precisely as a theologian. He wants scripture to be the word of God, not just another historical text, as we shall see in the next chapter.

Chapter 3

POPE BENEDICT AND SCRIPTURE

Pope Benedict had long shown that he privileges the testimony of scripture far above the contemporary emphasis on the historical-critical method. What is perhaps paradoxical about his approach to scripture was that this man, who had been so careful to define Catholic theology over against Protestant in his own work, comes close to a classical Protestant *sola scriptura* position, though from a decidedly Catholic perspective.

Indeed, as a member of the subcommission that assisted in the development of Vatican II's Dogmatic Constitution on Divine Revelation, *Dei Verbum*, he noted the paradox that the strongest opposition to the efforts of its authors to leave room for a Catholic idea of *sola scriptura* came from Protestant theologians who "seem to have moved dangerously away from the meaning and intention of the Protestant idea of *sola scriptura*."[1] Almost twenty years later he made a similar point when he observed that the "classical criterion of *sola scriptura* is hardly ever still applied" by those formulating ecumenical agreements, particularly the World Council of Churches' Lima text, *Baptism, Eucharist and Ministry*.[2]

To gain an insight into Pope Benedict's approach to scripture, we will consider how he sees the relation of scripture to theology and his critique of the historical-critical method. We will also try to situate his critique within the contemporary use of scripture in theology and church.

Scripture and Theology

Like the Reformers, Benedict approaches scripture precisely as a theological reality; it is first and foremost God's word to the church. He sees the Bible, read as a narrative, as witnessing to a special revelation that reaches its fullness in the incarnation and subsequent mission of the church; it is unique, transcending what humans can know in light of natural reason. He wants always to preserve the priority of the divine initiative and to distinguish revelation from what is merely human wisdom. He sees the Second Vatican Council as having moved from a legalistic concept of revelation to a more personal one, "founded not only in the word that Christ preached, but in the whole of the living experiences of his person, thus embracing what is said and what is unsaid."[3] Benedict approaches scripture not in a literalist or proof-texting sense but with a finely tuned sensitivity to the biblical themes and images, which he traces effortlessly through both Testaments.

To gain an appreciation of Benedict's understanding of scripture and its place in the theological enterprise, we will have to consider those who from early on shaped his views, particularly Friedrich Wilhelm Maier, from whom he learned the centrality of scripture for theology; Bonaventure, who helped him come to a less propositional understanding of revelation; and Romano Guardini, whose use of scripture closely resembles his own.

Friedrich Wilhelm Maier

When Ratzinger moved to Munich in the fall of 1947 to begin his theological studies at the Herzogliches Georgianum, much of its famous university was still rubble, its library inaccessible and its lecture halls in ruins. To continue their studies, the theological students moved with their faculty to Fürstenried, the former royal hunting lodge just south of the city. While their faculty was impressive, with several professors added to the faculty from faculties in Silesia and East Prussia, both now part of Poland, its star was an experienced professor of New Testament exegesis, Friedrich Wilhelm Maier. As we saw earlier, Maier had very early made his mark by advocating the "two-source theory" to explain the development of the Synoptic tradition; Mark, rather than Matthew, was the first written Gospel, the source of both Luke and Matthew, who also drew on another source for the sayings of Jesus, known as "Q" (from *Quelle*, source). While the two-source theory is almost universally accepted today, Maier's pioneering work in the early part of the twentieth century drew the attention of Rome, then in the midst of its crusade against Modernism, and Maier became one of its victims. He was dismissed from his position, served as a military chaplain in the First World War, then as a prison chaplain, and finally returned to a university faculty in Breslau in 1924. His lectures years later at Fürstenried were so popular that they filled to overflowing the greenhouse that was being used as a temporary lecture hall.

Ratzinger was fascinated by Maier's lectures, though he soon found his approach to exegesis too reminiscent of the theological liberalism that had earlier dominated German universities. In his memoirs he says that Maier looked on dogma as a "shackle" or "limit," not as a shaping force in the more constructive work of theology, clearly his own approach. Still, Ratzinger was obviously impressed by his professor's facility with the scriptures; he gave his full attention to Maier's lectures, discovering in the biblical text an immediacy and freshness that were new to him. For Ratzinger and his fellow seminarians, scripture was "the soul of our theological studies," and he acknowledges that it has remained the center of his own theological work.[4]

Bonaventure

Ratzinger's work on Bonaventure was also to shape his understanding of the nature of revelation as well as its relation to both scripture and tradition. In the first half of the twentieth century, scripture was simply identified with revelation, as still is the case for much of conservative Protestant theology. What Ratzinger learned from his study of Bonaventure was that such a facile identification was completely foreign to theologians in the high Middle Ages as well as at Trent. Revelation must be received, which demands a person to apprehend it. In other words, what was becoming clear to him was the personal dimension to revelation that would be so important later in *Dei Verbum*. Bonaventure's approach also brought the essential meaning of scripture and tradition into focus:

> If Bonaventure is right, then revelation precedes Scripture and becomes deposited in Scripture but is not simply identical with it. This in turn means that there can be no such thing as pure *sola scriptura* ("by Scripture alone"), because an essential element of Scripture is the Church as understanding subject, and with this the fundamental sense of tradition is already given.[5]

Using a wonderful simile, Ratzinger argued that revelation was not like a meteor fallen to earth, from which samples could be taken and then analyzed. Revelation is an act of God's self-disclosure; it precedes scripture and becomes embodied in it. For Bonaventure, "Scripture alone is theology in the fullest sense of the word because it truly has God as its subject; it does not just speak of him, but is his own speech. It lets God himself speak." But at the same time, the authors of scripture also speak as human beings, as those through whom God enters into history.[6] Thus, scripture witnesses to revelation, while revelation itself always requires a living person to whom it is communicated. "Its goal is always to gather and unite men, and this is why the Church is a necessary aspect of revelation."[7]

This personal understanding of revelation also underlies Ratzinger's later objections to what he saw as Karl Rahner's collapsing special revelation into a universal revelation, discernible in human nature. Rahner's move, of course, has important implications for scripture. "If the teachings of Christianity are the universally human, the generally held views of man's reason, then it follows that these generally held views are about what is Christian." This means that Christianity could be interpreted in terms of what is human, or what is thought to be human, and then "the materialistic reading of the Bible" becomes something quite normal.[8]

Ratzinger insists that scripture is to be read against the rich background of the apostolic tradition as it comes to expression in the fathers of the church, the liturgy, and the sacraments. He takes the witness of the New Testament as revelatory of God's will for the church and for the Christian life. In his work on Bonaventure, he states that what raises scripture to the status of "revelation" is "not to be taken as an affair of the individual reader, but is realized only in the living understanding of Scripture in the Church. In this way the objectivity of the claim of faith is affirmed without any doubt."[9]

Romano Guardini

When Ratzinger began his theological studies after the war, one of the first books he read was Romano Guardini's *The Spirit of the Liturgy*. Its impact on the young student was profound. Years later, Ratzinger gave the same title to his own reflections on the liturgy. According to John Allen, Guardini is Ratzinger's favorite modern theologian.[10]

An Italian who grew up in Germany and became a German citizen in 1910, Guardini, like Ratzinger, wrote a dissertation on Bonaventure. A scholar with wide-ranging interests, Guardini had an impact in the areas of liturgy, youth ministry, what we refer to today as faith and culture, and helping the laity to become more familiar with the Bible. His *The Spirit of the Liturgy* introduced the modern liturgical movement to Germany, while he himself experimented with saying Mass facing the people and using German for some of its important parts. He wrote on literary figures such as Pascal, Dostoevsky, and Rilke and led a Catholic youth movement in Germany before it was closed by the Nazis. If he addressed cultural issues in his writings, he remained silent on the social and political issues that were often implicated, though in 1935 he lost his university position because of his implicit criticism of the Nazi cult of Hitler, expressed in the greeting "Heil Hitler," in his *Der Heiland*, which showed that salvation or well-being (*Heil*) could come only from Jesus Christ. After the war, he argued that the Germans had an obligation to seek reconciliation with the Jews.

Guardini's most famous book, *The Lord* (1937), represented an extended biblical meditation on the person of Jesus so powerful that it drew many Catholics to a new desire to study the Bible. For Ratzinger, it marked a decisive break with the rationalist character of liberal theology and exegesis, which attempted to discover the true "historical" Jesus behind the "veneer of dogma" by stripping or "cleansing" the gospel portrait of Jesus from the supernatural elements in which it was presented, losing in the process the mystery of God. Especially important for Ratzinger was Guardini's emphasis that the liturgy was the true context for understanding the Bible as well as the living context in which its texts first emerged.[11]

Guardini's Christology was enormously influential. However, both his Christology and his approach to scripture suffered from his reluctance to use historical criticism. At the time he wrote *The Lord*, the historical-critical method was still considered suspect by the Catholic Church. But even after Pius XII's encyclical *Divino Afflante Spiritu* (1943), encouraging Catholic scholars to use critical methods, Guardini continued to reject them. Thus, he takes texts such as the infancy narratives and the story of Jesus before the doctors in the temple (Luke 2:41–47) as historical rather than symbolic. Even if he was more interested in the "fuller sense" of scripture, his approach remained precritical.[12] In some ways, Ratzinger's approach to scripture is similar to Guardini's, though Ratzinger, of course, is fully aware of the methods and uses of historical criticism.

Historical Criticism

In his commentary on *Dei Verbum*, Ratzinger quotes with approval a sarcastic comment by the great New Testament scholar Ernst Käsemann, warning about being too dependent on historical-critical exegesis: Käsemann suggested that it would be safer to walk through a minefield blindfolded, adding that "our scholarship has gradually degenerated into a world-wide guerilla warfare."[13] Ratzinger does not treat biblical interpretation specifically in his work *Principles of Catholic Theology*, perhaps because he writes primarily as a dogmatic theologian and the book is a collection of essays.

Perhaps the best source for gaining an insight into his understanding of the historical-critical method is a lecture he gave in 1988 entitled "Biblical Interpretation in Crisis: On the Question of the Foundations and Approaches of Exegesis Today." The talk took place at a conference on Bible and Church held at St. Peter's (Lutheran) Church in New York at the invitation of Richard John Neuhaus, then still a Lutheran pastor.[14] We will consider his arguments in this talk as well as a response by Father Raymond E. Brown, the premier Catholic New Testament scholar at the time.

Ratzinger's lecture was basically a critique of the rationalist presuppositions of much of contemporary exegesis, at least in its European and particularly its German expressions. He clearly rejects fundamentalism, with its efforts to brand any use of the historical-critical method as "false in itself and contradictory" (3). His principal concern is the rationalism he sees as informing much of contemporary exegesis. He identifies the root problem as the attempt to find the "real history" or the more original sources behind the biblical texts, thus removing from the exegete's concern the "irrational residue," that is, anything that has to do with faith or with the action of God in history (2). In other words, many exegetes, in his opinion, are no longer approaching the biblical text as the inspired word of God; instead, they tend to approach the text as a source for historical information about Israel or Jesus or the primitive church, from the more original sources that then become the criterion for interpretation. But the net effect of this method is the disintegration of interpretation. The Bible is dissected into discontinuous pieces that are then used for new methods of exegesis interested not in what the text originally intended but in ideological reconstructions serving only the agenda of the interpreters (5).

Behind this exegetical approach lies the attempt to find in matters biblical or theological the same kind of certainty that might be found in the natural sciences; indeed, they give the appearance of "a quasi-clinical-scientific certainty" (6). But Ratzinger challenges this confidence by reminding us of Heisenberg's principle that an experiment is always influenced by the point of view of the observer (7). He is not unaware of the genuine insights that have been uncovered by the historical method. He acknowledges this, but his lecture seeks to disclose what he sees as the limitations of the method, particularly those evident in some of its methodological presuppositions. Some of them are literary-historical; the more fundamental is philosophical.

In what he calls "a self-criticism of the historical-critical method," he critiques a number of presuppositions of the form-critical method developed by Dibelius and Bultmann, specifically the principle of discontinuity, which assumes that what is simple is original and what is more complex must be a later development.[15] In its many manifestations, this principle allows the exegete to prune away as later developments much of what is presented by the biblical author, judging it to be based on later theological reflection, representing Hellenistic rather than Judaic thought, event rather than original word, or eschatological rather than apocalyptic imagery. For example, many of those using such a principle of discontinuity are unable to find any continuity between the pre-Easter Jesus and the formative period of the early church. For Ratzinger, such judgments represent arbitrary choices based largely on the theological or philosophical presuppositions of the exegete.

> The consequence is simple: what is Hellenistic cannot be Palestinian, and therefore it cannot be original. Whatever has to do with cult, cosmos, or mystery must be rejected as a later development. The rejection of "apocalyptic," the alleged opposite of eschatology, leads to yet another element: the supposed antagonism between the prophetic and the "legal," and thus between the prophetic and the cosmic and cultic. It follows, then, that ethics is seen as incompatible with the eschatological and the prophetic. In the beginning there was not ethics, but simply an ethos. (12)

One can see here how certain biases of the interpreter—whether a Lutheran contrast of law and gospel; a disinterest in liturgy, sacraments, or eschatology; or some liberationist or feminist agenda—begins to color what the exegete finds and thus the interpretation that emerges.

From this Ratzinger moves to a critique of historical reason itself, locating the "philosophic presupposition of the whole system" in the work of Immanuel Kant. Kant presupposes that "the voice of being-in-itself cannot be heard by human beings." In other words, God cannot be heard or known, except in the postulates of the practical reason (15). Human intelligence can know only the realm of the categories—in other words, its own knowing—for the noumenal, or thing in itself, continues to escape. The result is that a split has opened between the "exact" sciences and theology, and what was thought to be a direct proclamation of the divine can be only myth (16).

Thus, modern exegesis for Ratzinger, built in the last analysis on this fundamentally Kantian philosophical presupposition, has "completely relegated God to the incomprehensible, the otherworldly and the inexpressible in order to be able to treat the biblical text itself as an entirely worldly reality according to natural-scientific methods" (7). This "scientific" approach in principle excludes God and what God might speak in human words or how God might personally enter into human history (19). Ratzinger cites Guardini to the effect that modern exegesis "has produced very significant individual results, but has lost sight of its own particular object and generally has ceased being theology" (18).[16]

At the end of his lecture Ratzinger calls into question any pre-supposition that determines in advance what might be or what God might do. He calls for a reexamination of the relationship between event and word since an event can itself be "a word." He insists that the New Testament cannot be cut off from the Old. And while certain texts may have to be traced back to their origins and interpreted in their proper historical contexts, the exegete must also view them in light of the total movement of (biblical) history and in light of its central event, Jesus Christ.

Thus, he does not deny the importance of philological, historical, and literary methods for the exegetical task; he reaffirms them again at the end. But he emphasizes that the exegete cannot "stand in some neutral area, above or outside history and the Church." He or she must approach the Bible as the product of a coherent history, which, if not approached with a certain *sympathia* that comes from faith, will remain theologically a closed book (22–23).

One of the three responders to Cardinal Ratzinger's talk at the conference was Raymond Brown. In general, Brown was more positive in his attitude toward the influence of historical-critical biblical scholarship, suggesting gently that Ratzinger's concerns more accurately reflected his European, particularly his German, background than it did the situation in the United States. He emphasized that the rationalist origins of historical criticism to which Ratzinger so strongly objects had not been evident in the ecumenical dialogues in which he had been personally involved, and he held up the *Jerome Biblical Commentary* as an exemplary work of Catholic scholars, hardly the product of "the over-influence of enlightenment rationalism."[17] In his 2000 conversation with Peter Seewald, Ratzinger acknowledged that American theology "has made new breakthroughs in exegesis, in overcoming the one-sidedness of the historical-critical method by so-called canonical exegesis, that is, by reading the Bible as a whole."[18]

Ratzinger has raised critical questions about contemporary biblical exegesis in some of his other works.[19] But he does not ignore the historical-critical method. Most helpful was his spelling out of the broad outlines of his biblical methodology in his book *Jesus of Nazareth*. He states, first of all, that the historical-critical method is and remains an indispensable dimension of exegetical work because of the intrinsic nature of theology and faith. Precisely because Christian faith is based on real historical events, the historical-critical method is necessary; furthermore, its importance has been recognized by the church.[20]

But he adds two cautions. First, for those who properly understand the biblical writings as a single corpus of divinely inspired scripture, the exegetical task is not exhausted by using the historical-critical method. This is crucial for Ratzinger. The limits of the historical-critical method must be recognized. Its proper task is to investigate the historical context out of which the texts emerged and, thus, what the biblical authors intended to say. It is concerned with the human words as human. But the words of the biblical authors often take on new meaning, transcending their original meaning, gaining a "deeper value." Historical-critical exegesis cannot really tell us what the text means for us today. That is a theological task. Scripture is not simply literature; nor can it be reduced to history. Only when understood within the community of faith, the "people of God," the church, does the present meaning of the texts emerge.[21]

Second, the unity of scripture is a theological datum. It is a single corpus of writings inspired by God, shaped by a rereading of texts in new contexts, adding to their meaning. "Older texts are reappropriated, reinterpreted, and read with new eyes in new contexts. They become Scripture by being read anew, evolving in continuity with their original sense, tacitly corrected and given added depth and breadth of meaning," a process Ratzinger calls "canonical exegesis."[22] The process is not linear, but one that unfolds in the light of Christ. Therefore, exegesis must remain a properly theological task.

Ratzinger's Approach

Just as he is far from a biblicist, proof-texting approach, so Ratzinger refuses to reduce the sacred text to mere literature, or to the history behind the text, or to the theology of an individual author. He wants to approach the biblical text in its full integrity as the inspired word of God, respecting what the biblical authors have given us, whether it is the theology of Paul, Luke, John, or their communities, receiving each as God's inspired word.

For example, particularly concerning the Gospel of John, he speaks of the "remembering" that lies behind the text, not as a private affair but as the Spirit-assisted memory of the "we" of the church. Inspiration works not just through the individual author but also through the community "because the author thinks and writes with the memory of the Church."[23] Similarly, a "saying of Jesus reported in the Bible is not made binding on faith because it is acknowledged as Jesus' word by the majority of contemporary exegetes, and it does not lose its validity when the opposite is the case. It is valid because Holy Scripture is valid and because Scripture presents it to us as an utterance of Jesus."[24] If the discourses in John are not like recorded transcripts, they cannot be dismissed as mere "Jesus poems." What they convey is the substance of Jesus's teaching, so that the readers encounter the decisive content of his message.[25]

Ratzinger's reverence for the word of God as something constitutive of the church and Christian life makes him stand out from many theologians today, both Catholic and Protestant. Thus, Christology is to be based on the biblical authors themselves, not on the original apostolic preaching or what can be reconstructed from the earliest levels of the Q community, which remains, of course, a hypothesis. Ecclesiology is founded on the gospel portrait of Jesus as the patriarch of a new Israel, with the Twelve as its origin and foundation. The Eucharist is the foundation of a new covenant for a new people; through it Jesus draws the disciples into communion in his body and blood and with God.[26] A developed ecclesiology must find its foundation in Paul's theology of the apostolic ministry and the New Testament understanding of the apostle's role, not on critical reconstructions of the development of the concept of apostleship from the work of the early Christian missionaries.

For example, the concept of the *successio apostolica*, or apostolic succession, emerges from the efforts of the authors of Luke-Acts, 1 Peter, and the Pastoral Epistles to link the ministry of second-generation church leaders with the original apostolic ministry and its development in the succeeding centuries.[27] It cannot be deconstructed by arguing that the concept of apostle is a later theological development, or that the Twelve did not exercise actual leadership or pastoral supervision, or that their role was merely symbolic, or that there is little evidence that the apostles appointed others to take their place, or that the picture of succession painted by the author of *1 Clement* is more theological than historical. For Pope Benedict, *1 Clement* is specifying a doctrine that is already evident in scripture: "The laws that regulate this derive from God himself in an ultimate analysis. The Father sent Jesus Christ, who in turn sent the apostles. These then sent out the first heads of the communities and established that they would be followed by worthy men."[28]

Ratzinger also insists on the fundamental unity and continuity of the two Testaments, "an inner unity-in-diversity," an insight he attributes to his teacher at Munich, Gottlieb Söhngen.[29] He credits one of his early teachers, Friedrich Stummer, with opening up the Old Testament, so that he came to see that "the New Testament is not a different book of a different religion that, for some reason or other, had appropriated the Holy Scriptures of the Jews as a kind of preliminary structure. The New Testament is nothing other than an interpretation of 'the Law, the Prophets, and the Writings' found from or contained in the story of Jesus." He adds that both Judaism, which begins after the formation of the Jewish canon, and Christianity are "two ways of appropriating Israel's Scriptures, two ways that, in the end, are both determined by the position one assumes with regard to the figure of Jesus."[30] In other words, Christianity and Judaism are virtually contemporary religious movements, and the Old Testament is essential to the church's self-understanding.

Thus, Ratzinger takes the scripture, both Old and New Testament, in its integrity as the inspired word of God. Like St. Paul, like the fathers of the church, he reads the scriptures typologically. Such an approach is evident in Origen:

In the Scriptures Jericho is often represented as an image of the world. There can be no doubt that the man whom the Gospel describes as going down from Jerusalem to Jericho and falling into the hands of brigands is an image of Adam being driven out of paradise into the exile of this world. Likewise the blind men in Jericho, to whom Jesus came to give sight, signified the people in this world who were blinded by ignorance, to whom the Son of God came.[31]

For Ratzinger, such typologies are more than homiletic. The parallels, foreshadowings, and analogies between the two Testaments have obvious import for our theology. For example, as early as the year 96, the author of *1 Clement* could compare the high priest, priests, and Levites in the Jerusalem temple (40–41) to the order of the Christian community with its apostles, bishops, and deacons (42). Similarly, Ratzinger argues that the New Testament interpretation of the office of presbyters, using the images of shepherd and flock, means that "the office of priest is in this way incorporated into the traditional line of sacral ministries among the ancient people of God."[32] In the words of St. Augustine, "The New Testament lies hidden in the Old; the Old Testament is enlightened through the New."[33] This principle of the continuity of the two Testaments will have important consequences when we consider Ratzinger's understanding of the cultic and liturgical tradition of the church.

Of course, most theologians would claim to be doing theology on the basis of scripture. But it is not clear that all of them take scripture as a text that is truly inspired, what Sandra Schneiders calls the "revelatory word."[34] For many it has become simply history. Here Benedict's insistence on taking scripture as God's word is a message that needs to be heard.

Does He Have Legitimate Concerns?

Ratzinger is not the only theologian to raise critical questions about how the Bible is to be interpreted. Perceptive commentators, both Catholic and Protestant, have called attention to a crisis in the area of biblical interpretation. Brevard Childs, a Protestant biblical scholar, has traced how the Reformation principle of "the clarity of scripture," which meant that scripture was able to interpret itself (*scriptura sui ipsius interpres*), gradually began to break down.[35] Gerhard Ebeling argues that, under the influence of the Enlightenment in the eighteenth century, biblical theology was transformed from a normative discipline into a critical one.[36] Like other critical disciplines, it sought to investigate religion "objectively." Neither faith nor church nor biblical canon played an important role in this process. As James Sanders suggests, Enlightenment scholarship took the Bible away from the church's lectern and put it in the scholar's study.[37]

Once the biblical canon no longer served as the context within which scripture was to be interpreted, theologians and exegetes sought to ground what was normative in it on some ontology, ethical theory, or secular humanism, or in some theory such as Oscar Cullmann's "salvation history," Rudolf Bultmann's "self-understanding," or Gerhard Ebeling and Ernst Fuchs's "linguisticality of being," in other words, in some hermeneutical principle outside the text.[38] But this is precisely the fragmentation or ideologizing of the biblical text to which Ratzinger so strongly objects. A purely secular, scientific approach to scripture cannot encounter it as the word of God, as a theological reality.[39]

The most obvious example of this trend is to be found in the work of the Jesus Seminar. Its members follow such a purely secular, supposedly "scientific" approach, reducing the whole, rich story of Jesus in the Gospels to a collection of discrete sayings, without the narrative and later New Testament preaching that are the foundation for the church's christological faith. They reject the narrative of Mark's Gospel, claiming that it is based not on history but on theological interests. To recover the earliest strands of the Jesus tradition, they vote on the sayings of Jesus, using color-coded beads.[40] They reject 82 percent of the sayings of Jesus as inauthentic, including all those eschatological sayings that refer to judgment, reward, and punishment beyond death. What remains are several disconnected sayings, from which they reconstruct the "real" Jesus, who has little resemblance to the Jesus of the Gospels. For John Dominic Crossan, whose argument is based on a few noncanonical texts, Jesus becomes a Jewish cynic philosopher and "magician," not a miracle-worker in the gospel sense, while Burton Mack presents him as a wisdom teacher whose story was later retold by some of those associated with his movement in terms of divine power.[41] Some of Mack's motives are clearly political. He claims that the story of the conflict between Jesus and the Jewish leaders of his day was invented by Mark, making them the villains. This "myth of innocence" has had disastrous effects on Western culture, particularly American culture, giving rise to the myth of America as "the innocent redeemer of the world."[42]

Of course, it is not fair to compare the tendentious work of the Jesus Seminar to that of mainstream biblical scholars. While the Seminar's concern is supposedly historical—to discover the "real" Jesus hidden behind the texts and Christian preaching—it is not really theological. Nevertheless, not a few professors in Catholic colleges and universities and even teachers in Catholic high schools regularly use the work of members of the Seminar in their own courses. It also remains true that a good many contemporary theologians, both Catholic and Protestant, have moved beyond the priority of scripture. Their exegesis too often reduces scripture to something less than the canon of inspired texts received by the church, let alone to an inspired portrait of Jesus. What is important to them is the history that lies behind the text, or some "canon within the canon," or some interpretative principle outside of the scripture itself.

Thus, in Christology, Hans Küng takes as normative the early exaltation Christology, stressing the humanity of Jesus the Messiah, who was exalted by his resurrection as Son of God. But gradually, he argues, this was superseded by a theology of incarnation in the later New Testament and still later clothed in Hellenistic categories of divine sonship.[43] The church's Christology is the result of a later Hellenization. Roger Haight opts for a wisdom Christology, such as one finds in John and Paul, though one pruned of its preexistence motifs. In the Fourth Gospel, *logos* (word) has been substituted for *sophia* (wisdom), thus transcending other wisdom Christologies in the direction of the incarnation of a hypostatized being. Haight sees this as poetry and metaphor, not to be taken literally.[44] Some feminist scholars such as Elisabeth Schüssler Fiorenza seek to "reconfigure the Christian New Testament discourses about Jesus not as 'scientific' but as rhetorical."[45] Her Christology presents a Jesus who saw God not as Abba, despite multiple attestations of this in the tradition, but as Divine Sophia, a female Wisdom figure (Gestalt), and himself as Sophia's prophet. She criticizes even Rosemary Radford

78

Ruether for a "heavy reliance on the historical Jesus," which to her is "troublesome" because it remains bound to an understanding of Jesus in masculine terms.[46] Nor will she allow an approach focused on "the option of the historical Jesus for the poor and outcast," for she argues that "we must ground feminist theology on wo/men's struggles for the transformation of kyriarchy" (her term for the rule of some men over others).[47]

In ecclesiology, scholars like Ernst Käsemann, confronted with an emphasis in the postapostolic generation on the ritual transmission of office, the teaching responsibility of the presbyter/bishops, the importance of preserving the apostolic tradition, and apostolic succession, reject all this as "early Catholicism." Though Käsemann acknowledges that this early Catholicism is evident in some of the later New Testament books, he dismisses it as illegitimate, an attempt to bind the Spirit to ecclesial structures, settling instead for a canon within the canon, Paul's doctrine of justification by faith.[48] James D. G. Dunn rejects the idea that any normative form of Christianity can be found in the New Testament; what the canon gives us is the irreducible diversity of Christianity.[49] Leonardo Boff analyzes the church from the perspective of liberation theology, interpreting the emergence of church offices in Marxist categories.[50] Ratzinger would see all these approaches as driven not by theological interests but by ideology.

Reading the Bible within the Church

Against such contemporary, often ideological exegesis, Ratzinger calls for "an exegesis rooted in the living reality...of the Church of all ages."[51] Christology is always the key. He argues that two hermeneutical principles govern theological research for the Catholic Christian. First, doctrine is to be based on scripture, "not on hypothetical reconstructions which go behind it," and, second, he stresses that scripture is always read within the living community of the church.[52] At the end of his lecture on the crisis in biblical interpretation that we considered earlier, he says simply that Christian faith itself is a hermeneutic that "allows the solitary possibility for the Bible to be itself."[53] Brown says something similar in his response to Ratzinger's lecture, arguing that "the Bible is the book of the church and that liturgy, church history, and the *sensus fidelium* are major hermeneutical tools."[54]

This emphasis on reading the Bible within the living tradition of the church has been a constant for Benedict throughout his career. In his *Jesus of Nazareth*, he calls attention to the process of "rereading" scripture through which older texts are reappropriated and reinterpreted in new historical contexts.[55] The Pontifical Biblical Commission made a similar point in its important 1993 document "The Interpretation of the Bible in the Church." Catholic exegetes, it argues, "approach the biblical text with a pre-understanding which holds closely together modern scientific culture and the religious tradition emanating from Israel and from the early Christian community."[56] Refusing to honor this principle risks turning the inspired books of scripture into a collection of disconnected historical texts no longer able to convey God's revelatory word to the Christian community. Since the Bible is not merely a collection of historical documents, the church that receives it as the word of God must continually turn to the work of "actualizing" and "inculturating" the biblical message within the living tradition of the community of faith, particularly in the liturgy, in a meditative reading of the texts (*lectio divina*), and in the church's pastoral ministry.[57] The conclusion states that Catholic exegesis must remain a properly theological discipline; it "does not have the right to become lost, like a stream of water, in the sands of a hypercritical analysis."[58]

In the introduction to another important instruction of the Pontifical Biblical Commission, "The Jewish People and Their Sacred Scriptures in the Christian Bible," Ratzinger appeals to the fathers of the church, who insisted on the internal unity of the Bible, and to Origen, who taught that Christ was the meeting point for all the Old Testament pathways. It was precisely this view, which saw Christ as the key to "the scriptures," rooted in the New Testament itself (cf. Luke 24:27), that was lost by the triumph of the historical-critical method, since it presupposed that the biblical texts "could have no meaning other than that intended by their authors in their historical context."[59] The instruction is careful to note in light of the horrors of the Shoah that Christians are not monopolizing the Jewish Bible by reading it christologically. Both a Jewish and a Christian reading of the Jewish Bible are possible, as the latter developed in a parallel fashion (no. 22).

Conclusion

Pope Benedict's works display a reverence for the priority of the divine initiative and thus for the integrity of the biblical witness in its fullness. He roots the possibility of communication between humans and the divine in the Logos, a term that affirms not just that meaning, reason, and intelligible communication characterize the divine, but also that the divine Logos has become human in the person of Jesus, entering into time and space. Thus, the gap between time and eternity has been bridged, and we are brought into relationship with God. This is what makes prayer possible. It is also the central article of the Christian Creed.

In many ways Benedict comes close to a Protestant reverence for scripture as God's inspired word at a time when many theologians, both Catholic and Protestant, are treating it more as a historical source of theology. He has serious concerns about how the use of the historical-critical method has lost a sense of the unity of the biblical tradition, dissolving it into a vast multiplicity of competing interpretations and ideological reconstructions, reducing it simply to literature. By training, he is a dogmatic theologian, not an exegete, but he is well acquainted with biblical scholarship and has been insightful in critiquing the rationalist biases of much contemporary exegesis. Familiar with the historical-critical method, he rejects a literalist, "proof-texting" approach, that is, "drawing final conclusions from isolated texts," rather than taking a comprehensive approach to scripture that respects its integrity. Thus, he argues,

> Neither the New Testament as a whole nor its individual authors follow a strict system of terminology. They grasp a thought from a particular perspective, but they do not systematize it. They speak in examples and with the finding force of the exemplary but also with the limitations inherent in the example, which can always be expanded by other examples and by other trains of thought. This means, of course, that its statements are not all equally pertinent.[60]

While Ratzinger's vast knowledge of the biblical tradition enables him shrewdly to characterize the motifs and themes in the scriptures, he seems unable to find anything of real value in the study of the development of the biblical texts. He is more interested in what the text says to the church today. But for systematic or dogmatic theology, for example, in the area of ecclesiology, the history that lies behind the texts is important. Such knowledge may indeed put a received meaning in a new context. To fail to pay careful attention to the situation in life of a text can miss its intended meaning. The church's ministerial office developed only gradually within the New Testament communities, which were able to live with considerable diversity in structure and theology. His concept of the apostle is more theological than strictly historical, though it is a theology rooted in the New Testament. Certainly, Mary Magdalene meets Paul's concept of apostleship (to have seen the risen Lord and have been "sent" on a mission to represent him), and many judge that Junia is identified as an apostle by Paul (Rom 16:7), as Ratzinger himself acknowledges.[61]

Similarly, the New Testament does not use the Greek word for "priest" (*hiereus*) of any Christian minister. Thus, to say, based on the linking in 1 Peter of the word *presbyter* with the apostle Peter as copresbyter and both with Christ as shepherd and bishop, that by the "end of the apostolic era there is a full-blown theology of the priesthood of the New Covenant in the New Testament" is at least questionable.[62] The development of the church from its roots in the Jesus movement and its different expressions in the various New Testament communities could have implications for the church of today. Benedict's insistence on basing theology on the received interpretation of scripture, without taking into account the history that may lie behind the text, risks ignoring the development evident within the New Testament.

In many ways, Ratzinger's approach is like that of Hans Urs von Balthasar, a critical theological reflection on the themes, metaphors, and images emerging from the New Testament tradition. Like von Balthasar, Benedict tends to describe the church using traditional sexual typologies, as Christopher Ruddy has perceptively noted: "The church is to be like Mary: receptive before active, contemplative and not bureaucratic, seeking only to let God's will be done."[63] It is these metaphors, typologies, and themes that provide the inspired basis for his theology, not mere history.

Still Benedict's insistence that the Christian faith itself, with its christological center, is the hermeneutic that allows the Bible to be itself is one that needs to be acknowledged today. Scripture is God's revelatory word; it needs to be approached in its integrity, not reduced to some a priori determination of how God interacts with the world or to a mere historical record of developing religious ideas. He insists on the unity of the biblical tradition, even if this is a theological principle, not "an immediate historical datum."[64] If the Bible is to be understood as God's word, it must be read and reread within the context of the life and liturgy of the church from which it originated. Only in this way can it be for the church a revelatory text.

Chapter 4

CHRISTOLOGY

Christology has always been a crucial concern for Pope Benedict. As we saw in the last chapter, long before he became pope, he had voiced objections to the way the historical-critical method was being used by contemporary scholars, particularly liberal Protestants in Germany in the fifties and sixties. In *Called to Communion*, a book on the church, he called attention at the very beginning to "the tangled thicket of exegetical hypotheses" concerning Jesus and the initial form of the Church with "a kind of aerial photograph" of biblical exegesis in the twentieth century. It is particularly interesting because it charts how christological interpretations have shifted and changed as a result of historical criticism.

First, the liberal exegesis of the late nineteenth century transformed the Jesus of the tradition into a noncultic individualist who reduced religion to ethics. "Such a Jesus, who repudiates cultic worship, transforms religion into morality and then defines it as the business of the individual, obviously cannot found a church."[1] When this liberal worldview collapsed after the First World War, what came next was a rediscovery of the church even among Protestants. No longer was Jesus seen as a critic of cultic worship, and there was a growing awareness that the Messiah could not be conceived of without his church. With this came a new recognition of the community-forming meaning of the Last Supper, while first Russian Orthodox and then Catholic scholars developed a eucharistic ecclesiology that saw the Eucharist as foundational to the church.

Finally, after the Second World War, a new variant of the old liberal theology reappeared with a new version of the earlier individualism. Jesus's message was interpreted eschatologically, based on Jesus's preaching of the liberating kingdom of God. He was seen as proclaiming the end of institutions, setting prophecy, charism, and creative freedom against priesthood, cult, and institution. The kingdom of God was interpreted in terms of political and liberation theologies, which in turn led to the opposition of a "popular" to an "official" church, little more than a Marxist-oriented interpretation of the kingdom to which Ratzinger has remained so opposed.

If Ratzinger's overview focuses primarily on European, particularly German, theology, still that theology continued to exercise a considerable influence on theology in the United States at least until into the eighties. The ever-finer distinctions produced by critical scholarship between the "Jesus of history" and the "Christ of faith," that is, the chasm between the Jesus of history and the Christ presented by the Gospels written in light of Easter faith, meant for Ratzinger that the figure of Jesus himself was receding further and further into the distance. We have already seen how the members of the Jesus Seminar dismiss the Markan narrative as theological rather than historical and discard more than 80 percent of the sayings of Jesus as inauthentic, pruning away any that speak of judgment, reward, or punishment beyond death. Their Jesus becomes a wandering cynic philosopher and social critic (Crossan), a charismatic sage and spirit person (Borg), or a wisdom teacher divinized by his followers (Mack). Other, more responsible scholars speak easily of a Hellenization of Christology in terms of divine sonship (Küng) or settle for a wisdom Christology, pruned of preexistence motifs (Haight).[2] But what is lost in this process is the Christ of the Christian tradition.

Concerned about this loss of the real Jesus, Pope Benedict presented his own Christology, developing it in three volumes. He began the work in 2003 and brought it to completion after his election as pope. *Jesus of Nazareth: From the Baptism in the Jordan to the Transfiguration* was published in 2007. Within the first five months of its appearance the book sold over two million copies. Two other volumes followed, *Jesus of Nazareth: From the Entrance into Jerusalem to the Resurrection* (2011) and *Jesus of Nazareth: The Infancy Narratives* (2012).

General Approach

In his 1968 *Introduction to Christianity*, Ratzinger began his Christology not from the Jesus of history but from the Apostles' Creed. He rejected attempts to establish Christology on a secure historical basis, arguing that such efforts were restricted to the phenomenal or demonstrable and were thus unable to produce faith or, in reality, they were based more on personal opinion than historical research.[3]

Yet from the beginning of *Jesus of Nazareth*, Pope Benedict makes clear that he takes for granted everything that the Second Vatican Council and modern exegesis teaches about literary forms and authorial intention. In the introduction he describes it as "in no way an exercise of the magisterium" but rather an expression of his personal search "for the face of the Lord."[4] The resulting book is a mixture of scholarly analysis, biblical commentary, polemic, and homiletic reflections. We will focus on the first volume, considering his general approach, his treatment of the preaching and ministry of Jesus, and his position on Jesus's self-understanding.

He spells out his method in the foreword. The historical-critical method remains "indispensable" (xvi), but he stresses the need to recognize its limits. He takes the unity of the Bible as a given, even if this is a theological datum, presupposing an act of faith, not immediately a historical one. He applauds the American method of "canonical exegesis," seeking "to read individual texts within the totality of the one Scripture, which then sheds new light on all the individual texts" (xviii; cf. *DV* 12). This recognition of the unity of scripture leaves room for a meaning that may go beyond the "precise sense the words were intended to convey at their time and place of origin" (xix), thus a properly theological interpretation, what biblical scholars often refer to as the "fuller sense." Since scripture is not simply literature or history, it must always be read within the living tradition of the people of God or the church. His own intention is to try to portray the Jesus of the Gospels as the real, "historical" Jesus "in the strict sense of the word" (xxii). Thus, he takes faith as his starting point, though he will read the texts with the help of historical methodology.

His approach, arguing that the Jesus of the Gospels is the historical Jesus, is controversial. Modern scholarship has presumed, at least since the time of Martin Kähler (1835–1912), a difference between the Jesus of history and the Christ presented by the Gospels. The church recognizes that the Gospels are the end product of a long process of development, from the words and deeds of the historical Jesus, through the oral preaching of the early Christian communities, to the actual writing of the Gospels by the evangelists.[5] Thus, most contemporary scholars regard much of what is attributed to Jesus in the Gospels as representing the oral preaching of the early communities or the theologies of the individual evangelists, even if this material preserves faithfully the sense of Jesus's words. Over the years they have developed criteria or principles for identifying the words and deeds that go back to the historical Jesus.[6] Benedict, of course, is fully aware of this and is generally careful not to assume that whatever is attributed to Jesus in the Gospels represents his *ipsissima verba*, his very words. History, however, is not his principal concern.[7] Important as it is, it cannot tell us what the text means today, as we saw earlier. As he says, "Historical-critical exegesis does not transmit the Bible to today, into my present-day life."[8]

One might say that the leitmotif of *Jesus of Nazareth* is the parallel the pope draws between the person of Moses in the Old Testament and Jesus in the New. The Book of Exodus presents Moses as one to whom the Lord used to speak "face to face, as one speaks to a friend" (Exod 33:11). The Book of Deuteronomy promises that God will raise up a new Moses, "a prophet like me from among your own people; you shall heed such a prophet" (Deut 18:15). But the book ends with a "melancholy" conclusion: "Never since has there arisen a prophet in Israel like Moses, whom the LORD knew face to face" (Deut 34:10). Here his principle of the continuity of scripture is engaged. The implication is that the promised "prophet like me" would be even greater than Moses, with an even more personal vision of God. Jesus of course is that prophet. This is the context in which the conclusion to the Prologue of John's Gospel is to be read: "No one has ever seen God. It is God the only Son, who is close to the Father's heart, who has made him known" (John 1:18).[9]

A Johannine Perspective

In many ways, the Gospel of John becomes the lens through which Benedict reads the Synoptic tradition, while that tradition is represented largely by Matthew. He shows how Jesus emerges from the Gospels as one who in giving the new Torah becomes the Torah in person, just as he is the Word of God, the true paschal lamb, the real temple, the true bread. Thus, he can find a high Christology not just in John but in the Synoptics as well. For example, the story of the transfiguration presents Jesus not just as the realization of the Feast of Tabernacles, with its themes of God's action in creation, history, and in the fulfillment of history, but also as "the living Torah, the complete Word of God" (317). While he acknowledges that the discourses in John are not historical, in the sense of something like recorded transcripts, nevertheless they cannot be reduced merely to later compositions of the Johannine School—"Jesus poems" as he calls them. The Gospel claims that "it has correctly rendered the substance of the discourses" of Jesus (229), which Benedict situates, following Martin Hengel, as coming from a group of disciples associated with the priestly aristocracy of Jerusalem (see John 18:15), part of the Hellenized Jewish upper class in that city (221).

Benedict finds good evidence to see Zebedee's son John, who he believes is identified in the Gospel as the bystander (John 19:35) or the disciple whom Jesus loved (John 19:26; 21:20ff.), as the true author of the Gospel. The "literary executor" or "transmitter" is the one Eusebius of Caesarea (d. ca. 338) identifies as Presbyter John (225–26); in the New Testament he appears as the sender and author of the second and third letters of John. Cardinal Carlo Martini, himself a biblical scholar who generally praises the pope's book, notes that "not everyone" would agree that "the current state of research perfectly allows us to see in John, son of Zebedee...the true author of the Gospel." He also observes that Pope Benedict is not an exegete but a professor of theology.[10]

Baptism and Temptations

The Gospel picture of Jesus coming from Galilee to the Jordan where John was baptizing, joining the sinners waiting on the banks, is for Benedict a sign of his solidarity with all people who have incurred guilt and yet yearn for righteousness. Already Jesus is entering into the sins of others, anticipating his death on the cross. Benedict's interpretation of the baptism is admittedly ecclesiastical, though he takes the words of John, referring to Jesus as "the Lamb of God who takes away the sin of the world" (John 1:29), as the actual words of the Baptist (21). He rejects as illegitimate psychologizing the idea that Jesus's baptism was for him a personal moment of discovery. The baptism reveals instead Jesus as the "beloved Son." He does not mention that Jesus may have been originally one of John's disciples, ultimately breaking with John and beginning his own movement, as a number of scholars today would maintain.[11]

The story of the temptations of Jesus takes the theme of Jesus's solidarity with sinners a step further; Benedict relates it to the descent "into hell" of the Apostles' Creed as something Jesus experienced, not just in his death, but rather throughout his life. The first temptation, to change stones into bread, challenges Jesus to offer evidence for his claims, providing bread for the hungry world as God fed the people of Israel with bread from heaven. The second tempts him to provide "bread and circuses," extravagant displays of power to convince the multitude of the truth of his teachings. The third, offering him kingship over the entire world, is the temptation to see his mission as political. And for Benedict this is not a new one in the church's history:

> This temptation to use power to secure the faith has arisen again and again in varied forms throughout the centuries, and again and again faith has risked being suffocated in the embrace of power. The struggle for the freedom of the Church, the struggle to avoid identifying Jesus's Kingdom with any political structure, is one that has to be fought century after century. (40)

So are efforts to establish a perfect society on earth through human effort, for humans cannot achieve that alone. The kingdom is God's work through those who open themselves to grace.

There is a subtlety to the temptations as Benedict interprets them. They are not temptations directly to evil but suggest a false realism to which we also can fall prey, substituting work for a better world rather than putting God first, as Jesus must do. The struggle over his own mission in the temptation stories touches something we must all confront: "At the heart of all temptations, as we see here, is the act of pushing God aside because we perceive him as secondary, if not actually superfluous and annoying, in comparison with all the apparently far more urgent matters that fill our lives" (28).

Jesus's Preaching and Ministry

Pope Benedict argues that *euangelion*, the Greek word for *gospel*, means far more than the traditional "good news." Originally a word used for an imperial decree, it means a saving message, or, in terms of contemporary linguistic theory, the gospel is *performative* speech, an action or power that enters the world to save and transform it. At its core is Jesus's proclamation that the kingdom of God is at hand (47).

The Kingdom of God

Benedict surveys three different dimensions to the interpretation of the kingdom in the fathers. The christological interpretation saw Jesus as the kingdom in person (Origen); the mystical or idealistic interpretation located the kingdom in human interiority; and the ecclesiastical related it in different ways to the church. While the last interpretation has tended to dominate in modern times, more recently the kingdom has been given an individualistic (Adolf Harnack), eschatological (Albert Schweitzer, Jürgen Moltmann), or most recently, secularist interpretation that sees the kingdom as the goal of history itself ("regnocentrism"), with religiously inspired peoples working to bring about a world of justice, peace, and environmental sustainability. Benedict, of course, rejects such regnocentric or secular-utopian interpretations of the kingdom because, in his view, they ultimately eliminate the divine, leaving the human person as the only actor on the stage (54).

Benedict's *Jesus of Nazareth* stresses Jesus's preaching of the kingdom of God more than his earlier works. At the same time, without attention to the social conditions that may have helped shape his teaching, viewing the Jesus of history through Johannine lenses risks overlooking Jesus's concern for the poor and the marginalized that is so evident in the Synoptics; we catch sight of it in parables where "the poor, the crippled, the blind, and the lame" are invited to the feast (Luke 14:21) or in the criticism of Jesus as "a friend of tax collectors and sinners" (Matt 11:19; Mark 2:16). It is difficult to overlook the social dimensions of the kingdom in the preaching of Jesus or his call to discipleship in the service of the kingdom.

For Benedict, the kingdom is like a grain of mustard seed, a small leaven within history; it means the lordship of God breaking in through Jesus's life and action (Luke 11:20). Thus, what is distinctive in Jesus's message is to be found in Jesus himself: "Through Jesus's presence and action, God has here and now entered actively into history in a wholly new way. The reason why *now* is the fullness of time (Mark 1:15), why *now* is in a unique sense the time of conversion and penance, as well as the time of joy, is that in Jesus it is God who draws near to us" (60–61). The entire preaching of Jesus, for Benedict, is about the mystery of his person (63).

The Sermon on the Mount

Benedict focuses on Matthew's account of the Sermon on the Mount, which presents Jesus as the new Moses, echoing the promise in Deuteronomy, and his teaching as the new Torah. Like Luke's version, Jesus's Sermon is addressed to the whole world yet demands discipleship as the *way* of following him. Central to the Sermon are the Beatitudes, which "might be called the actual condition of Jesus's disciples" who are poor, hungry, hated, and persecuted (71). There is a paradoxical quality to the Beatitudes; they are eschatological promises that, like Paul's teaching on the cross and resurrection and John's on "exaltation," turn the values of the world upside down, transposing the mystery of the cross into a lesson on discipleship as well as in Matthew's version, a "kind of portrait" of Jesus himself (74).

Similarly, Benedict sees the relationship between the two sets of petitions in the Our Father as comparable to the relationship between the two tablets of the Decalogue; both stress the primacy of the love of God, leading to the right way of being human, which necessarily entails love of neighbor (134). He argues that "the social commandments are theological commandments, and the theological commandments have a social character—love of God and love of neighbor are inseparable, and love of neighbor understood in this context as recognition of God's immediate presence in the poor and the weak, receives a very practical definition here" (125–26).

Thus, the Sermon on the Mount, while not without social relevance, is not a social program; it is not about poverty as such but about what it means to live from and for God. What did Jesus bring, asks Benedict? He brought neither world peace, nor universal prosperity, nor a better world. "The answer is very simple: God. He has brought God." The gradual revelation of the divine mystery, first to Abraham, then to Moses, to the prophets, and later in the wisdom literature, now has reached its fullness in Jesus; Jesus has brought God and the truth about our origin. Now we know God and can call on him. God alone is to be worshiped, not any earthly kingdom, not the tempter's promise of a future that offers hope to all (44).

A Rabbi Talks with Jesus

In one of the most moving sections of his book, Pope Benedict turns to Jacob Neusner's book *A Rabbi Talks with Jesus*. Neusner, imagining himself among Jesus's disciples on the mountain in Matthew's Gospel, finds himself able to follow Jesus's interpretation of the Torah, save for one point, the very centrality of Jesus himself in his message. He turns to Jesus's words to the rich young man (Matt 19:21) as evidence. As Benedict summarizes Neusner's argument: "Perfection, the state of being holy as God is holy (cf. Lev 19:2; 11:44), as demanded by the Torah, now consists in following Jesus" (105).[12] This Neusner cannot accept. He uses the dispute over the Sabbath (Matt 12:1–8) as further evidence of Jesus placing his own authority beyond that of the Torah. "He [Jesus] and his disciples may do on the Sabbath what they do because they stand in the place of the priests of the Temple; the holy place has shifted, now being formed by the circle made up of the master and his disciples" (108).[13] In Benedict's words: "Jesus understands himself as the Torah—as the word of God in person."

> The tremendous prologue of John's Gospel—"in the beginning was the Word, and the Word was with God, and the Word was God" (Jn 1:1)—says nothing different from what the Jesus of the Sermon on the Mount and the Jesus of the Synoptic Gospels says. The Jesus of the

> Fourth Gospel and the Jesus of the Synoptics is one and
> the same: the true "historical" Jesus. (110–11)

Note how Benedict conflates the Synoptic accounts with John's.
The heart of his argument in *Jesus of Nazareth* can be seen here. The
Jesus of the Gospels is the historical Jesus.

The historical-critical scholar might object that Matthew has
rearranged the Jesus material to portray Jesus as the new Moses,
even arranging his speeches in five great discourses to recall the
five books of the Torah. The pope's conclusion that Jesus understands himself as the Word of God in person, and thus that the
Jesus of the Synoptic authors and of the Fourth Gospel are essentially the same, goes beyond what strict historical-critical interpretation would allow.

Nevertheless, the pope has recognized that Jesus *does* put his
authority ahead of the law, behind which stands God, and he draws
the necessary conclusions. He notes that according to Matthew, the
people were "alarmed" at his way of teaching, claiming an authority that belongs to God, not simply "astonished" as modern transla-
tions like the RSV (and NAB) render it (Matt 7:28; cf. Mark 1:22;
Luke 4:3) (103). Few mainstream scholars would deny the authenticity of Jesus's Sabbath words, and many argue, correctly, that
Jesus himself is inseparable from the message he proclaims. Efforts
to reduce Jesus to a liberal rabbi mitigating Jewish "legalism" make
no more sense to Benedict than they do to Neusner, who as a Jew
recognizes clearly what is entailed by the claims of Jesus discernible
in the Gospels. Furthermore, Jesus's redefinition of family relationships (Matt 12:46–50) in his claim that his community of disciples
forms a new Israel constitutes for Neusner a violation of one of the
great commandments on which the social order of Israel is based.
Neusner concludes, "I now realize, only God can demand of me
what Jesus is asking" (115).[14]

The Fuller Sense

While recognizing the importance of the historical meaning of
the text, Benedict insists that biblical interpretation must go beyond
it to a properly theological interpretation (xxiii). He frequently
makes use of what scholars call the "fuller sense" (*sensus plenior*)

of scripture, as we saw earlier.[15] Again, this points to the properly theological task of telling us what the words mean today, as we saw earlier in considering his approach to scripture.

For example, in his discussion of the Our Father, he raises the question of the meaning of the difficult word *epiousios* in the fourth petition, translated as our "daily" bread. While it is most often understood as a petition for the bread we need to live, the fathers of the church almost unanimously understood it in a eucharistic sense. Benedict argues that "it is necessary to keep in mind the larger context of Jesus' words and deeds" (155). From this perspective, when one considers the important place bread holds in Jesus's message, from the temptations in the desert, through the multiplication of the loaves, to the Last Supper and the Bread of Life discourse in John 6, a consideration of Jesus's message in its entirety cannot exclude the eucharistic dimension of the petition (156).

Similarly, in Mark's account of the calling of the apostles, the text reads, "And he appointed [literally 'made'] twelve, whom he also named apostles" (Mark 3:14). Noting that the strange "made twelve" represents Old Testament terminology for appointment to the priesthood, Benedict concludes that the evangelist's words "thus characterize the apostolic office as a priestly ministry" (171). Arguing, as many do, that the language of priesthood does not appear until the early third century misses the point; what counts for Benedict is not historical development but what the language of scripture affirms. Similarly, the parable of the Good Samaritan is not merely a lesson on who is one's neighbor, though, of course, it is also that. But in a deeper sense it can be understood from the christological perspective so typical of the church fathers, who saw the half-dead man as humanity itself and the Good Samaritan as Christ (200). Benedict picks up what so many contemporary commentators miss: the evangelists' finely tuned references to the biblical tradition. Particularly in dealing with the Fourth Gospel, he traces out the christological meanings of images such as water, vine, wine, bread, and shepherd.

The Self-Understanding of Jesus

The New Testament authors used various titles, rooted in the biblical tradition, to express the meaning of Jesus. The title "Christ" (Hebrew *messiah*) is understandable only within a Semitic culture. Though Jesus most probably did not use this title himself, it was later so identified with his role that it was conjoined to his name, Jesus Christ, showing the inseparability of the person of Jesus and his work. The titles "Lord" and "Son" suggest his relationship to God. Lord (Greek *kyrios*) had become in the late Old Testament period a paraphrase for the divine name, Yahweh. Benedict focuses on the titles "Son of Man" and "Son," which, according to the Gospels, Jesus used for himself, as many mainstream scholars would acknowledge.

Son of Man

The title "Son of Man" is found only on Jesus's lips, with one exception (Acts 7:56). It was Jesus's preferred self-designation. Scholars divide the Son of Man sayings into three types: the first occurs in an apocalyptic context, speaking of the Son of Man who is to come in judgment; the second refers to the earthly ministry and authority of the Son of Man; and the third refers to his suffering and resurrection. Benedict notes the tendency of many scholars to consider only the first as authentic, though they argue for a distinction between Jesus and the one who is to come. He finds this approach questionable. Just as Jesus spoke in riddles and parables, his use of the title Son of Man both concealed the mystery of his identity and gradually made it accessible. The saying "the Son of Man is lord even of the sabbath" (Mark 2:27) is, as we saw earlier, evidence of the authority he claimed. In Benedict's Johannine reading of the text, "The magnitude of Jesus's claim—which is an authoritative interpretation of the Law because he himself is God's primordial Word—becomes fully apparent here" (325). Though he reserves discussion of the texts about the Son of Man coming in judgment to the second volume of his book, he argues on theological and

95

patristic grounds—against the judgment of many critical scholars—
that the sayings about the coming of the Son of Man, the authority
with which he acts, and his words about the "ransom for many"
(Mark 10:45) are essentially authentic, without insisting on the his-
toricity of any individual saying.

The Son

The title "Son of God" was widely used in the political theology of ancient Egypt, Babylon, and Rome as a term for the king or
emperor. In Israel, the notion of Israel as "firstborn son" was transferred to the Davidic kingship (2 Sam 7:12ff.; Ps 89:27ff.). The early
Christians saw this promise of a future king who would be adopted as
God's son as fulfilled in the resurrection of Jesus (Acts 13:32), citing
Psalm 2:7: "You are my son; today I have begotten you." But this was
more than simply New Testament theology; Jesus referred to himself
as "the Son," which, according to Benedict, gives the political title
"Son of God" its definitive Christian significance (338).

If "the Son" occurs most often in the Gospel of John (eighteen times), it also occurs in the Synoptics, in an often-remarked-on
passage that reflects the Johannine tradition: "All things have been
handed to me by my Father; and no one knows the Son except the
Father, and no one knows the Father except the Son and anyone
to whom the Son wills to reveal him" (Matt 11:27/Luke 10:22).
While Benedict argues that this passage "already contains the entire
Johannine theology of the Son" (343), he is not alone in judging
that the words here find their origin in Jesus. Walter Kasper sees
Matthew 11:27/Luke 10:22 as a "reworking of authentic words of
Jesus" who referred to himself as son in a unique way.[16] In addition,
Marinus de Jonge maintains that, in Matthew, Jesus "is portrayed
above all as the Son who operates in union with the Father."[17] Cer-
tainly Benedict is correct in stating that the term "the Son" finds its
true origin in Jesus's prayer (344).

I Am

More controversial from the perspective of the Jesus of history
is Benedict's argument that the "I am" sayings of John and one that
he finds in the Synoptics come from Jesus himself. Just as the Old

Testament uses "I am" to interpret the enigmatic name of Yahweh
(Exod 3:14; Isa 43:10ff.), so the author of the Gospel of John several
times puts the absolute revelatory formula "I am" (John 8:24, 28,
58) on the lips of Jesus. In addition, he uses the formula in at least
seven other passages where Jesus says, "I am the Bread of Life,"
"the light of the world," "the resurrection and the life," and so on.
Benedict sees even "It is I" of Mark 6:50 in the story of Jesus walk-
ing on the water as part of this same tradition, particularly as the
context in which it appears is a theophany (352).

Again, these "I am" formulas represent for Benedict not the
theology of the evangelists but, like the titles "Son of Man" and
"Son," terms at once concealing and revelatory that he says are possible only on the lips of Jesus (354). In other words, they are authentic sayings of Jesus that reveal his awareness of his oneness with the
Father. Jesus is claiming the uniqueness of his origin, his right to
utter the Father's self-designation and to speak the Father's revelatory word in his own name as Son (348). At the end of the book,
Benedict returns to reject again the charge that Nicaea Hellenized
Christian faith. The council's use of the Greek *homoousios*, or con-
substantial, represents not the adoption of an alien philosophy but
rather the capturing in a stable formula what emerged in Jesus's new
and different way of speaking with the Father (355).

Some Critical Questions

Jesus of Nazareth was written in large part to bridge what Benedict sees as the chasm opened by critical scholarship between the
Christ of faith and the historical Jesus (xi–xii). He argues, for example, that in various ways, the disciples were able to sense in Jesus
the presence of the living God himself during Jesus's ministry, thus
establishing the foundations for their post-Easter faith (302–3).

Some scholars will object that he asserts more than critical
scholarship can support. For example, without denying that Jesus
interpreted his death as an offering to inaugurate a new family under
God, Gerald O'Collins asks if he did so "precisely in the light of the
Suffering Servant of Isaiah 53? It is not clear that Jesus consciously
identified himself 'with the suffering and dying Servant of God.'"[18]

Jack Miles observes that Benedict breaks with the critical majority of scholars in treating the "floridly mythological episode" of the transfiguration as a historical event.[19] Others will question Benedict's readiness to place the Johannine "I am" sayings on the lips of the historical Jesus. Richard Hays says that the "total portrait of Jesus that Benedict draws stands in serious tension with the findings of historical criticism."[20] If he is rightly concerned about an overly critical approach to the historical Jesus, he overlooks careful efforts by scholars such as Richard Bauckham, Raymond E. Brown, James D. G. Dunn, Joseph A. Fitzmyer, Daniel J. Harrington, Luke Timothy Johnson, and N. T. Wright, four of them American.[21] Thus, his work remains Eurocentric in its orientation.

Woven through his treatment of Jesus's preaching is a thinly veiled polemic against using power to secure faith or identifying the kingdom with any messianic ideology or political structure. Again, in the story of the temptations, for Benedict it is the temptation to construct a kingdom "of this world" that Jesus rejects. This is a constant theme. But there is more to his position here than a deep antipathy toward political theologies. As Nichols says, the kingdom is not irrelevant to politics; "it is supremely relevant, but as an ethical, not an eschatological reality."[22] Benedict believes firmly that the kingdom of God cannot be established in history; it is God's work and lies beyond it. He contrasts Barabbas, whose name means "son of the father," with Jesus: "The choice is between a Messiah who leads an armed struggle, promises freedom and a kingdom of one's own, and this mysterious Jesus who proclaims that losing oneself is the way to life" (41). In a similar way, in his 2007 encyclical, *Spe Salvi*, he says, "Christianity did not bring a message of social revolution like that of the ill-fated Spartacus, whose struggle led to so much bloodshed" (no. 4).

Benedict has argued that one of the threats to democracy today "is the inability to come to terms with the imperfection of human affairs. The longing for the absolute in history is the enemy of the good in it."[23] Such efforts lead too easily to the state totalitarianisms such as we have seen in the twentieth century, with their social engineering that substitutes pragmatism for morality. Or they can result in various theocratic attempts to govern according to a religious ideology, as is often evident in Islamic societies. If the church becomes a political force, as has happened unfortunately in the past, it can

Christology

fall into either of these traps. D. Vincent Twomey, a former student
of Ratzinger, describes his teacher's political philosophy this way:

> All attempts to establish a perfect society (the kingdom
> of God on earth) are rejected by the New Testament. The
> New Testament rejection of justification by one's own
> effort is likewise a rejection of political theology, which
> would claim that a perfect society based on justice could
> be established by human effort alone. Perfect justice
> is, rather, the work of God in the hearts of those who
> respond to his love (grace). Justice in society cannot be
> achieved simply by changing the structure of society. It
> is, instead, the temporary result of continued imperfect
> efforts on the part of society's members.[24]

In *Spe Salvi*, Benedict stresses that structures are necessary and
important, but at the same time, "since man always remains free
and since his freedom is always fragile, the kingdom of good will
never be definitively established in this world" (no. 24).

If Benedict strongly resists the tendency in some liberation
christologies to turn Jesus into a latter-day prophet preaching God's
concern for the poor or a social reformer critiquing dehumanizing
structures and social sin, the Johannine perspective that so influences his presentation of the Jesus of the ministry risks ignoring
the social context that shaped his preaching and is reflected earlier
in the Synoptic Gospels. Commenting on the social divisions that
were growing in Jesus's time, Ben Witherington observes, "In such
a situation, parables about unlucky tenant farmers, day laborers in
vineyards, absentee landlords, unscrupulous middlemen and the
like would hardly have sounded like pious platitudes. They would
have rung true to the realities of life, a social commentary on how
the coming Dominion of God could ultimately change the situation."[25] But Benedict tends to spiritualize the Beatitudes and overlooks the repeated warnings against the danger of wealth in Jesus's
preaching (Mark 10:23, 25; Luke 12:15, 21; Matt 6:19–20). The parable of Lazarus and the rich man (Luke 16:19–31) becomes in his
interpretation not a condemnation of the rich man for his lack of
compassion but the rejection of his demand for a sign, while Jesus
himself becomes "the sign of Jonah" (214–17).

As Richard Hays has pointed out, "Benedict's portrait of Jesus is strongly Johannine: grounded in high-christological claims that Jesus was one with God, claiming a universalism that breaks the boundaries of Judaism, proclaiming a realized eschatology, and sketching a Jesus whose kingdom is not of this world and whose teaching contains minimal social ethics."[26] He focuses far more on the full christological meaning of Jesus as the Logos, the Torah in person, and the new temple than he does on the Jesus of the ministry and his call to discipleship in the service of the kingdom. Harvey Cox made a similar point long before *Jesus of Nazareth* was written. "In his thoughtful writing on Jesus, the prefect prefers to concentrate not on the prophet of Nazareth, but on the passion and sacrificial death of the divine Son of God." Although the difference is more one of emphasis, Cox's point was that the dispute between Rome and the liberation theologians was "about just how much the earthly life of Jesus should shape the church's work today."[27] The question is not insignificant.

Conclusion

Pope Benedict's first volume, *Jesus of Nazareth: From the Baptism in the Jordan to the Transfiguration*, is eloquent testimony to his christological faith. Written from the perspective of canonical criticism, it is a profoundly biblical work that seeks the face of Jesus in the fullness of the biblical tradition, though with special emphasis on John and Matthew. He is impatient with much of contemporary exegesis, which he says has been used "to put together the most dreadful books that destroy the figure of Jesus and dismantle the faith," an impatience evident in his sarcastic reference to the work of Russian writer Vladimir Soloviev, who portrays the Antichrist receiving an honorary doctorate in theology from the University of Tübingen (35). His concern is the faithful exposition of the Christ of the Gospels.

While he presupposes the importance of historical-critical scholarship and makes some use of it, his Christology is not critically grounded in the historical Jesus. He often ascribes more to the historical Jesus than many scholars would be able to acknowledge.

Because his primary concern is the meaning of the text for today, he is less interested in the history that lies behind the text. Nevertheless, his book is more spiritual and theological than critical. Constructing a Christology in this way, without grounding it in the Jesus of history, leaves it open to the often-heard charge that the church's christological doctrine underwent a "Hellenization," divinizing Jesus the teacher and healer by turning him into a god. Similarly, his concern to depoliticize recent interpretations of the kingdom of God may cause him to overlook the special concern for the poor and the marginal that is evident in Jesus's ministry and the warnings against the dangers of wealth found so often in his sayings. One risks losing the Jesus who proclaims good news for the poor and liberty for captives, so unmistakable in the Synoptic tradition (Luke 4:18).

Nevertheless, Benedict is fundamentally correct in arguing that the post-Easter faith could not have developed as it did if Jesus had not laid its foundation before Easter (303). His book goes a long way toward demonstrating the impossibility of separating the mission of Jesus from his person. It does not get lost in problematic reconstructions but traces the christological metaphors and images of the New Testament back to their Old Testament roots and forward to their fuller meaning in the ecclesial and sacramental tradition of the church.

He shows how Jesus's teaching and ministry are rooted in his filial relationship with the one he called Abba, Father. Thus, Benedict continues to work against any facile reduction of Jesus's preaching of the kingdom of God to a social gospel of human betterment. Nor can Jesus himself be reconstructed as a liberal rabbi replacing the prevailing "politics of purity" with a "politics of compassion." Still less can Christology be relativized for the sake of dialogue with other religions, particularly in Asia, a charge he makes against the work of John Hick and Paul Knitter.[28] For Benedict, Jesus is the kingdom of God in person. He came to give us a share in God's life, which is his own deepest identity.

Chapter 5

ECCLESIOLOGY

The church has always been at the center of Ratzinger's theological reflection, the point of departure for his theology. If his ecclesiology began with his dissertation on Augustine,[1] *Lumen Gentium*, the Second Vatican Council's Dogmatic Constitution on the Church, constitutes its focus. He has been described as "an exemplar of moderate universalist ecclesiological tendencies," which means that he stresses the universal church over its local or particular expressions.[2] He objects to any horizontal ecclesiology that reduces the church to a sociological entity or a merely human community.

For Ratzinger, the church is a *communio* (*koinonia*) founded on the Eucharist that is at once vertical, with God in Christ, and horizontal, among the believers themselves. The church's "permanent structure is not *democratic*, but *sacramental*, consequently *hierarchical*,"[3] since each particular church is presided over by a bishop who maintains its unity with the Bishop of Rome and thus with the universal church. His ecclesiology is more christological than pneumatological, since he argues that the work of the Spirit cannot be separated from that of Christ in establishing the church on its apostolic and Petrine foundations. We will begin with his early ecclesiological reflections.

The Church

Ratzinger developed his work on Augustine's ecclesiology in his 1969 book on the new people of God.[4] In this work, he sought to reconcile what he identified as the traditional ecclesiological polarities, either a stress on the church's visible, external side or an emphasis on her invisible, interior aspects. His approach was to develop a "eucharistic ecclesiology." Though this concept was first expressed by theologians in the Russian Orthodox tradition,[5] it was developed particularly in the work of Henri de Lubac and then by Ratzinger himself. It is the one Eucharist that binds Christians together into the one, indivisible Body of Christ, thus the one catholic and apostolic church. From de Lubac, Ratzinger also drew his patristic understanding of the mystery of Christ as a mystery of unity that heals the separations and divisions that are the results of sin. Ecclesial unity, the nature of the church, as a real *communio*, is a key theme.

Ratzinger has also long been interested in how the church should carry out its mission regarding the world. But as we saw earlier, he was critical of what he felt was the overly optimistic approach of Vatican II's Pastoral Constitution on the Church in the Modern World, *Gaudium et Spes*, which seemed to see the church and the world as equal partners. In Ratzinger's view,

> there is only one legitimate form of the Church's open-
> ness to the world, and so must it certainly always be. That
> form is two-fold. It is: mission as the prolongation of
> the movement of the Word's procession, and the simple
> gesture of disinterested serving love in the actualizing of
> the divine love, a love which streams forth even when it
> remains without response.[6]

Thus, the church turns its face toward the world in terms of mission and charitable service. Dialogue, while not unimportant, is more than a conversation between equals. What the church brings is the gospel, the word of salvation that is to be proclaimed. Already in 1964, he contrasts "the Few" (*die Wenigen*) of the church, entrusted with Christ's mission of bringing the good news of salvation in Christ, to "the Many" (*die Vielen*) of the world. This contrast will surface again in his sense that the church might well have to decrease in members if it is to carry out its true mission.

For Ratzinger's mature ecclesiology, we will rely on several of his works: his essay "The Church's Nature and Structure" in his book *Church, Ecumenism and Politics*; his little book *Called to Communion*, particularly the opening chapter, "The Origin and Essence of the Church"; and his extensive treatment of the *successio apostolica*, or apostolic succession, in his *Principles of Catholic Theology*.[7] *Called to Communion* explores the nature of the church as a *communio* in word and sacrament, the relation between a eucharistic ecclesiology and the episcopal office, with the bishop's responsibility to maintain the local church in the *communio* of the whole church, and the foundation of the ministerial office of bishops and priests as a participation in the mission of Christ.

The Origin of the Church

For Ratzinger, the church has its origins in Jesus's gathering of the community of the new covenant. He sees historical analogies to Jesus's work in both John the Baptist and the community at Qumran; these also gathered communities of the end times, but as he says, in Jesus the imminent eschatology of John the Baptist passes into the "now" of Christology. He rejects any sharp contrast between the kingdom of God and the church, cleverly reversing Loisy's famous dictum, "Jesus preached the Kingdom; what came was the Church," by saying, "The Kingdom was promised, what came was Jesus."[8]

From the beginning, this new people of God had a structure; it was not "an amorphous mob," but centered on the Twelve, representing the twelve tribes of Israel. After the resurrection, the Twelve received the title "apostles."[9] The night before his passion Jesus transformed the Passover of Israel into an entirely new worship, breaking with Israel and the temple and establishing a people of the new covenant. The eucharistic words of institution look back to Sinai and forward to the new covenant. As we will see in considering Ratzinger's view of liturgy, "The Body of the Lord, which is the center of the Lord's Supper, is the one new temple that joins Christians together into a much more real unity than a temple made of stones could ever do."[10] Thus, the Eucharist becomes both the origin of the church and its center. This principle is foundational to Ratzinger's ecclesiology.

From apostolic times, this new people of God adopted the designation *ekklesia*, derived from the Old Testament root *qahal*, meaning "assembly of the people." However, the New Testament use was different from the term in the Greek world, where it meant only men who alone could serve as political agents; in the Hebrew it was inclusive of women and children. In the late Jewish period, a constant component of Jewish prayer was a supplication for a new *qahal* coming from God.[11] The early Christian community adopted the term *ekklesia* (in contrast to "people of God"), seeing itself as this new assembly, gathered by God in Christ. It signifies the church as a cultic gathering or local community, the church in a larger geographical area, or the one church of Christ itself.

Eucharistic Ecclesiology

Paul's doctrine of the church as the Body of Christ roots the church in the sacraments of baptism and Eucharist that, in turn, opens Christology up into Trinity. "The bread that we break, is it not a sharing in the body of Christ? Because there is one bread, we who are many are one body, for we all partake of the one bread" (1 Cor 10:16–17). Paul's formula, the church as the Body of Christ, "thus states that the Eucharist, in which the Lord gives us his body and makes us one body, forever remains the place where the Church is generated, where the Lord himself never ceases to found her anew."[12] Aidan Nichols calls this "the central motif" of Ratzinger's ecclesiology, which he along with Henri de Lubac adopted as "a full-scale, systematically elaborated, 'eucharistic ecclesiology.'"[13] The concept of the church as a *communio* is key:

> The Church is *communio*; she is God's communing with men in Christ and hence the communing of men with one another—and, in consequence, sacrament, sign, instrument of salvation. The Church is the celebration of the Eucharist; the Eucharist is the Church; they do not simply stand side by side; they are one and the same.[14]

Thus, Ratzinger argues that the Last Supper is the actual foundation of the church; it provides the church with its fundamental constitution, "for the Church lives in eucharistic communities."[15]

There is also what he calls a "nuptial" dimension to his ecclesiology; he sees the church as the Body of Christ, not in virtue of an identity without distinction but rather in the way "a man and woman are one flesh, that is, in such a way that in their indissoluble spiritual-bodily union, they nonetheless remain unconfused and unmingled," that is, by a "pneumatic-real act of spousal love."[16] This means that there is a tenuous dimension to this mystery of love; it is not simply given, but is a personal event challenging the church constantly to become what it must be and from which it can always fall short.

Ratzinger concludes his chapter by turning to Luke's narrative ecclesiology in his Acts of the Apostles. Here the church is portrayed as an assembly with diverse orders from its earliest moments in the upper room, as a community adhering to the teaching of the apostles, the breaking of the bread, and to the prayers (Acts 2:42). The church is thus united by word and sacrament, though the word is tied to the institutional role of witness, a preview of the apostolic succession. The Pentecost event reveals a church that is already both catholic and universal, both key themes as we will see later.

The Apostolic Office

Ratzinger sees the concept of the apostle as one who is sent, rooted in Jesus's being sent by the Father and his sending of the apostles (see Luke 10:16; John 20:21).[17] "The Twelve," the first of those later called apostles, represent the origin and foundation of the new Israel. In the post–New Testament period, particularly as the church struggled against the anti-institutional model of the free development of the word, the church looked to the apostolic succession in certain key churches, Rome, Antioch, and Alexandria, among which Rome, where both Peter and Paul had suffered martyrdom, was seen as truly normative. For Ratzinger, the apostolic succession has a sacramental efficacy in mediating the tradition. Holy Orders is the sacramental expression of the principle of tradition.[18] While the teaching ministry (papal and episcopal) acts against the background of the faith of the whole church, interpreting and expressing it, it can also anticipate or demand assent: "there resides in the teaching ministry, under certain conditions, the possibility of authentically and therefore bindingly distinguishing true faith from false."[19]

Episcopal Collegiality

The college of bishops is the successor to the community of the twelve. Ratzinger points to the concept of episcopal collegiality as one of the main pillars of Vatican II's ecclesiology. He singles out the work of the Belgian liturgical theologian Bernard Botte as opening the door for the council's development of collegiality, stressing that its origins lie not in concerns over power sharing but in worship, with its liturgical orders. Collegiality works on two levels. Each bishop is surrounded by a council of presbyters, and the bishops together form an *ordo* or *collegium* (the terms are virtually interchangeable); later the term *ordo* was used for the sacrament of orders, or ordination. Thus, this collegiality in succession belongs to the essence of the bishop's office.[20]

Collegiality does not mean that the church universal has a central government, for according to *Lumen Gentium* (no. 22), the college has plenary power only when gathered in an ecumenical council or in the agreement of all bishops with the pope. According to Nichols, Ratzinger believes that making the episcopal college the church's central government would introduce a centralism more burdensome than the present papal Curia, while giving increased power to the synod of bishops would result in bishops being absent from their churches for considerable periods of time. Bishops perform their responsibility toward the universal church best when they guide their particular churches and keep them in communion with one another.[21]

The Petrine Primacy

Although Ratzinger acknowledges that the primacy of Peter and its continuance or "succession" in the bishop of Rome is the most difficult ecumenical problem, he argues that the primacy is necessary for the unity and community of the universal church, with which every particular church and bishop must be in communion. "The Roman Primacy is not an invention of the popes, but an essential element of ecclesial unity that goes back to the Lord and was developed faithfully in the nascent Church."[22] Roman centralism is dispensable. "What is, however, indispensable to the Church's unity is the attentive obedience of all to the definitive interpretation of faith offered at the chair of Peter."[23]

Ratzinger seeks to show how the primacy of Peter, with its origin in the Lord, is recognized by all the major New Testament traditions; even the great Rudolf Bultmann agrees. However, the Petrine texts have meaning for the church and its constitution not because one or another scholar acknowledges them as authentic but because they are included in the canon, which the church recognizes as the word of God. He rejects the Protestant view that the succession is merely in the words of scripture and not in any "structures," for in the New Testament and the fathers of the church the word is always tied to specific witnesses, something already evident in the Acts of the Apostles and the Pastoral Letters.[24] Nor do these witnesses speak simply on their own; there is a "threefold" binding of word, witness, and Holy Spirit and Christ already recognized within the New Testament by the laying on of hands. Here lies the root of his understanding of the apostolic succession.[25]

The Church as Communio

The rediscovery of the eucharistic character of the church has helped retrieve the notion of *communio*, a notion that, for the church fathers, united two important aspects of life in Christ—*ekklesia*, or the gathering of people, and *communio*, their communion in Christ and with one another. Ratzinger writes,

> The Church is communion; she is the communion of the Word and Body of Christ and is thus communion among men, who by means of this communion that brings them together from above and from within are made *one* people, indeed, one Body.[26]

Thus, the "center of the oldest ecclesiology is the eucharistic assembly—the Church is *communio*."[27] Because *communio* is anchored in the Eucharist, the church is not born as a "federation of communities." It is born of the one bread that makes it one body.[28] Ratzinger is careful to distinguish the traditional concept of church as *communio* from what he sees as a popular misunderstanding of *communio* ecclesiology today, reducing it to an emphasis on the church as an aggregate of self-sufficient local churches. For him, the key is always to be found in the concept of the apostolic succession, which sees the bishops precisely as successors to the apostles maintaining the two dimensions of *communio*: the vertical communion with the apostolic church, and the horizontal communion of the bishops and their churches with one another. The horizontal communion, however, must be "diachronic" as well as "synchronic." In other words, it includes communion not just with all the believers at any moment in the church's life but also with all the faithful of all times. He appeals to this double dimension of communion to reject what he sees as a misuse of the concept of the people of God, arguing for change on the basis of what some group or generation of the church wants: "The Church lives her life precisely from the identity of all the generations, from their identity that overarches time, and her real majority is made up of the saints."[29]

At times one hears the argument that Ratzinger has substituted an emphasis on *communio* for Vatican II's metaphor of the church as the people of God. But Ratzinger is a careful scholar who, because of his vast knowledge of biblical studies, uses terms with a rare precision. Noting that some seized on the council's discovery of "people of God" to turn the church into a sociological entity, he argues that the biblical evidence does not support this. In fact, in the New Testament "people of God" rarely means "church," probably only in two cases. Its ordinary reference is to Israel. As a consequence, he argues that chapter 2 of *Lumen Gentium* on the people of God does not lay a foundation for a theology of the laity; it refers to the church as a whole, which the subsequent chapters treat in its different classes, hierarchy (chapter 3), laity (chapter 4), and religious (chapter 6). This attempt to interpret people of God from a sociological and political perspective is not new in Christian history but goes back as far as Eusebius of Caesarea (263–339 CE). In more modern times, it has been used to construct an antihierarchical and antisacral view of the church.[30] Ratzinger finds this especially in what he calls the "ecclesiological relativism" of Leonardo Boff. According to Boff, there were at the beginning only different local churches with different theologies and different offices. Therefore, no institutional church can declare itself the one church willed by

God, as all churches are human constructions arising out of socio-logical imperatives.[31]

If Ratzinger is critical of ecclesiologies that overemphasize the horizontal dimension of communion, others argue that his own ecclesiology neglects it. According to Philip Franco, he "puts little emphasis on the horizontal bonds of human community and therefore has little to say in terms of social justice and other issues of human solidarity."[32] Dennis Doyle observes that "Ratzinger scarcely refers to human solidarity and makes no ecclesial claims about it."[33]

Church Local and Universal

We noted earlier that Ratzinger maintains the ontological and temporal priority of the universal church over the local or particular church. For example, he has written that "the priority of the universal church always preceded that of particular churches."[34] This position was later reaffirmed by a letter of the CDF (1992) entitled "Letter to the Bishops of the Catholic Church on Some Aspects of the Church Understood as a Communion" (no. 9). Similarly, *Apostolos Suos*, John Paul II's 1998 apostolic letter on the theological and juridical nature of episcopal conferences, maintains that being a member of the college of bishops precedes the office of being head of a particular church (no. 12). Though Ratzinger insists that the priority of the universal church does not identify the universal church with the Roman church, especially with the pope and the Curia,[35] a number of theologians have taken issue with his view.

Part of the problem stems from Vatican II's failure to develop an adequate theology of the local church. Walter Kasper, while agreeing with Ratzinger and the CDF that the universal church cannot be seen simply as the sum of the particular churches, argues that declaring that the universal church is ontologically and temporally prior to the particular churches moves beyond how Vatican II understood the relationship of the particular church to the universal church. Specifically, in reference to the particular churches, modeled on the universal church, the council taught that "it is in and from these that the one and unique catholic church exists" (*LG* 23).[36] Others have argued that Vatican II's ecclesiology remains universalist, emphasizing the universal church at the expense of the local church. According to Hermann Pottmeyer, a "fear of shared governance by the bishops" at Vatican II led to a one-sided emphasis on the pope's freedom to act; "it is striking that nothing is said with comparable clarity about the obligation of the pope to involve the bishops in decisions affecting the universal church."[37] Christopher Ruddy maintains that because the council failed to resolve the relationship between the local churches and the universal church, its documents remain universalistic: "In short, a juridical ecclesiology triumphs over an ecclesiology of communion, and the question of priority, which seemed at first to be a minor, even esoteric academic exercise, shows itself to be of the highest importance for the life and ministry of the church."[38] The differences between these two views are not insignificant; they have practical as well as theoretical consequences.

Richard Gaillardetz has written that the universalist ecclesiology emphasized by the Vatican since 1985 has resulted in many bishops putting the priority on their relationship with the universal church, meaning Rome, to the detriment of their accountability to their local churches and corresponding responsibility to represent their churches' concerns. This unilateral vision of their role, prioritizing their relationship to the Bishop of Rome, is rooted in the council's ambiguity over a bishop's relationship to the episcopal college and to the local church that he serves.[39] As Killian McDonnell says, "The ontological and temporal priority of the universal Church becomes completely problematic when by some secret unspoken assumption (*unter der Hand*) the Roman church is de facto identified with the pope and the curia."[40] From a practical perspective, "the model of an ontologically prior universal church has meant that the voice of human experience rising up from local communities has found little echo in Rome."[41] Even questions such as how bishops are selected—chosen by the local church or simply appointed by Rome—are all consequences of emphasizing the universal church at the expense of the local. Addressing this overemphasis on a universalist ecclesiology could help restore the proper relationship between the universal and the local.

Apostolic Succession

For Ratzinger, the *successio apostolica* is the essence of the church's catholicity and apostolicity; this is another of his foundational ecclesiological principles. While the celebration of the Eucharist, the administration of the sacraments, and the proclamation of the word are all elements of the concrete identity the church takes in history, he argues that "since the confrontation with *gnosis*, the *successio apostolica* has consistently been regarded as the basic form of this identity."[42] For him, apostolic succession means guaranteeing the continuity and unity of the faith in a continuity that is sacramental and seeing that the church retains its universality and unity, rather than lapsing into a sort of federation of local churches.[43]

Ratzinger has frequently identified apostolic succession as the key question between Catholics and Protestants. Because Luther reduced the Eucharist to an "assurance to the individual's troubled conscience that his sins have been forgiven," the Reformation lost the sense of the eucharistic context of *communio* as constitutive of the church as well as of Christ's "gathering together of the dispersed Adam into the *communio* of *agape*."[44]

Ratzinger credits Vatican II with retrieving the recognition of the episcopate as the fundamental form of the sacrament of orders, as well as making clear again that the *successio* structure is a sacramental (and not merely organizational) link with tradition. But it can't be reduced to a mechanical theory, a pipeline of sacramental power. "The *successio*-structure is the expression both of the link with tradition and of the concept of tradition in the Catholic Church."[45] He dismisses attempts to supply the succession through an arranged imposition of hands as "apocryphal," as though the rite could be separated from the church, an attempt to "dig one's own private channel to the apostles. It is, rather, an expression of the continuity of the Church, which, in the communion of the bishops, is the *locus* of tradition."[46] One cannot be a bishop alone, without entering into the *successio* or the episcopal college. The bishops (unlike the pope) succeed not individual apostles but the apostles in general.[47] In this way, the bishops link their churches with the *communio* of the entire church and with the apostolic church, as we have seen.

112

The lack of the *successio apostolica* clearly affects the ecclesial status of an ecclesial community. He asks, "Can the essential character of the word and the essential character of the Church be present where there is a break with the concrete continuity of the Church that celebrates the Eucharist with the bishops?"[48] In an article responding to the recent debate about "a community's right to the Eucharist," implying that lacking a priest, a community could simply provide its own Eucharist, Ratzinger makes several interesting arguments. First, he argues that neither Catholic theology nor Vatican II used the term *community*, which is originally a Protestant concept. The council speaks of the concept of church on three levels—universal, local, and particular. Though some of the later conciliar texts do refer to the *communitas Christiana* (*AG* 15), the meaning of this term is not fixed. He traces the concept of church as community to Martin Luther, who used *church* to designate a pagan shrine in his translation of the Old Testament but regularly used the word *community* (*Gemeinde*) for church.[49] For Luther, "the Church withdrew into the local community. Only the congregation that hears the word of God on the spot is the Church. Hence it substituted the word congregation or community for that of Church, which became a negative concept."[50]

Second, because he sees catholicity as the formal principle of Christianity, Ratzinger argues that unity with the universal church is not something added on but is a constitutive element of the eucharistic celebration:

> To celebrate the Eucharist means to enter into union with the universal Church—that is, with the one Lord and his one Body....The outward sign that one cannot manipulate the Eucharist at will and that it belongs to the universal Church is the *successio apostolica*: it means that no group can constitute itself a church but *becomes* a church only by being received as such by the universal Church.[51]

Third, when the concept of catholicity is reduced or removed from the concept of church, the understanding of the Eucharist itself is changed: "Its theological meaning is then sought primarily in the meals Jesus took with sinners, which deprives these meals of their great symbolic function as the expression of Jesus's divine power to forgive sins and of the coming of the kingdom."[52]

Ecumenism

Ratzinger's ecumenical vision is based on the primitive church's life as *ecclesia in ecclesiis*, the one church existing in many (local) churches, though he specifically excludes equating this with the present plurality of denominational churches.[53] With a nod to Oscar Cullmann, he accepts descriptions such as "unity through diversity," "unity in diversity," and "a reconciled diversity."[54] But always the concept of the apostolic succession is central, as is communion with the Bishop of Rome; in reference to the Orthodox churches, the CDF said, "Since...communion with the universal Church, represented by Peter's Successor, is not an external complement to the particular Church, but one of its internal constituents, the situation of those venerable Christian communities also means that their existence as particular Churches is *wounded*."[55]

In commenting on the debate over ecumenism in his 1966 report on Vatican II, Ratzinger summarized the views of Protestant professor Edmund Schlink of Heidelberg, given in Rome in October 1963. Schlink objected to the "Roman Church" identifying itself in an exclusive manner with the one, holy, catholic, and apostolic church, suggesting instead that the church of Jesus Christ exists in a plurality of churches. Ratzinger's response was to agree that indeed a multiplicity of churches exists within the one, visible church, but to be church, each must be in communion with the other churches that make up the church. This view, which he maintains is that of the New Testament, does not mean separated denominational communities but rather the many worshiping communities, or what today are referred to as particular churches, which are united in the one church. Ecumenism from a Catholic perspective does not mean the absorption of the other denominational churches but rather the hour when "'the Churches' that exist outside 'the Church' will enter into its unity. But they must remain in existence as *Churches*, with only those modifications which such a unity necessarily requires."[56]

Ratzinger's position has not essentially changed since his post-conciliar reflections, but he developed them at greater length in *Church, Ecumenism and Politics*, reflecting on the Anglican–Roman Catholic International Committee (ARCIC) and on relations with the Lutherans, primarily in Germany.[57] "The real goal of all ecumenical efforts must of course remain the transformation of the plural [sic] of confessional churches separated from one another into the plural [sic] of local Churches that are in their diversity really one Church."[58] Nichols teases out from his articles here three unacceptable solutions.[59] The first is an ecumenism "from below," a kind of "grassroots ecumenism" that tries to bring about unity from the base but ends up only with splinter groups of the like-minded that further divide communities. The second is "from above," a decision by church authorities to join separated churches, in the hope that the faithful would follow their lead, as suggested by the proposal of Heinrich Fries and Karl Rahner.[60] The third Nichols calls a "horizontal ecumenism," based on a false egalitarianism that reduces Christian confessions to different "traditions" without serious regard for whether they are grounded in scripture and the apostolic tradition. I find also a fourth, the Protestant view that unity is an eschatological rather than a historical quality. Ratzinger raises and rejects this view; the "true Church" is not a utopia that may emerge at the end of time but is a reality that exists now, "without...having to deny that other Christians are Christians or to dispute an ecclesial character on the part of their communities."[61]

In responding to a request for an article on the present state of the ecumenical movement in 1986 from the editor of the *Tübinger Theologische Quartalschrift*, Ratzinger sketched briefly his understanding of ecumenism as a "unity in diversity," urging that Catholics not pressure Protestants into recognizing the papacy and the Catholic understanding of apostolic succession, while Protestants should refrain from pressuring Catholics toward intercommunion:

> For us the twofold mystery of the body of Christ—the body of Christ as the Church and the body of Christ as sacramental gift—is a single sacrament, and dissociating the bodiliness of the sacrament from the bodiliness of the Church means crushing both the Church and the sacrament underfoot.[62]

115

He has consistently argued that the separation between Rome and Constantinople did not negate the basic form of the church that had developed prior to Nicaea, for the apostolic succession belongs essentially to this structure. Because of this fundamental unity, he once argued (though has since revised) that

> Rome must not require more from the East with respect to the doctrine of primacy that had been formulated and was lived in the first millennium....Reunion could take place...if, on the one hand, the East would cease to oppose as heretical the development that took place in the West in the second millennium and would accept the Catholic Church as legitimate and orthodox in the form she had acquired in the course of that development, while, on the other hand, the West would recognize the Church of the East as orthodox and legitimate in the form she has always had.[63]

Resolving the differences with the Protestant communities, which lack the unity of doctrine and structures of the ancient church, is much more difficult. Taking the Lutheran churches as a model, Benedict advocates not the dissolution of the Protestant confessions but precisely strengthening them in their ecclesial reality so that they are truly binding. The proposal that the Catholic Church recognize the Lutheran Augsburg Confession (CA) on its 450th anniversary as reconcilable with Catholic faith as it was originally intended to be represented one example. Ratzinger rejected this proposal, arguing that the Lutheran emphasis on *sola scriptura* meant that the CA remains only theology; it does not have for Lutherans the authority that would indicate that the church can teach precisely as church. Does it, for example, as the oldest personal statement of Protestant faith, stand as a normative interpretation against later, more polemical confessions such as the Schmalkaldic Articles, which speak of the pope as the antichrist? Thus, a prerequisite for Catholic recognition of the CA would be its Protestant recognition.[64] He also has some objections to its content—that it is not concerned chiefly with "certain traditions and abuses" but rather addresses a wide range of ecclesial forms of life and doctrine in a way that is not compatible with Catholic faith.

Protestant Eucharists

Ratzinger's position on the validity of the Protestant Eucharist is not always clear. He apparently holds that the Protestant Eucharists are not valid and yet that Christ is truly present. Thus, he writes that the Catholic teaching in regard to the Eucharist recalled in *Mysterium Ecclesia* (1973) "does not in any way deny that Protestant Christians who believe in the presence of the Lord also share in that presence."[65] In 1993, he wrote to Lutheran bishop Johannes Hanselmann as follows:

I count among the most important results of the ecumenical dialogues the insight that the issue of the eucharist cannot be narrowed to the problem of "validity." Even a theology oriented to the concept of succession, such as that which holds in the Catholic and in the Orthodox church, need not in any way deny the salvation-granting presence of the Lord [*Heilschaffende Gegenwart des Herrn*] in a Lutheran [*evangelische*] Lord's Supper.[66]

At the same time, in his commentary on Pope John Paul II's apostolic letter *Ad Tuendam Fidem* (1998), he stated that among those truths "to be held definitively" was the 1986 judgment of *Apostolicae Curae* that ordinations carried out according to the Anglican Rite are "absolutely null and utterly void" (no. 36).[67] As Michael Root has argued, what Catholic theology needs is a category that recognizes a "more or less," different from the absolutely valid or invalid, "a flexible, scalar category to apply to the episcopacy and ministries of the ecclesial communities, especially to the churches of the Lutheran and Anglican communions that affirm and practice episcopal succession."[68]

What seems for Ratzinger to be missing is not sacramental grace but union in the faith, tradition, and communion of the church of which the apostolic succession is the expression. He writes, "Unity with all other communities is not just something that may or may not be added to the Eucharist at some later time; rather, it is an inner constitutive element of the eucharistic celebration. Being one with others is the inner foundation of the Eucharist without which it does not come into being."[69] His argument against sacramental sharing is not based on the invalidity of the Protestant sacrament, but "because communion in the body of Christ is the bodily form of communion in the truth, in the unity of faith. Sacrament and faith are inseparable; if communion is not communion in faith then it is nothing."[70] Reconciliation demands communion in the apostolic faith, which is why joint agreements such as the 1998 Joint Declaration on the Doctrine of Justification between Lutherans and Catholics are so important for him; indeed, he played an important role in winning its acceptance.[71]

Ratzinger's focus on Lutheranism reflects his own German background.[72] While he is more comfortable with the confessional churches, he seems to have little personal contact with Evangelical and Pentecostal Christianity. This is regrettable, as these communities represent the most rapidly growing expression of the church today. But many of them are not liturgical communities centered on the Eucharist, and few would understand apostolic succession in the way that he does. Regardless, he recognizes that Evangelicals have discovered a new commonality with Catholicism, particularly as the traditional Protestant churches make an accommodation with secularization that the Evangelicals and Pentecostals often see as a betrayal.[73]

Conclusion

Pope Benedict's ecclesiology sees the church's structures as christologically grounded in Jesus's choice of the Twelve and their role in the primitive church. Key concepts include the constitutive nature of the Eucharist, the church as *communio*, the *successio apostolica*, and the Petrine ministry. The concept of *communio* informs all of his theology. His ecclesiology is biblical and christological, rooted in the picture of apostleship, Petrine ministry, church, and *communio* that emerges from the New Testament authors and the canon itself.

Ratzinger and now Pope Benedict's emphasis on the Eucharist as the foundation of the church, without denying the work of the Spirit, results in the Spirit's role being much less evident in his ecclesiology. Following his teacher, Augustine, he identifies the Spirit with what is shared by the Father and the Son. Thus, the Spirit can also be known as love (*caritas*) and gift (*donum*). Its fundamental activity is to unite and draw into an abiding unity.[74] Given the Spirit's unitive task, he rejects any opposition between Spirit and institution, an idea he attributes to certain heretical movements in the Middle Ages and to the Reformation as well as to modern romanticism. "For Augustine, the idea that the Spirit manifests himself only in what is discontinuous, only in the chance eruptions of self-taught and self-formed groups, is utterly inconceivable."[75]

Throughout his long career, Benedict has emphasized the apostolic succession as the basic form of the church's identity, linking the interpretation of scripture to the church's episcopal teaching authority, a linkage he sees the Reformation as rejecting. A document from the CDF in July 2007 reaffirmed that because those Christian communities born of the Reformation in the sixteenth century "do not enjoy apostolic succession in the sacrament of Orders," they "cannot, according to Catholic doctrine, be called 'Churches' in the proper sense."[76] The language could have come from what Ratzinger has written over the years, just as the 1992 CDF letter on the church as communion repeats his emphasis on the ontological and temporal priority of the universal over the local church.[77] Even if he does not identify the universal church with Rome, his emphasis on the ontological and temporal priority of the universal church does not help resolve Vatican II's failure to explain adequately the relationship between the local churches and the universal church, giving the bishops a true participation in its government.

Though Benedict stated in an address the day after his election as pope that his primary task was "the duty to work tirelessly to rebuild the full and visible unity of all Christ's followers,"[78] the ecumenical landscape is going through a process of rapid change, as Cardinal Walter Kasper, then president of the Pontifical Council for Promoting Christian Unity, noted in a November 2006 address.[79] The changes, of course, cannot all be laid at the door of Benedict. Kasper pointed to a new emphasis on denominational identity; lack of agreement on the foundations and goals of ecumenism; the rapid growth of Evangelical, charismatic, and Pentecostal communities; and Konrad Reiser's "new paradigm," a secular ecumenism that stresses collaboration for justice, peace, and freedom rather than visible unity through theological dialogue.

119

In the immediate future, more ecumenical progress seems possible with the Orthodox than with the Protestant communities. The Orthodox are increasingly concerned about the growing secularism of Europe, both East and West, as well as with the influence of Islam, and the former Russian patriarch Alexi II was much more comfortable with Pope Benedict XVI, a German, than he was with Pope John Paul II, a Pole. However, Patriarch Kirill's support of Vladimir Putin's brutal 2022 invasion of Ukraine has complicated ecumenical relations considerably. Catholics and Protestants will continue to work together, but full communion, with sacramental sharing, will remain a more distant goal. Ecclesiological differences are still significant, with many Protestants stressing diversity not just in ministerial and theological expression but in the nature of the church itself.[80]

In Germany, the expression "ecumenism of profiles" describes such a juxtaposition of diverse if not contradictory forms of church, seen not as an obstacle to unity but as an important source of religious identity. For example, the World Council of Churches' document on ecclesiology, "Called to Be One Church," states, "Each church is the Church catholic and not simply a part of it. Each church is the Church catholic, but not the whole of it."[81] In responding to the July 2007 CDF response on the doctrine of the church, Clifton Kirkpatrick, stated clerk of the General Assembly of the Presbyterian Church (USA), affirmed this WCC statement as part of his critique. Pope Benedict would consider such an egalitarian approach to ecclesiology an example of the relativism he is so much against.

There are also new issues that have immeasurably complicated the ecumenical agenda. Recently Kasper made clear that the elevation of women to the episcopacy in the Church of England would destroy any chance for full unity with the Catholic and Orthodox churches, adding that the Catholic Church would inevitably refuse to recognize the validity of Anglican orders.[82] Moreover, there is little evidence that the Anglican and Protestant churches will reverse themselves on these questions. Thus, agreement on the nature of the church and its ministry remains perhaps the most pressing ecumenical problem.

Chapter 6

LITURGY

The liturgy has shaped Pope Benedict's experience of the faith since his boyhood in Bavaria. Very early he became enchanted with the rituals and drama of the Mass. He has left us a lyrical description of his appreciation of liturgical time while he was still a boy living in Aschau:

> The Church year gave the time its rhythm, and I experienced that with great gratitude and joy already as a child, indeed, above all as a child. During Advent the "liturgy of the angels" [Rorate Mass] was celebrated at dawn with great solemnity in the pitch-black church illuminated only with candles. The anticipated joy of Christmas gave the gloomy December days their own particular character.... Then, on Holy Saturday evening, the celebration of the Resurrection was especially impressive. Throughout Holy Week black curtains had covered the windows of the church so that even during the day the whole space was filled by a mysterious darkness. When the pastor sang the words "Christ is risen!" the curtains would suddenly fall, and the space would be flooded by radiant light.[1]

Ratzinger has always had this sense for the mysterious, even cosmic character of the liturgy. It is always something received, "a reality that no one had simply thought up, a reality that no official authority or great individual had created." This "givenness" of the liturgy means that it is not to be tinkered with. Its texts were mysterious, something that had developed over the centuries, reflecting the ancient faith of the church: "It bore the whole weight of history within itself, and yet, at the same time, it was much more than the product of human history. Every century had left its mark upon it."[2] His love for the liturgy was enhanced by Romano Guardini's work, *The Spirit of the Liturgy*, one of the first books he read as he began his theological studies after the war. Guardini, who introduced the liturgical movement to Germany, saw the liturgy as the expression of the church's inner essence.

As Eamon Duffy notes, there is a certain element of nostalgia in the way Ratzinger writes about his early experience of the liturgy, the smell of flowers and the freshness of the birch trees, the young men firing their guns in salutes at the village Corpus Christi procession, his perhaps uncritical gratitude for the Bavarian Catholicism that formed him.[3] At Vatican II he had supported efforts to reform the liturgy. He referred to the Latin Mass of his youth as "archaeological," arguing that its meaning was "a closed book to the faithful" and that the saints of the Catholic reformation such as John of the Cross and Teresa of Avila drew none of their spiritual nourishment from it. He also called for the "active participation of the faithful" and suggested that Latin, at least in seminaries, "is no longer the vehicle of movement for the human spirit."[4]

But Ratzinger has not been happy with what he sees as the current state of the liturgy. One of the only changes in his own thinking that he has been willing to acknowledge comes in regard to liturgical renewal. He says, "At the beginning of the Council, I saw that the draft of the Constitution on the Liturgy, which incorporated all the essential principles of the liturgical movement, was a marvelous point of departure for this assembly of the whole Church....I was not able to foresee that the negative sides of the liturgical renewal movement would afterward reemerge with redoubled strength, almost to the point of pushing the liturgy toward its own self-destruction."[5]

Though he does not criticize what he calls the missal of Paul VI, the normative liturgy introduced after the council, he has bitterly objected to the fact that Pope Paul prohibited the use of the old missal created by Pius V (1570) after the Council of Trent. He saw this as unprecedented, a move that set one missal against the other without allowing for the process of growth and purification, making the new missal appear not as a living development but as the work of scholars and juridical authority. Vatican II needs to be understood as a stage of development, not as a breach: "I am convinced that the crisis in the Church that we are experiencing today is to a large extent due to the disintegration of the liturgy."[6] He goes on to speak of the need for a new liturgical movement, using at times the phrase a "reform of the reform."[7]

The Feast of Faith

Ratzinger's first book on the liturgy was a collection of his essays, published in 1981 in German as *Das Fest des Glaubens* (*The Feast of Faith*). He begins by responding to what he sees as a widespread view that human beings have outgrown the need or even the possibility of calling on a transcendent God and instead are challenged to a self-transcendence, perhaps best understood as working for a better future. He does not, however, see these arguments as particularly novel; he reduces them to three: first, the rejection of metaphysics, and with it the idea of a creator; second, the modern scientific and technological worldview, which rules out any idea of a divine intervention; and finally, the more serious argument of Aristotle about the impossibility of the eternal entering into relationship with the temporal. Each of these would seem to rule out the possibility of prayer. In response, Ratzinger argues that Christianity's trinitarian doctrine reveals that relationship, speech, and Logos are present in God; this is the ontological foundation of prayer.[8] We can address God because God has already addressed us in Jesus, the Word made flesh.

Having established the theological basis for prayer and liturgy, he turns to its form and content in the Eucharist. But those formed in the post–Vatican II liturgical tradition will sense a discordant note here. Pointing out that the liturgical studies between the wars had focused not on rubrics but on the form (*Gestalt*) of the liturgy, he turns to the work of Joseph Jungmann to show that the basic structure of the Eucharist was not the meal but, from the end of the first century, has been *eucharistia*, a term used as early as Ignatius of Antioch (d. 110), the prayer of *anamnesis*, or memorial, in the shape of a thanksgiving. Indeed, he argues that, after 1 Corinthians 11:20, the Eucharist was not referred to as a meal again until the sixteenth century. Luther's use of the word "Supper" (*Abendmahl*) was a complete innovation. Though there are meal elements to the

Eucharist, "the eucharistic prayer is an entering-in to the prayer of Jesus Christ himself; hence it is the Church's entering-in to the Logos, the Father's Word, into the Logos' self-surrender to the Father, which, in the Cross, has also become the surrender of mankind to him."[9] Thus, he sees the basic structure of the Mass not as meal but as *eucharistia*, a thanksgiving for a spiritual sacrifice, Jesus's self-offering to the Father into which we enter through the eucharistic prayer. The Eucharist is first and foremost prayer and worship. This has implications for posture at Mass. Because it is prayer, it is neither necessary nor appropriate for those in the congregation to be able to look at each other while praying or receiving holy communion. All should face the image of the crucified.[10]

He rejects the view that the Last Supper should be seen as the basis of the Christian liturgy; "the Last Supper is the foundation of the dogmatic content of the Christian Eucharist, not of its liturgical form. The latter does not yet exist."[11] Nor does the Eucharist develop out of Jesus's table fellowship tradition, an idea he sees as reflecting a Lutheran identification of Eucharist with the doctrine of justification as a pardoning of sinners. He argues that the Eucharist cannot be reduced to an inclusive meal of hospitality. This was not the understanding of the early church. "Whereas Paul says that those who approach the Eucharist in sin 'eat and drink judgment' upon themselves (1 Cor 11:29) and pronounces an anathema to protect the Eucharist from abuse (1 Cor 16:22), proponents of this view see it as the essence of the Eucharist that it is available to all without distinction and without conditions."[12] He specifically rejects the idea that the Eucharist was originally a simple meal of fellowship with the disciples or that it was a continuation of the meals Jesus shared with sinners. On the contrary, the "Eucharist is not itself the sacrament of reconciliation, but in fact it presupposes that sacrament. It is the *sacrament of the reconciled*, to which the Lord invites all those who have become one with him." Thus, there are conditions for participating in it.[13] It is in his critique of the meal as the heart of the Eucharist that Ratzinger's liturgical views appear most at odds with much of popular liturgical thinking. As Duffy says, "Reject the paradigm of the meal as the interpretative key to the Mass and the inner logic of many of the post-conciliar changes collapses, from the reorientation of sanctuaries to the deliberate cultivation of community in such institutions as the holy handshake."[14]

For Ratzinger, the origins of the Eucharist are to be found in the specifically eucharistic action, which was not identified with Passover but was placed within the new context of the "Lord's Day," the day marking both the first day of creation and the new creation represented by Christ's resurrection.[15] Thus, there is a cosmic dimension to the liturgy, which he describes with reference to Romans 3:24–26 as a "tearing open the closed-up heavens."[16]

The Spirit of the Liturgy

Ratzinger's next liturgical book, *The Spirit of the Liturgy*, is deliberately reminiscent of Guardini's book of the same title.[17] Though he observes that it is less a systematic treatment of the liturgy than a collection of insights, it has an advantage over *The Feast of Faith* in that it is not just a collection of occasional essays but develops many points more thoroughly.

He begins by comparing the liturgy at the time Guardini wrote in 1918 to a fresco that had been completely overlaid with whitewash. The liturgical movement and the council uncovered it again, but since the council, it has been endangered by climate, restoration, and reconstruction. Ratzinger's book is eloquent, even lyrical in describing the liturgy in the church's tradition as he surveys history, culture, theology, and art with a remarkable familiarity, but as he reveals his own views on questions of participation, practice, and posture, he continues to deconstruct much of what has become the received liturgical wisdom since the council.

To summarize, he argues that because of the ancient tradition, both churches and congregations, including the priest (he does not like the term presider), should face east, that turning the priest toward the people has turned the community into a self-enclosed circle (80), and that the cross should stand in the middle of the altar as a common point of focus (83). He maintains that the Eucharist is primarily a sacrifice, not a meal, that contrasting a personal rather than a "thing-centered" view of the Eucharist is "nonsense," since the only presence is that of the whole Christ (98), and that the greatness of the liturgy depends on its "unspontaneity" (*Unbeliebigkeit*) (166). Creativity, for him, cannot be an authentic liturgical category

(168). He sees the "active participation" of the faithful of which Vatican II spoke as meaning, not multiple "parts," but entering into the action of God taking place through the words spoken by the priest (171–72). Kneeling remains indispensable to liturgical prayer, especially at the "Consecration" (212), and dancing is not a form of expression for Christian liturgy, while applause means that it has become entertainment (198). The priest need not always say the eucharistic prayer or canon aloud but might just say aloud the first words of each prayer, leaving a space for reverent silence (215).

Each of these positions needs to be more carefully considered. We need to look at what we might call the "foundations" of his liturgical theology and then at some of its characteristic themes or "principles."

Foundations

Ratzinger begins by arguing that the cultic history of Israel leads "by its inner logic to Jesus Christ, to the New Testament."[18] Israel's worship was distinctive in that it was directed not at subordinate "principalities and powers," which the Israelites increasingly saw as alienating humans from God and themselves, but at the one God, whom they worshiped through an extensive sacrificial system. His analysis builds on the biblical narratives, which must be taken in their integrity. First, Genesis tells the story of Abraham's willingness to sacrifice his only son, Isaac. The lamb that God provides as a substitute at the last moment becomes the type of Christ, the true Lamb of sacrifice who comes from God, a theme traced through the Fourth Gospel (John 1:29; cf. 1 Pet 1:19) and Revelation, where the lamb once sacrificed is at the center of the heavenly liturgy (Rev 5). Second, Exodus recounts the institution of the Passover. Here also the focus is on the Passover lamb at the center of Israel's liturgical year and memorial of faith, as well as on the "firstborn," which was to be consecrated to God (Exod 13:2).

In reviewing worship in the Old Testament, Ratzinger illustrates convincingly how Israel's whole sacrificial system underwent a transformation, a critique from within the tradition. What was developing was a purification of the concept of sacrifice. The prophets especially stressed that obedience or submission or love of God was better than sacrifice (1 Sam 15:22; Hos 6:6; cf. Ps 50:12–14;

Amos 5:25–27; Matt 9:13; 12:7), a theme that would be taken up by Jesus. Thus, sacrifice does not necessarily consist in the destruction of a victim or the transfer of property. Ratzinger links this critique with the charge brought against Jesus at his trial, the claim that he said, "I will destroy this temple that is made with hands, and in three days I will build another, not made with hands" (Mark 14:58). This charge points in turn to Jesus's action in the temple, the so-called cleansing of the temple, which Ratzinger interprets as an attack on the whole cult of the temple with its system of animal sacrifice. With the resurrection, he notes,

> The new Temple will begin: the living body of Jesus Christ, which will now stand in the sight of God and be the place of all worship. Into this body he incorporates men. It is the tabernacle that no human hands have made, the place of true worship of God, which casts out the shadow and replaces it with reality.[19]

The story in the Synoptic Gospels of the tearing of the veil of the temple, from top to bottom, symbolized that the time of the old temple has come to an end.

Here emerges into view the foundational principle of Ratzinger's understanding of the liturgy. From now on, the body of Christ made present in the Eucharist in his self-offering to the Father, his spiritual sacrifice, becomes the new temple, the true place of meeting between God and God's people. It is the Eucharist that constitutes the church, as we have seen. Ratzinger sees this idea of a spiritual sacrifice or worship, *logike latreia*, already growing in the exilic and postexilic periods, particularly in the Hellenistic era, when "the word of prayer" came "into prominence as the equivalent of exterior sacrifice."[20] But there are other principles that stand out in his liturgical theology.

Continuity of the Testaments

The foundation for Ratzinger's theology of the liturgy rests on his presumption of the fundamental unity and continuity of the Testaments, as we saw earlier.[21] This is not at all a given today. Many Protestants and not a few Catholic theologians—though they recognize that the Old Testament points toward the New—argue for a radical discontinuity between the two Testaments. In a sense, they have gone beyond the replacement theology of the Hellenist Jewish Christians, reflected in the Letter to the Hebrews. What the Christ event means is that temple, priesthood, sacrifice, and altar all belong to the past, to the first covenant. With the Christ event comes a spiritualizing of the tradition. The temple is now the New Testament community, "a holy temple in the Lord...a dwelling place for God" (Eph 2:21–22). Priesthood is finished with Christ's sacrifice; the New Testament knows a priestly people (1 Pet 2:5–9), but only ministers. Christ the high priest has offered the once-and-for-all sacrifice for sins (Heb 9—10); there are no more sacrifices. The Eucharist is thus not a sacrifice but a "festive" or inclusive meal, the altar more properly a table, the priest a presider. The sacred itself is secularized; it is not to be found in a place but in the people themselves. Ratzinger is familiar with these arguments and rejects them.

Active Participation

Key to the modern liturgical movement and the liturgical reforms of the Second Vatican Council was the principle of the "active participation" of the faithful in the liturgy: "Mother Church earnestly desires that all the faithful be led to that full, conscious, and active participation in liturgical celebrations which is demanded by the very nature of the liturgy" (SC 14).

The council was reacting in part to the tendency that had developed in the church of the second millennium and especially in the period after the Council of Trent in which the faithful were reduced largely to spectators at the liturgy. The language, Latin, was for most of them foreign. They did not respond to the priest's prayers; rather, altar servers responded for them. Nor did they take the parts of lectors or extraordinary eucharistic ministers. They received only the consecrated bread, not the cup, and most received infrequently. The kiss of peace had been reduced to a sign exchanged by the priest, deacon, and subdeacon at a solemn high Mass.

Ratzinger rejects the idea that "active participation" should be understood to mean that as many as possible should be visibly engaged in the liturgical action. The *actio* to which the sources refer, he argues, is the eucharistic prayer, the true liturgical act, the *oratio*, or "solemn public speech," spoken in the person of Christ by the priest. This is the real action in which all, priests and faithful, participate, the great action of the liturgy in which God is acting through Christ and the faithful are drawn into that action by God.[22] It is Christ's self-surrender to the Father, and thus, that of humankind, as we have seen.[23] He acknowledges that the readings, singing, and bringing up of the gifts can be distributed among the faithful, but these are secondary matters. He is correct that sometimes too much business or even theatricality can empty the liturgy of its dignity and sense of mystery.

But the faithful are not to be mere spectators. It is not enough to insist on an inner, spiritual participation. He does not quote the section of the Constitution on the Liturgy that says, "By way of promoting active participation, the people should be encouraged to take part by means of acclamations, responses, psalmody, antiphons, and songs, as well as by actions, gestures, and bodily attitudes. And at the proper times all should observe a reverent silence" (*SC* 30).

To the East

One of Ratzinger's most radical arguments is that the decision to redirect the position of the priest at Mass *versus populum*, toward the people, rather than with them, toward the altar, was seriously misconceived. The result "has turned the community into a self-enclosed circle. In its outward form, it no longer opens out on what lies ahead and above, but is closed in on itself."[24] The priest has now become the focus, as though the whole liturgy depended on him, and the community risks celebrating only itself. But this emphasis on community's action forgets that the community is not the primary subject; it is God who truly acts in the liturgy. The liturgy should be "*opus Dei* in which God himself first acts and we become redeemed people precisely through his action."[25] He notes with approval that, in spite of their great emphasis on the community character of worship, "when it is a question of praying together, Protestants, people and leader, together turn to the image of the Crucified."[26] "Where a direct common turning toward the east is not possible, the cross can serve as the interior 'east' of faith. It should stand in the middle of the altar and be the common point of focus for both priest and praying community."[27]

His argument rests on his reading of history, specifically, the principle that the church has always prayed toward the east, toward the rising sun, a tradition that goes back to the beginning. One early exception was Rome, where, for topographical reasons, the basilica of St. Peter was built facing west. "Thus, if the celebrating priest wanted—as the Christian tradition of prayer demands—to face east, he had to stand behind the people and look—this is the logical conclusion—toward the people," an arrangement that was apparently replicated in other churches in St. Peter's sphere of influence.[28] John Baldovin, a liturgical historian, acknowledges that he is at least in part correct in arguing for an eastern orientation:

> The current situation of priest and people facing one another makes it possible for the liturgy to depend too much on the personality of the priest. The argument that priest and people faced one another in the early church does not hold water in the face of the overwhelming evidence of praying toward the East. On the other hand, the evidence from the early church is extremely complex and there were almost certainly instances in "Westward oriented" churches where priest and people did face each other during prayer.[29]

Many would argue that the posture of the priest facing the people better accords with a deeper sense of the communal dimension of the liturgy and its origin in the meal Jesus shared with his disciples the night before he died. But Ratzinger has difficulties with these views as well.

Sacrifice Not Meal

Despite the fact that the earliest evidence we have for the church's celebration of the Eucharist identifies it as the "Lord's Supper" (1 Cor 11:20), Ratzinger insists that to see it as "assembly" or as "meal" seizes on individual elements while failing to grasp their historical and theological connections.[30] He maintains that seeing the essence of the liturgy as a communal meal is based on a mistaken idea of meals in antiquity, in which people faced not toward each other but away from one another around a "C" or horseshoe-shaped table. Indeed, he says that to "speak of the Eucharist as the community meal is to cheapen it, for its price was the death of Christ."[31] The word *Eucharist*, in pointing to the form of worship that took place in the incarnation, cross, and resurrection of Christ, is an appropriate designation for Christian worship. Its deepest meaning is to be found not in the meal, despite its establishment within the framework of the Passover meal, but in the fact "that the Eucharist refers back to the Cross and thus to the transformation of the Temple sacrifice into worship of God that is in harmony with *logos*."[32]

In many ways, *The Spirit of the Liturgy* is an eloquent testimony to Ratzinger's love for the liturgy. As a thinker of remarkable complexity and depth, he moves easily from comparing the nuance of a particular term in the Hebrew or Greek texts of the Old Testament, or from tracing the development of Augustine's theory of music, from the early influence of Pythagoras to his rethinking the celestial harmonies in terms of the angelic choirs and the creative power of the Logos, or to identifying modern rock concerts as a secular form of worship that gives expression to elemental passions.[33] One can only learn from this book.

At the same time, the book fails to explore adequately other important aspects of liturgical theology. Neither this nor Ratzinger's earlier book develops the pneumatological dimension of the Eucharist, a common failing of Western theology, which tends to slight the work of the Spirit. While *The Spirit of the Liturgy* gives an eloquent defense of the practice of kneeling in the tradition, he does not explain the reference in the Roman Canon to the *circumstantes*, those "standing around" the altar. Some would dispute his interpretation of the twentieth canon of Nicaea, which outlawed the apparently novel practice of kneeling during the Sunday Eucharist. Ratzinger interprets this as a special dispensation for standing during the Eastertide.[34]

Sacramentum Caritatis

In 2007, Pope Benedict published *Sacramentum Caritatis*, his post-synodal apostolic exhortation on the October 2005 Synod of

Bishops on the Eucharist. Many had awaited this document with some anxiety, seeing it as a test case of the direction the pontiff would take on matters liturgical. There had been some discouraging signs. Recent Vatican instructions had emphasized the differences between the ordained and the nonordained. A 1997 instruction from eight Vatican dicasteries tended to reserve the term *minister* to the ordained and forbade the laity to use titles such as pastor, chaplain, coordinator, or moderator, while the nonordained should be referred to as extraordinary ministers when helping to distribute communion.[35] In October 2005, the president of the United States Conference of Catholic Bishops received a letter that stated, at the direction of Pope Benedict, extraordinary ministers of holy communion would no longer be permitted to assist in the purification of the sacred vessels at Masses. Long-standing rumors that the pope would extend broader permission for use of the Tridentine Mass were realized on July 7, 2007, when he released a motu proprio, a document released "on his own initiative," granting permission for priests to celebrate the 1962 missal of John XXIII "as an extraordinary form of the single Roman rite."[36]

Some feared that the pope would use the expected post-synodal letter to address his concerns about priest and people facing "toward the east" in the liturgy. Yet others like Eamon Duffy noted that Benedict "has more than once indicated his sensitivity to the dangers of liturgical fatigue among the laity, and he has said that constant change, even change back towards the traditional ways of doing things, can be very destructive."[37]

Benedict's exhortation, released on March 13, 2007, proved to be far more pastoral than prescriptive. Treating the Eucharist in three major sections, "The Eucharist, a Mystery to Be Believed," "The Eucharist, a Mystery to Be Celebrated," and "The Eucharist, a Mystery to Be Lived," the exhortation weaves together doctrine, liturgical practice, and what Benedict calls "spiritual worship" (*logike latreia*). What emerges here is the new voice of Pope Benedict as universal pastor, not that of the professor, who in his earlier book *The Spirit of the Liturgy*, occasionally lapsed into sarcasm. While responding to specific concerns raised by the bishops at the synod held in Rome, the exhortation also seeks to draw out some of the themes addressed in his first encyclical, *Deus Caritas Est*. It stresses Benedict's view of the Eucharist as constitutive of the church's being and activity precisely as a mystery of communion (no. 15) and reaffirms both the practice of priestly celibacy (no. 24) and the inadmissibility of those who are divorced and remarried without an annulment to the sacraments (no. 29).

In the first part of the letter, "The Eucharist, a Mystery to Be Believed," Benedict stresses that Jesus in the Eucharist "does not give us a 'thing,' but himself" (no. 7). The Eucharist makes us sharers in God's own life, received as a free gift (no. 8). Instituted at the Last Supper in the context of a Jewish ritual meal (no. 10), it is truly something new, so the ancient Hebrew sacrificial meal does not need to be repeated. The ancient rite has been surpassed by the gift of the incarnate Son, who draws us into his act of self-oblation or sacrifice and into himself (no. 11). Indeed, the word *sacrifice* appears over forty times in the letter. The pope calls for a "renewed awareness of the decisive role played by the Holy Spirit in the evolution of the liturgical form and the deepening understanding of the sacred mysteries" (no. 12) and especially with regard to transforming the gifts into Christ's body and blood and the faithful into one Body (no. 13).

In treating the Eucharist as a mystery to be celebrated, in the encyclical's second part, Pope Benedict introduces the term *ars celebrandi*, the art of proper celebration, as a way of ensuring the active participation of the faithful. It notes, in contrast to his earlier words in *The Spirit of the Liturgy*, which seemed to redefine active participation, that Vatican II taught that the people take part not "as strangers or silent spectators" (*SC* 48). Non-Catholic Christians, lacking full communion with the Catholic Church, generally may not receive the sacraments of Eucharist, reconciliation, or the anointing of the sick, though he notes that the *Catechism of the Catholic Church* and its *Compendium* admit of certain exceptional situations, and he asks Christians who are not Catholic to understand and respect Catholic conviction, which is grounded in the Bible and tradition (no. 56). He calls special attention to the need of the sick, prisoners, and migrants to share in the Eucharist and suggests that for certain large-scale celebrations Latin might be used (no. 62).

The final section on living out the eucharistic mystery reaffirms the practice of eucharistic adoration, nuancing it with a citation from Augustine, who said, "No one eats that flesh without first adoring it; we should sin were we not to adore it" (no. 66). The section includes five paragraphs drawing out the social implications of the sacrament, stressing the demands of justice, the church's social teaching, and concern for the environment (nos. 88–92), though emphasizing again that it is not the proper task of the church to be engaged in political action (no. 89).

The exhortation very much reflects Benedict's own thinking. Rich in citations from scripture and the fathers of the church, it is far more pneumatological than his earlier books on the liturgy. His frequent use of the terms *worship* and *liturgy* reflects his understanding of the Eucharist as God's work, as our incorporation into the sacrifice of Christ. The emphasis is on the Eucharist as the work of Christ; there is less emphasis on how the faithful join in the celebration beyond their uniting themselves with Christ's sacrifice. Only once does he use the term *thanksgiving* in reference to the eucharistic prayer, and there is little on the theology of the assembly. He refers to the ministerial priesthood six times, but only twice does he mention the royal or baptismal priesthood.

Summorum Pontificum

Benedict's motu proprio relaxing restrictions on the use of the 1962 Latin *Missale Romanum* appeared in July 2007. It was a carefully balanced document. He argued that the 1962 missal of John XXIII, the last revision of the earlier missal (often referred to as the "Tridentine Mass"), had never been abrogated, and he explained in an accompanying letter to the bishops of the world, "What earlier generations held as sacred, remains sacred and great for us too, and…cannot be all of a sudden entirely forbidden or even considered harmful." The pope gave priests permission to celebrate according to the Roman missal promulgated by Pope John XXIII as an extraordinary form of the liturgy of the church (art. 1).[38] The accompanying norms in the motu proprio decreed that priests of the Latin Rite celebrating Masses without the faithful could use the 1962 missal without special permission on any day except in the Sacred Triduum (art. 2); that communities or institutes could use this missal in their own oratories, "often, habitually, or permanently" (art. 3); that members of the faithful who desire to attend the liturgies mentioned in article 2 could be admitted (art. 4); that in parishes where

Liturgy

a group of faithful attached to the previous tradition "exists stably," pastors could accede to their requests (art. 5.1) on any weekday but at only one such celebration on Sundays or feast days (art. 5.2); that such celebrations could be requested for special occasions such as weddings, funerals, or occasional celebrations such as pilgrimages (art. 5.3). At Masses celebrated with the faithful, the readings could be proclaimed in the vernacular, using approved editions (art. 6); and groups of faithful who do not obtain their request from their pastor are encouraged to inform the diocesan bishop, who in turn should refer the matter to the pontifical commission, *Ecclesia Dei* (art. 7).

The pope's letter to the bishops explained that the two editions of the missal were not to be considered two different rites; rather, the one Roman missal has two forms, the normal form, the missal of Paul VI (1970), and an extraordinary form, that of John XXIII (1962). Since the use of the old missal presupposes special liturgical formation and some knowledge of Latin, he found fears of disarray or division within parish communities unfounded. The motive behind the motu proprio was the desire, first expressed by Pope John Paul II, to reconcile to full unity with the successor of Peter those in the Society of Saint Pius X, the movement begun by Archbishop Marcel Lefebvre, though the pope acknowledges reasons deeper than liturgical ones behind the break. The reason motivating his decision is to come to "an interior reconciliation in the heart of the Church." He makes clear that priests ordained for communities following the former usage "cannot, as a matter of principle, exclude celebrating according to the new books," which would not be consistent with the new rite's value and holiness. In perhaps his most personal statement, his letter refers to a lack of fidelity to the liturgical prescriptions in the celebration of the new missal:

> The latter actually was understood as authorizing or even requiring creativity, which frequently led to deformations of the liturgy which were hard to bear. I am speaking from experience, since I too lived through that period with all its hopes and its confusions. And I have seen how arbitrary deformations of the liturgy caused deep pain to individuals totally rooted in the faith of the Church.[39]

135

Benedict hoped that allowing two forms for the use of the Roman Rite might prove to be "mutually enriching," with the sacrality of the former usage leading to the missal of Paul VI being celebrated with great reverence, bringing out its spiritual depth.

Conclusion

Pope Benedict's liturgical interests come together in his eucharistic ecclesiology. The Eucharist constitutes the church as a real communion in the body of Christ. "The Church is Eucharist."[40] In the Eucharist, the body of Christ becomes the new temple, the true place of meeting between God and God's people, who are caught up into Christ's self-offering to the Father, which through the cross becomes their own surrender to God. Therefore, the celebration of the Eucharist should be deeply prayerful and contemplative, relying more on silence, adoration, and music in the great tradition of the church than on spontaneity, creativity, and music more Dionysian in spirit.

He criticizes attempts of individuals or groups to adapt the liturgy, comparing "any kind of self-initiated and self-seeking worship" to the story of the children of Israel dancing around the golden calf.[41] He takes exception to the contemporary concern for "the experience of togetherness" and fostering community at the expense of the deepest meaning of the sacrament. Typically, his emphasis is on the "objectivity of the Eucharist," rather than on the "subjectivity of experience," for when experience is placed above sacramental reality, the congregation ends up celebrating itself,[42] forgetting that the liturgy is God's work, the *opus Dei*. His stress on the Eucharist as sacrifice and prayer rather than meal (thus his preference for a more formal, priest-centered liturgy with the congregation kneeling), his concern to emphasize the differences between the ordained and the nonordained, as well as his views on facing east, inclusive language, creativity, dancing all suggest a much more traditional approach to liturgy.

But the Eucharist is a multifaceted mystery. It could be argued that the term *meal* can help illumine the mystery of faith that we celebrate as much as *sacrifice* and *thanksgiving*. If the Mass is thanksgiving for the sacrifice of Christ, it is also the meal that nourishes us in our reception of his body and blood and unites us as his Body for the world; it is a sign and foretaste of the banquet we look forward to in the kingdom. Though Benedict's encyclical *Sacramentum Caritatis* develops the social implications of the Eucharist more than his earlier writings do, his approach risks a one-sided emphasis on Eucharist as including us in something already accomplished in Christ's sacrifice. Contemporary liturgists stress more the *ad extra* dimension of the liturgy, drawing us outside of ourselves through Christ's presence in assembly, presider, word, and sacrament, into his own mission: "It calls and empowers Christians to participation in what has not yet been completed, namely Christ's proclamation of the Kingdom of God."[43]

Many did not see Benedict's July 2007 motu proprio making the wider use of the 1962 missal as a positive sign. One noted that it would increase the occasions when women were not allowed in the sanctuary or that allowing the use of the preconciliar rites for all the sacraments except ordination meant that parents whose infants were baptized according to the Tridentine Rite would no longer be asked to respond.[44] Others observed that since the motu proprio makes use of the revised lectionary optional, some Catholic communities would no longer be hearing the same readings heard by most Catholics every Sunday or by the many Protestant communities that have adopted the revised Catholic lectionary. Certainly, Benedict's initiative reflected his own personal tastes as much as they did his desire to reconcile those who had been alienated by its loss. One senses a certain nostalgia for the style of liturgy and eucharistic piety he experienced in his youth. He writes frequently about adoration of the Blessed Sacrament. And while it is difficult to translate the Corpus Christi processions—he remembers so fondly blessing the farms and fields of Bavaria—into our urban or suburban communities today, he hopes that wider celebration of the "extraordinary form" of the Roman missal will help restore a greater sense of reverence to the "ordinary" form of the liturgy.

More positively, Benedict's liturgical initiatives may help the church recover some of the mysterious sense of the presence of the holy, which too often has been lost in contemporary liturgies. His calls for greater reverence and more silence in the liturgy are well taken. An overemphasis on the Eucharist as a communal meal has led to a loss of its sacrificial dimensions. If the experimentation of the 1970s and early 1980s is behind us, the language of lectors and presiders, at least in the United States, too often focuses on celebration, community, ministry, and hospitality, with far less attention to worship, entering into the holy, or approaching the altar of God. Too often our liturgies have become overly wordy, didactic, and even banal. Those coming to worship from a highly sensate culture, overstimulated, constantly connected electronically to iPods, cell phones, and computers easily tire of repeated liturgical formulas and eucharistic prayers. Ritual prayer no longer satisfies; they want variety:

> This is why, here especially, we are in such urgent need of an education toward inwardness. We need to be taught to enter into the heart of things. As far as liturgy is concerned, this is a matter of life or death. The only way we can be saved from succumbing to the inflation of words is if we have the courage to face silence and in it learn to listen afresh to *the Word*. Otherwise we shall be overwhelmed by "mere words" at the very point where we should be encountering the Word, the Logos, the Word of love, crucified and risen, who brings us life and joy.[45]

We do need a greater sense of inwardness in our liturgy. Hopefully this can be achieved without reclericalizing the liturgy as the exclusive action of the priest, consigning again to limbo the theology of the liturgical assembly. If we need inwardness in our liturgy, we also need a sense that we are active participants, not spectators, as well as a renewed sense of mission for the sake of the kingdom.

Chapter 7

A Retrospective

Joseph Ratzinger will be numbered among those theologians and churchmen who helped creatively channel the enormous energy released by the Second Vatican Council. As a young theologian, he played an important role in the development of some of the council's most important documents, among them the Dogmatic Constitution on Divine Revelation (*Dei Verbum*), the Dogmatic Constitution on the Church (*Lumen Gentium*), the Pastoral Constitution on the Church in the Modern World (*Gaudium et Spes*), and the Decree on the Missionary Activity of the Church (*Ad Gentes*).[1] He continued to play a major role after the council, both as a theologian and later as prefect for the Congregation for the Doctrine of the Faith.

From the beginning of his papacy, Benedict sought to counter the popular view that Christianity is nothing more than a collection of rules or prohibitions. This was particularly obvious in his encyclical, *Deus Caritas Est*. His deepest conviction is that being a Christian is the result of entering into a relationship with the person of Jesus. The encyclical presents a personal God who is love itself and who loves human beings and creation itself passionately. John Allen characterized his style as one of "affirmative orthodoxy, a tenacious defense of the core elements of classic Catholic doctrine, but presented in a relentlessly positive key," stressing what it is for rather than what it is against.[2]

For example, after a visit to Spain in 2006 for the World Congress of Families, he was asked by a German TV reporter why he refrained from mentioning controversial issues such as gay marriage, abortion, or contraception, all stressed by Spain's Socialist government. His answer: "Christianity, Catholicism, isn't a collection of prohibitions: it's a positive option. It's very important that we look at it again because this idea has almost completely disappeared today. We've heard so much about what is not allowed that now it's time to say: we have a positive idea to offer."[3]

A Cautious Reformer

Many scholars find a consistent if distinctive theological vision in his work.[4] His *Theological Highlights of Vatican II*, first published as small booklets in Germany after each session of the council, showed him embracing the council's reformist agenda, though somewhat cautiously.[5] After the first session, he lamented that the 2,500 bishops and faithful present at the council's opening liturgy were mere spectators. He wrote in favor of more active participation by the faithful and applauded the decentralization that allowed the various episcopal conferences to formulate, within limits, their own liturgical norms. Arguing that Latin as a liturgical language was dead, he used the example of the Eastern Catholic churches as a corrective to Latin exclusivity.

As a *peritus* he contributed to the development of *Lumen Gentium* and its theology of collegiality. At one point he commented that so much attention was devoted to the relation between collegiality and primacy that the principle of collegiality itself had been obscured, especially its foundation in the structure of the early church. He saw Roman centralism as an obvious problem and an obstacle for ecumenism. Nor did he welcome Pope Paul VI anticipating the council by establishing the Synod of Bishops on his own with his motu proprio (September 14, 1965), making it "directly and immediately subordinated to the authority of the Bishop of Rome." Objecting that this was not how the council conceived the synod, Ratzinger commented that a collegial organ had been turned into an instrument of the primacy.

Among the schemas approved in the council's final months were two decrees, on missionary activity (*Ad Gentes*) and on the ministry and life of priests (*Presbyterorum Ordinis*). When some argued that a new rationale for missionary work was needed, he commented that at least as far as Asia was concerned, evangelization had failed, since "conversion to Christianity...for all practical purposes, meant conversion to Europeanism." In asking for an indigenous Asian Christianity, he was endorsing what would later be called a contextual theology and inculturation.[6] He qualified his positive appraisal of the decree on priestly ministry by noting that Paul VI's prohibiting debate on clerical celibacy could not avoid a future quiet review of the question, given the church's responsibility to preach the gospel in the context of the modern world.

Several times Ratzinger called attention to the need for a reform of the Curia. He noted that calls for reform did not originate at Vatican II but had already been debated at Trent. He also pointed out that Pope Paul VI had invited the fathers at Vatican II to make suggestions for curial reform, reserving for himself any final decisions.[7] Ratzinger brought the question up again in 1963 in the context of the schema on bishops, noting decentralization as one of its goals by granting bishops powers that up to now had been concentrated in the papacy, to be supplemented by the development of episcopal conferences. Closely related to this debate about curial reform was a speech he called "significant" by Cardinal Frings of Cologne, showing a readiness "to introduce the positive results of modern legal thinking into ecclesiastical structures."[8] Frings's statement was greeted with loud, sustained applause. John Allen maintains that Ratzinger was the principal ghostwriter for the speech, denouncing the methods of the Holy Office as "a cause of scandal to the world."[9]

Allen reports that in 1968 Ratzinger joined with Hans Küng, Karl Rahner, Edward Schillebeeckx, Yves Congar, J. B. Metz, and Roland Murphy in signing a statement originating at Nijmegen in the Netherlands, eventually signed by 1,360 Catholic theologians, arguing that the teaching office of pope and bishops "cannot and must not supersede, hamper and impede the teaching task of theologians as scholars."[10] So Ratzinger was on the side of reform. But that was to change.

Benedict's Legacy

After the 1968 student protests across Europe brought chaos to the universities and at Tübingen a caricaturing of both church and Christian theology, Ratzinger's thought began to move in a more conservative direction, both as a theologian and then in his later years as bishop, cardinal prefect of the CDF, and finally pope. If the record of his papacy is mixed, the church he leaves behind will treasure the legacy of his teaching, expressed in so many written works.

His work on ecclesiology has been enormously influential, shaping the life of the church as it moved into the third millennium. He exercised a care for the integrity of Catholic doctrine in an era of considerable pluralism, both in theology and in the postconciliar dialogue with other religions, though in this last area he was much more cautious than his predecessor, Pope John Paul II. As a reformer, he was the first in Rome to take serious steps to address the scandal of the sexual abuse of minors by clergy.

In the early years of his papacy, he was more directly engaged in governance. He made efforts to reform the Vatican bank, submitting Vatican finances to Moneyval for supervision. He sought bishops not for their ideological purity or personal connections but who were good pastors and effective leaders. One friend, who is well placed in Rome, told me that when Benedict received a list of episcopal appointments from a curial official, who waited at his desk for him to sign them, he asked for the dossiers and began to study them. But in the later years of his papacy the scholar won out over the administrator. Retiring to his study, much of his energy was addressed to his writing. Governance was left largely in the hands of the Curia. Episcopal appointments suffered as a result.

Benedict's theological vision was largely Eurocentric. In 2011, Robert Mickens reported that 76 percent of those whom Benedict appointed to the Vatican's highest positions were from Western Europe, while another 10.2 percent were North Americans, for a total of 86.2 percent, rather than from the developing world where the church is most obviously growing. Furthermore, nearly 90 percent of his appointees did their theological studies in Rome.[11] That meant that those governing the church spoke largely the clerical language of Rome. This was also evident in his appointment of cardinals. By the time he resigned the papacy, of the 115 cardinals who could vote for his successor, sixty were Europeans—twenty-eight of them from Italy—and twenty were from North America, with only thirty-five from the rest of the world. Thus, the election of Pope Francis, from Latin America, was a surprise.

More practically, many commentators in Europe and the United States expressed concern about a growing divide between an educated laity who expected to take an active role in the church and a younger, neoconservative clergy who seemed deaf to their concerns.[12] Still, Benedict's impact on the life of the church was substantial. We will briefly consider some of the areas that felt his influence.

Theology

Pope Benedict was a classic dogmatic theologian. Few of his contemporaries can approach the sheer number of his publications. And while his familiarity with the history of theology and the writings of contemporary theologians is difficult to equal, his approach puts him at some distance from many of his peers in the academy.

Following the modern "turn toward the subject," contemporary theology has long emphasized the need to ground its work in experience. Extremely influential has been the method of David Tracy that seeks to bring into a critical "correlation" the two principal sources for theology, the Christian tradition expressed in texts with common human experience and language.[13] In other words, in the task of theology, Christian tradition and human experience enter a dialogue as partners. In the search for truth, each has its own methods, each can learn from the other, and each must be evaluated critically. Human experience includes its intellectual culture and the social and political dynamics that shape it. For example, three important dimensions or "gifts" of American intellectual culture to the world church include a feminist perspective, openness to pluralism, and the rise of the laity.[14]

Benedict's tendency is to emphasize, not experience, but the church's inherited doctrine. In a book on the liturgy, he criticizes what he sees as the modern tendency to "switch from the objectivity of the Eucharist to the subjectivity of experience, from the theological to the sociological and the psychological."[15] While he wants the faithful to experience their faith as something real and vital, his primary concern as a dogmatic theologian is not experience as a theological category but the objectivity of the truth taught by the church.

His privileging of what he sees as objective truth over experience reflects his discomfort with German Enlightenment thinking, with its stress on the sensible and the empirical. His own thinking tends to be more Neoplatonic than Aristotelian, stressing the ideal over the historical and the developmental. His instincts are more hierarchical and tradition centered than creative, with an emphasis on *ressourcement* rather than *aggiornamento*, reflecting what seems to be a distrust for learning that is merely secular or worldly. He rarely cites women scholars. At times, he seems to defend positions that are simply "traditional" rather than expressing what is deepest in the tradition.

For example, he holds that the Latin church has emphasized the strictly charismatic character of the priesthood by linking it with celibacy. Without this linkage, the priesthood would no longer be regarded as a charism, but only as an office that can be assigned by the institution at will.[16] But this does not necessarily follow. A charism is freely given by the Spirit; it is not created by a rite. First, if celibacy is a charism, so also is ordained ministry. Much of the problem with living out priesthood today is that too many have been ordained who do not truly have the charism for preaching, presiding, and guiding a Christian community. The problems of ordaining those without a charism for celibacy are obvious. The Orthodox churches and Eastern Catholic churches have always been able to discern the charism for priesthood in those who are already married.

Purity of Doctrine

For Ratzinger purity of doctrine had long been a primary theological concern. As head of the CDF, he worked in partnership with Pope John Paul to strengthen the authority of the ordinary magisterium. Many scholars saw the flood of documents issued by the Congregation under his presidency as expressions of a doctrinal maximalism or "creeping infallibilism," maximizing the authority of the ordinary magisterium. These documents exhibit what Richard Gaillardetz calls "a pronounced magisterial activism."[17] They included firmly accepting what the church proposes "definitively" ("Profession of Faith," 1989), even if not revealed ("Instruction on the Ecclesial Vocation of the Theologian," 1990), because it is infallibly taught by the ordinary and universal magisterium (*Responsum ad Dubium*, 1995), with new penalties added to canon law for dissenting (*Ad Tuendam Fidem*, 1998). The result of these efforts only exacerbated the tension that had been developing between professional theologians and the hierarchical magisterium.[18]

144

Under Ratzinger's prefecture, the CDF was even more active in investigating and censuring theologians, among them Jon Sobrino, Roger Haight, Jacques Dupuis, Anthony de Mello, Ivone Gebara, Tissa Balasuriya, Edward Schillebeeckx, Johannes Brosseder, Leonardo Boff, Charles Curran, Carmel McEvoy, John Sachs, and Paul Crowley. Charles Curran and Carmel McEvoy were forced from their academic positions; Johannes Brosseder had his canonical mission revoked; Tissa Balasuriya was excommunicated, though after negotiations it was rescinded a year later. And there were others, less well known.[19]

Logos Christology

Though Benedict's earlier works had been critical of efforts to discover the historical Jesus, his book *Jesus of Nazareth* seeks to show that the Jesus of the Gospels is the real, "historical" Jesus "in the strict sense of the word."[20] He rightly stresses that post-Easter christological faith must be rooted in what Jesus did and said during his historical ministry. But his reluctance to anchor his Christology in competent scholarship on the historical Jesus, even to take positions contrary to the consensus of most mainstream scholars, means that some will find his arguments difficult to sustain from a historical-critical perspective. His Christology is more an eloquent restatement of Christian faith, read against the Old Testament story of God's people and the testimony of the evangelists, than one that is critically grounded.

At the same time, Pope Benedict argues convincingly that the mission of Jesus cannot be separated from his person. Jesus is the Logos, the source of meaning and truth. He cannot be reduced to a liberal rabbi or a social reformer, and he is more than a prophet. Benedict is right to insist that the kingdom cannot be secularized into a work of human achievement; it does not mean an earthly utopia or a just society. In his encyclical *Spe Salvi*, Pope Benedict warns that since human freedom is always fragile, the kingdom will never be definitively established in this world (no. 24). What the kingdom means is the lordship of God breaking in through Jesus, the only Son of God, who has come into the world. While these themes can also be found in the Synoptics, Benedict's Johannine optic means that he sees Jesus's preaching as centered on the mystery of his person,

145

even in the Synoptics. At the deepest level of his being, Jesus's identity is rooted in his union with the one he called Abba, Father.

Thus, Pope Benedict is concerned not with historical reconstruction but with the meaning of Jesus for Christians today. His book is more than a work of theology; it represents a loving meditation on the portrait of Jesus that emerges from the Gospels, the fruit of a lifetime of prayerful contemplation of the gospel texts and the works of the fathers of the church. It is a book to be prayed as well as studied.

Eucharistic Ecclesiology

Ecclesiology has always been at the center of Ratzinger's work. Two important themes stand out. One is a fundamentally *eucharistic vision of the church*. With appeals to Paul in 1 Corinthians 10:16–17, he argues that we become the one Body of Christ by sharing in the Eucharist: "The Church is the cerebration of the Eucharist: The Eucharist is the Church; they do not simply stand side by side; they are one and the same."[21] Sharing in the Eucharist breaks down the divisive walls of our subjectivity, gathering us into a deep communion with Christ and with each other.

From this eucharistic ecclesiology flows the second theme, the church as a communion (*communio*). The mid-twentieth-century recovery of this ancient concept has helped move Catholic ecclesiology from a juridical, institutional ecclesiology to a more theological one, based on a shared life in Christ and in the Spirit.[22] United by word and sacrament, especially the Eucharist, the church is a communion of men and women with the triune God and with each other, becoming truly one Body. The church is always more than a club or a circle of friends or even an ideal community; it is the people of God coming together, in all its diversity. Thus, "the center of the oldest ecclesiology is the eucharistic assembly—the Church is *communio*."[23]

Benedict stresses the Eucharist as the place where humans encounter the divine. In the Eucharist we are taken up into the Son's surrender in love to the Father and so into the very divine presence. But he does not always stress as clearly how encountering Christ in word, sacrament, and liturgical community draws us into Christ's mission for the world, to witness and service on behalf of the kingdom.

More often his emphasis is on eucharistic adoration, though in his homilies he is careful to link adoration to mission.

He has been critical of efforts to reduce the church to an aggregate of self-sufficient local churches. A church that does not live in visible, sacramental communion with other Christians or that does not seek communion with the worldwide communion of the *ecclesia catholica* may be an ecclesial community but not church in the proper sense. Hence his emphasis on apostolic succession, understood as the succession in the historic episcopacy. This is one of his foundational ecclesiological principles, the essence of the church's catholicity and apostolicity. He saw this as the key question between Catholics and Protestants, arguing that Luther's reduction of the Eucharist to an assurance that one's sins are forgiven resulted in the Reformation losing a sense of the eucharistic context that constitutes the church as a communion.[24]

Some see Benedict's biblical ecclesiology as uncritical and less open to reform. It is very different from a historical ecclesiology, sensitive to a diversity of ecclesial forms and the nuances of historical development, such as one finds in Roger Haight.[25] Benedict would see this as ecclesiological relativism. His holding for the ontological and temporal priority of the universal church over the local churches does not help remedy Vatican II's failure to explain adequately the relation between the local and the universal church. It risks perpetuating a universalist ecclesiology that will be unable to restore the proper tension between primacy and conciliarity, the universal and the particular, the global and the local. Nor will it address Orthodox and Protestant concerns about how papal authority might be complemented by the authority of bishops or local church leaders or show how they might share in the government of the universal church.

Collegiality

Like Pope John Paul II, Benedict XVI continued to recenter authority and decision-making in Rome. This countered Vatican II's efforts to emphasize a more collegial exercise of authority and give more decision-making authority to bishops and local episcopal conferences. Early in his pontificate, Pope John Paul II spoke of national episcopal conferences and the synod of bishops as "two new instruments of collegiality."[26] But the implementation of these new instruments was disappointing.

After reading an article by Henri de Lubac, Ratzinger rethought his position on the theological status of episcopal conferences, seeing them now as products of ecclesiastical rather than divine law.[27] In his lengthy interview with Vittorio Messori, he said that "episcopal conferences have no theological basis; they do not belong to the structure of the Church, as willed by Christ."[28] In his 1998 motu proprio, *Apostolos Suos*, prepared by the CDF, Pope John Paul wrote that episcopal conferences could make a doctrinal statement only with a unanimous vote of all the members, or by at least two-thirds of the members, provided that it would not be published without first receiving the *recognitio* from the Holy See (no. 22).

The establishment of the synod of bishops had led to hopes for a greater participation of the church's bishops in ecclesial governance and for a decentralization of authority. The synod began meeting every three or four years, but control of the agenda, process, and outcomes remained firmly in the hands of Rome. According to Michael Fahey, synods had "become rituals with little practical impact on the life of the Church."[29] Many bishops considered them not worth their time and energy. Nor did they contribute to a decentralization of authority.

Liturgical Renewal

Particularly unhelpful were Ratzinger's changed attitudes toward liturgical renewal. In his personal memoir, *Milestones*, published in 1997, he acknowledged that he had once seen the principles of the liturgical movement as a marvelous point of departure for the council, a point emphasized by Massimo Faggioli in his important book *Vatican II: The Battle for Meaning*.[30] Both were emphasizing that the eucharistic and *communio* theology of the Constitution on the Sacred Liturgy (*SC*) provided the theological foundation for the council's renewal and reform. However, Ratzinger later acknowledged that his views on the liturgy had changed, not foreseeing the negative side of the renewal, as we saw earlier.

In an attempt to restore communion with Archbishop Marcel Lefebvre's schismatic movement that refused to accept the teachings of Vatican II, Pope John Paul II surveyed the world's bishops in 1980 about giving limited permission to celebrate the pre–Vatican II "Tridentine" liturgy, using the 1962 pre–Vatican II edition of the Roman Missal promulgated by Pope John XXIII. Only 1.5 percent were in favor. But in 1984, he allowed diocesan bishops to authorize such celebrations under certain conditions. In 1988, consulting only the CDF, then under the direction of Cardinal Ratzinger, he broadened those conditions. Later as pope, Benedict went much further. His *Summorum Pontificum* of July 7, 2007, granted priests general permission to celebrate what he called the "extraordinary form" of the Roman Rite, including the Tridentine Mass and all the sacraments. But, as Faggioli has argued, these permissions "could not but weaken the theological impact of *Sacrosanctum concilium* on the living ecclesiology of Catholicism."[31]

Benedict's intentions were positive. He too had hoped to bring about reconciliation with Lefevbre's Society of St. Pius X and other traditionalists alienated by the Vatican II liturgy, and to allow the traditional liturgy to enrich the reformed one. Traditionalists were delighted, though Benedict had not consulted the bishops. Nor did he consult them in 2009 in lifting the excommunication of the four bishops consecrated by the schismatic Archbishop Lefebvre. One of them, Bishop Richard Williamson, was a Holocaust denier, later twice convicted on that charge in Germany, though Benedict was not aware of his background. The efforts of both John Paul II and Benedict to reconcile Archbishop Lefebvre's movement remained unsuccessful.

The greater availability of the Tridentine Mass unhappily resulted in what has often been described as the "liturgy wars."[32] Some traditionalist parishes began scheduling liturgies in the extraordinary form, and some monastic communities began using it exclusively. Birettas reappeared, as did "fiddle-back" vestments and traditional black chasubles for funerals rather than white ones, and some bishops or cardinals again began processing into church wearing the long, red-watered silk *cappa magna* or great cape, carried by two clerics. And there were no women in the sanctuary. New websites appeared, advocating a return to more traditional liturgical practices.

Under Pope Francis, the Tridentine liturgy became a symbol for traditionalists and too often a rallying point for those in opposition to his teachings. As Rita Ferrone has argued, the "broad availability of the older rites has been used as an opportunity to create a 'church within a Church,' a community apart from the mainstream," including a reactionary thought world. Not a few traditionalists have opposed Francis's teaching on marriage and the family, his calls for economic justice and ecological responsibility, liturgical reforms such as washing the feet of women at the Holy Thursday Mandatum, women and girl acolytes, receiving communion in the hand, and Mass facing the people, as well as Vatican II's commitment to ecumenism and interreligious dialogue.[33]

Opposition has come also from some in the hierarchy.[34] Cardinal Raymond Burke has been a leader of the opposition. Former Guinean Cardinal Robert Sarah, prefect of the Congregation for Divine Worship and the Discipline of the Sacraments, affirmed that a "reform of the reform" was underway and recommended that Mass be celebrated facing East (*ad orientem*), with the priest in the same direction as the congregation, rather than facing them, and he urged that communion in the hand be again forbidden. Former apostolic nuncio to the United States (2011–16) Archbishop Carlo Maria Viganò took the side of traditionalists and called for Francis to resign.

While demand for the Latin liturgy seems to be diminishing among the faithful, conservative younger priests, sometimes encouraged by their bishops, continue to turn their altars around again, restore communion rails, and stress the difference between priest and laity, often appealing to the so-called ontological difference after ordination. This increased attention to the role of the priest was contrary to the council's effort to teach that the entire assembly joins with the presider in celebrating the liturgy; it sought to simplify the rite, avoiding needless repetitions like the more than twenty-five signs of blessing and the five different kinds of bows made by the priest in the Mass, and to bring about a greater liturgical inculturation. Most of these were minor changes. But on a deeper level, the use of the unreformed Tridentine Mass disconnected both the liturgy and the council's teachings from the renewal the council intended, as noted earlier.

After a "detailed consultation" of the bishops conducted by the CDF in 2020, Pope Francis decided to intervene. In a letter accompanying his motu proprio *Traditionis Custodes* (July 16, 2021), he wrote that the responses to the questionnaire "saddened" him, noting that the use of the 1962 Tridentine liturgy "is often characterized by a rejection not only of the liturgical reform, but of the Vatican Council II itself." So, after consulting with the CDF, he abrogated the "extraordinary form" of the Roman Rite, declaring that as part of a "constant search for ecclesial communion," the liturgy reformed by Vatican II is "the unique expression of the *lex orandi* of the Roman Rite." He did not abolish the Latin liturgy, as some allege. By way of exception, after consulting with Rome, permission could be given by the diocesan bishop to celebrate according to the 1962 Roman missal for pastoral needs, but not in parochial churches or in newly erected personal parishes, with the provision that those celebrating according to the 1962 missal do not deny the validity of the liturgical reforms of the council. Of course, priests could still celebrate in Latin using the reformed liturgy.

Francis's letter paid tribute to Benedict's hope that *Summorum Pontificum*, with its broad permission to celebrate the Tridentine liturgy, would lead to a mutual enrichment of both rites and to greater unity. Unfortunately, that did not happen. At the end of his letter, Francis expressed his own hope that every liturgy would be celebrated with decorum and fidelity to the liturgical books promulgated by the council, attentive always to the real needs of the "holy people of God" rather than "the desires and wishes of individual priests."

Ecumenism

One of Ratzinger's important achievements was his facilitating the acceptance of the 1999 Lutheran–Catholic Joint Declaration on the Doctrine of Justification by the Catholic Church and the Lutheran World Federation, the issue on which the church was first divided in the sixteenth century. Relations between the Catholic Church and the Orthodox churches, particularly the Russian Orthodox Church, also warmed considerably during his pontificate. Both the Orthodox and Benedict were concerned with the secularism of Europe and the growth of Islam, though relations have cooled again with the Orthodox Church in Ukraine claiming autocephaly.

More controversial was the CDF's 2000 declaration *Dominus Iesus* as well as the 2007 CDF document, "Response to Some Questions Regarding Certain Aspects of the Doctrine of the Church," evidence that under Benedict Rome was not ready to acknowledge the full ecclesial reality of the Reformation churches. Evangelicals, however, appreciated the emphasis in *Dominus Iesus* on Christ as the universal savior. Benedict's *Anglicanorum Coetibus*, establishing a Personal Ordinariate for disaffected Anglicans who wanted to enter full communion with the Catholic Church while preserving some Anglican usages, took the Anglican Communion by surprise.

Other traditions were less open to his view of holy orders as the sacramental expression of the principle of tradition. For example, those in the Free Church tradition point to "the dynamic life and the orthodox faith" of their churches as evidence of their full ecclesiality, while Pentecostals claim that apostolicity is demonstrated not by episcopal succession but by a vital apostolic life on the model of the New Testament, particularly as evidenced by charismatic gifts and miraculous powers, the fruits of "Baptism in the Spirit."[35] But with his Eurocentric vision, Benedict did little to promote better relations with the exploding Evangelical and Pentecostal communities in the global South, part of a massive demographic shift as the Christian population of Europe and North America continued to diminish.

His view of the church as constituted by the Eucharist, while rooted deeply in the Catholic and Orthodox traditions, will not find a ready reception among many conservative Protestants who come from nonliturgical traditions that stress an individualist understanding of faith in which church or sacraments play little role. Others will see his emphasis on the Spirit as the worker of unity in the universal church through its institutional structures rather than as the creative Spirit that brings about new and vital expressions of Christian life as reflective of an ecclesiology that stresses Christology at the expense of pneumatology. Some scholars speak of such an overemphasis as christomonism: "This christological constriction of the flow of the Spirit in the church renders suspect charisms or purported manifestations of the Spirit outside hierarchical channels, unless they can be, somewhat begrudgingly, legitimated or coopted by the hierarchy."[36]

Interreligious Dialogue

While Pope John Paul II was generous in acknowledging the Spirit's work in other religions, Benedict stressed Christian faith as a supernatural gift; other religions have "beliefs," based on human wisdom and religious aspiration, but not faith, and their members are in a gravely deficient situation compared to those in the church (*DI* 7, 22). His concern about too positive an approach to religious pluralism led in 1998 to the investigation of Father Jacques Dupuis.

Then in September 2007, it became known that both the Vatican and the U.S. bishops had initiated an investigation of Georgetown University's Peter Phan, with close ties to the Federation of Asian Bishops' Conferences, concerned that Phan's work in the area of religious pluralism did not sufficiently acknowledge Jesus as the unique savior of the world.[37] Perhaps, as Aidan Nichols suggests, Benedict sees pluralistic theologies in India in the context of the Hindu tendency to reduce Jesus to one more manifestation of the Hindu absolute and thus as another manifestation of the relativism dominant in the West.[38] This goes against all of Ratzinger's theological instincts. Dialogue must be about more than encounter; it is concerned with truth, and therefore with critique. He writes, "Is it a presumption to talk about the truth of faith, or is it a duty?"[39]

In one of his more positive essays on the subject, "The Dialogue of the Religions," Ratzinger outlines three principles. First, dialogue takes place not by renouncing truth but by entering more deeply into it. Second, while looking for what is positive in the beliefs of the other, we must be willing to accept criticism of ourselves and of our own religion. Third, dialogue is always a dialogical process. It does not replace missionary activity but is always aimed at finding the truth, at conviction, so that mission and dialogue become not opposites but rather mutually interpenetrate each other. The "dialogue of religions should become more and more a listening to the Logos, who is pointing out to us, in the midst of our separation and our contradictory affirmations, the unity we already share."[40]

Political Philosophy

Much less well known is the depth of Ratzinger/Pope Benedict's work on political philosophy. According to political scientist Thomas Rourke, Benedict shows far more depth in this area "than one usually finds in the writings of political scientists and other social writers," a depth he attributes to his richer understanding of historical trends and developments in Western thought.[41] Ratzinger's public dialogue with Jürgen Habermas of the Neo-Marxist Frankfurt School after 9/11 showed him as a public intellectual. Their discussion was on the question of whether the modern democratic state could justify the human rights it presupposed without a metaphysical or religious foundation. Habermas answered affirmatively, based on social consensus. Ratzinger argued that such a grounding left those rights fragile. The shocking invasion of the U.S. Capitol, on January 6, 2021, is evidence of the fragility of that social consensus.

Without a metaphysical or religious foundation, civil law loses its grounding; it is reduced to a "juridical positivism" dependent on the "whim of the majority." What is really lost is the dignity of the human and life itself:

> Even human life is something that can be disposed of: abortion and euthanasia are no longer excluded from juridical ordering. Forms of manipulation of human life are manifested in the areas of embryo experimentation and transplants, in which man arrogates to himself not only the ability to dispose of life and death, but also of his being and of his development. Thus, the point has recently been reached of going so far as to claim the programmed selection and breeding for the continuous development of the human species, and the essential difference between man and animal is up for debate.[42]

Benedict has long been against any kind of political theology, seeing in modern attempts to find salvation through political activity or technological progress a secularization of Christian hope, separating the kingdom of God from the church, as not infrequently happens in some liberation or pluralist theologies. The 2000 CDF declaration *Dominus Iesus*, issued under his presidency, insists on the inseparability of the kingdom of God from Christ or from the church (no. 18). From the time of his *Habilitationsschrift* on Bonaventure's theology of history, he has contested any effort to "immanentize" the eschaton, to use the term of Eric Vögelin,[43] that is, to make it something *within* history rather than *beyond* it. This, in his view, was one of the mistakes of Marxism.

Benedict had always been allergic to political theologies, which he says makes the mission of the church primarily social, emptying theology of its transcendent dimension and reducing Christianity to an ideology. For Christians, the goal or end of history has already been revealed in the person of Jesus, "who is recognized as the last man or second Adam, that is as the long-awaited manifestation of what is truly human and the definitive revelation to man of his hidden nature."[44] He took up these themes again in his encyclical *Spe Salvi*.

Clergy Sexual Abuse

One of Cardinal Ratzinger's most significant reforms was in addressing the clergy sexual abuse scandal, the first in Rome to do so directly. As archbishop of Munich-Freising, he had been slow to recognize the enormity of the problem. Accusations later surfaced that he had failed to remove from ministry four priests accused of abusing minors, though the archdiocese attributed the responsibility to those reporting to him. After reviewing a lengthy 2022 report on sexual abuse in the Archdiocese of Munich that included his tenure as archbishop, the Vatican released a personal letter from Benedict acknowledging his deep sorrow for "the abuses and the errors" that occurred both in Munich and Rome under his administration, expressing the "deepest sympathy" for each of the victims. But an appendix released at the same time denied that he had any knowledge of sexual abuse or suspicions of sexual abuse on the part of the four cases in Munich he was accused of mishandling. His confession failed to satisfy his critics.

Later, as head of the CDF, he proved to be far more proactive than his predecessor or other Vatican officials. He took steps to centralize the labyrinthian way the Vatican dealt with accusations of sexual abuse. In 2001 he ordered that all cases be reported to the CDF, implemented in John Paul's motu proprio *Sacramentorum Sanctitatis Tutela*. Archbishop Vincent Nichols of Westminster credits Ratzinger with helping to initiate changes in church law, among them "the inclusion in canon law of Internet offenses against children, the extension of child abuse offenses to include the sexual abuse of all under 18, the case-by-case waiving of the statute of limitations and the establishment of a fast-track dismissal from the clerical state for offenders."[45]

Furthermore, as prefect of the CDF, he reviewed all these cases, initiating in the process a long and painful self-education. He began an investigation of Father Marcial Maciel Degollado, the founder of the Legionaries of Christ, against whom at least nine former seminarians had brought allegations of abuse, and shortly after becoming pope, ordered him to cease all public ministry and to retire to a life of prayer and penance. Though these allegations went back to at least the mid-nineties, Maciel had been repeatedly praised by Pope John Paul. Maciel was later found to have fathered several children.

Rather than a recognizing the scandal as a structural problem or the result of clericalism, however, Benedict seems to have seen it only as a spiritual problem, a crisis of faith brought on by secularization. He once described church reform as consisting, not in remodeling the church according to our tastes, but in clearing away subsidiary constructions, like the sculptor who allows the image hidden in the stone to be revealed.[46] He did not remove from office bishops who reassigned offending priests, nor did he require that they bring such cases to civil authorities.

A Final Concern

Finally, there remains for me the question of Pope Benedict's apparent inability to integrate new data into his thinking. I mentioned earlier Joseph Komonchak's comment that there are in his writings "very few positive references to intellectual developments outside the Church."[47] Similarly, Dennis Doyle once observed that while "Ratzinger acknowledges the good in modern developments that grant religious freedom and that recognize the relative autonomy of the state, he does not otherwise emphasize the positive impact of modern developments on Church teaching or on Church reform."[48] He also seemed impervious to criticism.

Thus, we need to ask, does the Platonic/Augustinian cast to his thinking make room for development and change? Was he able to accept new evidence and to admit historical fact as data? Was his thinking characterized by a concern for historical consciousness, or did it tend to be ahistorical?

Bernard Lonergan has described one of modernity's most important legacies as a shift from a classicist worldview to what he

calls "historical mindedness," usually referred to as historical consciousness.[49] The classicist worldview is basically static and essen-
tialist; it ignores the importance of history. Like classical Greek and
scholastic philosophy—Plato, Aristotle, Aquinas—it stresses the
abstract or universal. Its perspective assumes that the human person,
morality, theology, church, and sacrament are static, unchanging
realities, like Platonic forms or Aristotelian universals. Methodolog-
ically, it proceeds deductively, from the abstract or universal to the
particular case. It emphasizes a perennial philosophy, perfect defini-
tions (man is a rational animal), and absolute norms.

By contrast, historical consciousness stresses the concrete and
particular; it presumes development and change. Thus, it is open
to new insights, higher viewpoints, and reinterpretations of traditional positions. It proceeds not deductively from universal natures
(the human person, society, church) but inductively (from empirical
observation, critical investigation, historical evidence, and personal
experience). Meaning is not just discovered but refined by a historical process that is changing, developing, sometimes becoming fro-
zen and even going astray, but always capable of reinterpretation,
more accurate formulation, and the discovery of deeper meaning.
The Congregation for the Doctrine of the Faith acknowledged the
historically conditioned and therefore limited nature of all "expressions of revelation"—whether scripture, Creed, dogmas, doctrine,
or the teaching of the magisterium—in its 1973 instruction on Catholic doctrine, *Mysterium Ecclesiae*.[50]

From a theological perspective, historical consciousness presumes that the church's self-understanding develops and its structures emerge historically; they are not all given at the beginning.
Thus, ecclesiology is a historical discipline. Similarly, Christology
develops through stages: the preaching of the Jesus of history, the
proclamation of the early Christian communities, the constructive
work of the church fathers and the early councils.

Of course, as a scholar, an intellectual, and a man of his times,
Benedict was aware of the historical nature of consciousness. He
was intimately familiar with the history of the church. Still, historical consciousness did not seem to play an important role in
his work. For all his emphasis on reason working in consort with
faith, there remained a Platonic cast to his thought, an a priori,
conceptual dimension to his approach that seemed to leave little

room for theological development, whether the subject is Christology, ecclesiology, liturgy, or moral theology. He tended to dismiss the importance of historical studies for Christology. He spoke about the church, not as a historical reality, growing through its history, borrowing from the cultures in which it is embedded, but more like a Platonic idea existing eternally in the mind of God. He seemed reluctant to acknowledge how often the church has adopted time-conditioned forms and political structures from its surrounding culture.

Benedict was particularly reluctant to acknowledge any change in church teaching. If doctrine can change, then the ecclesial future might be more open than we might think. He resisted the idea that the Second Vatican Council moved the church in new directions, insisting that there is no "pre-" or "post"conciliar church but only one unique church that walks toward the Lord.[51] In an address to the Roman Curia the year he was elected pope, he contrasted a "hermeneutic of discontinuity and rupture" with a "hermeneutic of reform."[52] The former suggests a split between the preconciliar and postconciliar church; the latter, a willingness to acknowledge accidental changes, an apparent discontinuity in contingent matters, but no real change of principles, and thus, no genuine reversals, changes, or the emergence of anything really "new." As James Corkery says, "Continuity is his lens, 'going forward in continuity.'"[53]

For example, for Benedict the council's Declaration on Religious Freedom did not represent a change in church teaching on religious liberty, as many have argued. Rather, "with its new definition of the relationship between the faith of the Church and certain essential elements of modern thought," the council "has reviewed or even corrected certain historical decisions, but in this apparent discontinuity it has actually deepened and preserved her innermost nature and true identity."[54] John Courtney Murray, who drafted the declaration, writes that the real sticking point for those who opposed it at the council was the notion of development between it and the Syllabus of Errors of Pope Pius IX, something he said that would have to be explained by theologians.[55] In a later commentary he explained in language not unlike Benedict's that the development discarded "an older theory of civil tolerance in favor of a new doctrine of religious freedom more in harmony with the authentic and more fully understood tradition of the Church."[56] Yes, a development, but none the less one that reversed the teachings of earlier popes.[57]

Benedict long insisted that the ultimate goal of ecumenical dialogue is sharing a common faith; thus, dialogues can never be reduced to philosophical discussions or political negotiations. Truth is not a matter of consensus or a majority vote but is made manifest by an unanimity that can come only from God. We can work to become more worthy of unity, but we cannot bring it about by manipulation.[58] This is true, of course.

But still these questions remain: Can truth always be identified with such certainty, particularly when our own positions or institutional interests may be involved? Is what is judged to be true clearly revealed in Scripture, or is it more a matter of tradition and interpretation? Not all official teachings are matters of dogma. In reflecting on Pope Benedict's insistence that Vatican II represents not "discontinuity and rupture" but only reform, Richard Gaillardetz observes that both the pope and other church leaders are concerned about the maintenance of Catholic identity: "Yet no pastoral response that refuses to acknowledge the fact of historical change can offer a compelling long-term solution. Unqualified assertions regarding the certitude of all church teaching are ultimately futile." Rather than insisting that official church teachings (not dogmas) never change, Gaillardetz finds it more fruitful to emphasize the personal narratives of men and women living exemplary Catholic lives and the distinctive Christian practices that help shape a religious identity.[59]

Perhaps this concern for Catholic identity is most evident in Benedict's long effort to reinforce traditional teaching on divisive social issues, often referred to as questions in the "culture wars" or included among what Benedict himself once referred to as the "canon of issues,"[60] among them celibacy, abortion, homosexuality, women's ordination, divorce and remarriage, inclusive language, and so forth. Benedict's approach has been an attempt to hold the line.

Pope Francis, in his efforts to show a more welcoming face of the church, has a different approach. He has not sought to change doctrine, as some of his opponents frequently allege. Indeed, a pope is not able to simply change doctrine by himself. But Francis has encouraged a new attitude toward those who are different, greater tolerance, a changed stance.[61] His apostolic exhortation *Evangelii Gaudium*, setting out the agenda for his papacy, outlined some of

159

his pastoral principles, among them, time is greater than space (nos. 221–23) and realities are more important than ideas (nos. 231–33). In his post-synodal apostolic exhortation *Amoris Laetitia*, after the two synods on the family, he recommends the "law of gradualness"— appealed to earlier by Pope John Paul II. For those in "irregular situations" (nos. 295–96), Francis counsels accompaniment, avoiding hasty judgments, discernment, mercy, and pastoral care.

Conclusion

In the end, one might ask, despite all his brilliance and the positive way Pope Benedict sought to rearticulate Catholic doctrine in the context of secular culture, has his thinking really been characterized by historical consciousness, or does it represent a closed hermeneutical circle constituted by the teachings of scripture, the fathers of the church, and the magisterium? Was his thinking truly open to historical development, to new evidence, and to the knowledge that comes from experience? When all is said and done, these questions remain. Granted, the pope's mission is to keep the church faithful to the tradition it has received from the apostles; there was an essentially "conservative" dimension in the best sense to his ministry. However, to best serve the universal Church, one must also be able to read what Vatican II called "the signs of the times" (*GS* 4).

EPILOGUE

Having a pope who was also a world-renowned scholar was something new in the life of the church. Cardinal Joseph Ratzinger was elected to the Chair of Peter with at least sixty-six books (totals vary, as noted earlier) and countless articles. His astonishing range of interests extends from dogmatic theology to liturgy, culture and the arts, politics, ecumenism, and non-Christian religions. His *Introduction to Christianity*,[1] one of his most successful books, has been translated into at least nineteen languages, including Arabic and Chinese, while his three-volume work on Christology, *Jesus of Nazareth*, is a modern classic. Almost all comment that Pope Benedict was a good listener, and bishops always found visiting his congregation on their *ad limina* visits when he was the cardinal prefect the most fruitful.

He was not opposed to interreligious dialogue but insisted that dialogue must deal with real issues. It cannot compromise truth for the sake of a superficial tolerance. A particular concern for Benedict was Europe's loss of faith. He saw Europe as a continent in crisis. In the words of Jim Corkery, it was suffering from "a strange lack of confidence both about its past and about its future."[2] With negative birth rates, most countries in Western Europe seem to be depopulating themselves. The intellectual culture was determinedly secular. As Ratzinger wrote shortly before his election to the papacy, "For the very first time in history, we see a purely secular state that discards, as a mythical worldview, the idea that God is the ultimate guarantor of political life and that it is he who lays down the norms for its conduct. This state declares God himself to be a private matter that has no place in the public sphere in which the shared will of the citizens is formed."[3]

While the Western churches continue to lose members and practice has reached an all-time low, Islam seemed to be the only growing religion, its numbers increasing through immigrants, offspring, and converts. Perhaps this is why Benedict found the new ecclesial movements such as *Focolare*, the Neocatecumenate, Cursillo, and *Comunione et Liberazione* so promising. They touch people's hearts, though some bishops find the Neocatecumenate divisive and refuse to allow the movement in their dioceses.

At the same time, the church's center of gravity today has been shifting from Europe and North America to the global South. These Catholics have very different concerns from those of the West, and as these churches in Asia, Latin America, and Africa begin to find their own voices, developing their own "contextual" theologies to address local problems, there will be new tension between them and Rome.[4] A new language of evangelization will be increasingly necessary, and Pope Francis has initiated a global synodal process.

Benedict's Resignation

Benedict's sudden resignation on February 11, 2013, stunned the world. But it should not have been a surprise. He had several times raised the possibility of a pope resigning, telling journalist Peter Seewald in 2010 that "if a pope clearly realizes that he is no longer physically, psychologically, and spiritually capable of handling the duties of office, then he has a right and, under some circumstances, also an obligation to resign."[5] Still the news when it came was something of a shock.

Clearly, his concern was the good of the church and a sign of this remarkable man's humility and spiritual freedom. The office was never about him. Indeed, for this quiet but gracious scholar, it must have been a considerable burden. He had witnessed at close hand Pope John Paul II, once so vital, descend slowly into ill-health and disability. As he began to feel the effects of his own advancing years, he knew the church needed the strong leadership he could no longer provide.

Furthermore, intelligent as he was, he recognized that management was not his strong suit. Scholar and teacher, he was happiest in his study with his books. In the last years of his pontificate, he left governance largely in the hands of the Curia, and there had been continuing rumors that the Vatican was lacking clear leadership.

Stories multiplied after the 2012 "Vatileaks" scandal when the pope's butler, Paolo Gabriele, supplied the journalist Gianluigi Nuzzi with confidential documents alleging widespread corruption, financial mismanagement, and infighting within the Vatican. Confessing that he did it out of love for the pope and the church, Gabriele was sentenced to eighteen months in prison.[6] Benedict pardoned him after he had served just two, just before Christmas. Two months later, he resigned.

In the statement announcing his retirement, Benedict said, "In today's world, subject to so many rapid changes and shaken by questions of deep relevance for the life of faith, in order to govern the bark of Saint Peter and proclaim the Gospel, both strength of mind and body are necessary, strength which in the last few months, has deteriorated in me to the extent that I have had to recognize my incapacity to adequately fulfil the ministry entrusted to me."[7] And so, with remarkable courage, Benedict, often stereotyped as a conservative, took the unprecedented step of retiring, the first pope to do so on his own initiative since Celestine V in 1294.

To date, there are no protocols for a retired pope. Benedict established his own, not returning to Germany but retiring quietly to a former monastery for cloistered nuns in the Vatican gardens. Some have raised questions about the title "pope emeritus." They suggest that a retired pope should be called "bishop-emeritus of Rome" and not wear white. But as longtime Vatican watcher Tom Reese has observed, in his retirement, Benedict "had for the most part abided by his pledge to adopt a low profile and not speak out much." When he did, with some remarks on clergy sexual abuse and priestly celibacy, opponents of Francis were quick to exploit them, threatening Catholic unity.[8]

Regardless, Benedict's resigning his office may have been one of his most significant contributions to the church's life. In a sense he desacralized the papacy. The office was not a sacramental order into which one was initiated for life but a ministry that one took on and could give up for appropriate reasons, a move that will stand as an example for his successors. As Vincent Miller has noted, his resignation "is an act of magisterial teaching in its own right."[9]

Conclusion

Along with the Gregorian Reform in the eleventh century and the Lutheran Reformation in the sixteenth, Vatican II stands as one of three great reforming movements in the life of the church,[10] and Ratzinger played a major role in its success. His theological achievement was extraordinary. And if his theology moved in a more conservative direction in the postconciliar period, his concern was not so much the council itself but what he saw as its often uncritical reception. As he once acerbically observed, "They changed wine into water and called it '*aggiornamento*.'"[11]

He will be remembered as a public intellectual, being named a member of the Académie Française, the Rhineland-Westphalia Academy of Sciences, and the European Academy of Sciences and Arts. His encyclicals, relatively brief and very readable, are rich in references to philosophers, social scientists, and novelists, not all of them Christians, as well as to traditional works. *Spe Salvi* is particularly noteworthy.

His visit to the United States in April 2008 was highly successful, showing himself to be a gracious pastor. He did not chastise or rebuke, but with a pace that would have exhausted a man of fewer years, he repeatedly encouraged and exhorted American Catholics to witness to their faith in "Christ our Hope" in an increasingly secular and materialistic culture. At the United Nations, he called on international leaders to act jointly to resolve conflicts, warning that "a multilateral consensus should not be subordinated to the decisions of a few," implicitly ruling out unilateral action by one state against another, an important counsel when more politicians and countries are turning to ethno-nationalism. He also called for the protection of the environment.[12]

During his visit, he met with five men and women who had been abused by members of the clergy, praying with them, and grasping their hands. All accounts described the meeting as deeply moving. He also raised the scandal of sexual abuse by clergy at least five times, acknowledging to the bishops that it had been "sometimes very badly handled."[13] Later, he met with victims in Australia, Canada, and on the island of Malta. In his letter to the Catholics of Ireland, he expressed his willingness to meet with some of the victims.

His deepest interest was always to bring others to the love of God who is both reason and love. As he says in his encyclical *Deus Caritas Est*, "God is the absolute and ultimate source of all being; but this universal principle of creation—the *Logos*, primordial reason—is at the same time a lover with all the passion of a true love" (no. 10). Being a Christian cannot be reduced to morality, and it is more than theology; it means entering a relationship with the person of Jesus. As he says he learned from Romano Guardini, the essence of Christianity is Jesus himself, a principle later enshrined in *Dei Verbum*, Vatican II's dogmatic constitution on revelation that Ratzinger helped to draft.[14]

Thus, he easily adopted the language of his predecessor, Pope John Paul II, of a new evangelization because it so well embraced his own concerns. He continued to insist that evangelization remains essential to the church's mission. He has lived out his final years in retirement with remarkable grace. In his efforts to help others come into communion with the person of Christ, he will be remembered as a teacher for all the churches.

NOTES

Acknowledgments

1. Aidan Nichols, *The Thought of Pope Benedict XVI: An Introduction to the Theology of Joseph Ratzinger*, new ed. (New York: Burns and Oates, 2007), 245–75; first published in 1988 as *An Introduction to the Theology of Joseph Ratzinger*.

2. D. Vincent Twomey, "The Mind of Benedict XVI," *Claremont Review of Books* 5, no. 4 (Fall 2005): 66.

3. John L. Allen Jr., *Cardinal Ratzinger: The Vatican's Enforcer of the Faith* (New York: Continuum, 2000); reissued as *Pope Benedict XVI: A Biography of Joseph Ratzinger* (New York: Continuum, 2005).

4. John L. Allen Jr., *The Rise of Benedict XVI: The Inside Story of How the Pope Was Elected and Where He Will Take the Catholic Church* (New York: Doubleday, 2005).

Introduction

1. Karl Rahner and Joseph Ratzinger, *The Episcopate and the Primacy* (New York: Herder & Herder, 1962).

2. See "Service Requesting Pardon" held at St. Peter's Basilica on the First Sunday of Lent, March 12, 2000; *Origins* 29, no. 40 (2000): 645–48.

3. See Killian McDonnell, "Our Dysfunctional Church," *The Tablet* 225, no. 8 (September 8, 2001): 1661.

4. See John L. Allen Jr., *Cardinal Ratzinger: The Vatican's Enforcer of the Faith* (New York: Continuum, 2000), 298–99.

5. David Gibson, *The Rule of Benedict: Pope Benedict XVI and His Battle with the Modern World* (San Francisco: HarperSanFrancisco, 2006), 5–6.

6. Catholic News Service, April 20, 2005.

7. See Benedict XVI, "General Audience" (April 27, 2005), https://www.vatican.va/content/benedict-xvi/en/audiences/2005/documents/hf_ben-xvi_aud_20050427.html.

8. Joseph Ratzinger, *Milestones: Memoirs 1927–1977* (San Francisco: Ignatius Press, 1998), 136.

9. Ratzinger, *Milestones*, 137.

10. Joseph Ratzinger/Pope Benedict XVI, *Jesus of Nazareth: From the Baptism in the Jordan to the Transfiguration* (New York: Doubleday, 2007), xxiii–xxiv.

Chapter 1

1. Joseph Ratzinger, *The Spirit of the Liturgy* (San Francisco: Ignatius Press, 2000), 130.

2. John L. Allen Jr., *Cardinal Ratzinger: The Vatican's Enforcer of the Faith* (New York: Continuum, 2000), 11; reissued under the title *Pope Benedict XVI: A Biography of Joseph Ratzinger* (2005).

3. Ratzinger, *Spirit of the Liturgy*, 184.

4. Joseph Ratzinger, *Milestones: Memoirs 1927–1977* (San Francisco: Ignatius Press, 1998), 18–20.

5. Allen, *Cardinal Ratzinger*, 17–21.

6. Allen, *Cardinal Ratzinger*, 17.

7. Jeff Israely, "Pope Benedict's Auschwitz Prayer," *Time*, May 29, 2006.

8. David Gibson, *The Rule of Benedict: Pope Benedict XVI and His Battle with the Modern World* (San Francisco: HarperSanFrancisco, 2006), 137.

9. Johann Baptist Metz, *The Emergent Church: The Future of Christianity in a Postbourgeois World* (New York: Crossroad, 1986), 27.

10. See James Matthew Ashley, *Interruptions: Mysticism, Politics, and Theology in the Work of Johann Baptist Metz* (Notre Dame, IN: University of Notre Dame Press, 1998), 97–99.

11. Metz, *The Emergent Church*, 26–27.

12. Robert A. Krieg, *Catholic Theologians in Nazi Germany* (New York: Continuum, 2004), 175.

13. Joseph Ratzinger, *Theological Highlights of Vatican II* (New York: Paulist Press, 1966), 179.

14. Allen, *Cardinal Ratzinger*, 34.

15. Peter Seewald, in Joseph Ratzinger, *Salt of the Earth: The Church at the End of the Millennium; An Interview with Peter Seewald* (San Francisco: Ignatius Press, 1997), 55.

16. Ratzinger, *Milestones*, 108.

17. Ratzinger, *Milestones*, 121. Allen shows how his positions on collegiality, the authority of episcopal conferences, the role of the Holy Office, and the development of tradition, liturgy, and ecumenism have shifted since the council; see his *Cardinal Ratzinger*, 56–81.

18. Ratzinger, *Milestones*, 128.

19. Herbert Vorgrimler, ed., *Commentary on the Documents of Vatican II* (New York: Herder & Herder, 1967).

20. Ratzinger, *Milestones*, 134.

21. Ratzinger, *Theological Highlights of Vatican II*, 184.

22. Cited in Gianni Valenti, "The Difficult Years," *Thirty Days* 5 (May 2006): 42.

23. Ratzinger, *Salt of the Earth*, 77.

24. Allen, *Cardinal Ratzinger*, 116.

25. For Rahner's statement, see Allen, *Cardinal Ratzinger*, 125–26.

26. Allen, *Cardinal Ratzinger*, 149; Allen tracks the history of the struggle between Ratzinger and the liberation theologians in considerable detail.

27. Leonardo Boff, *The Base Communities Reinvent the Church* (Maryknoll, NY: Orbis Books, 1986; first published 1977), 13.

28. Leonardo Boff, *Church: Charism and Power* (New York: Crossroad, 1985), 112–13.

29. CDF, "Instruction on Certain Aspects of the 'Theology of Liberation,'" *Origins* 14 (1984): 193–204.

30. See Joseph Ratzinger, "Freedom and Liberation: The Anthropological Vision of the 1986 Instruction *Libertatis Conscientia*," in his *Church, Ecumenism and Politics* (New York: Crossroad, 1988), 255–75.

31. Allen, *Cardinal Ratzinger*, 166.

32. See Joseph Ratzinger, "Relativism: The Central Problem for Faith Today," EWTN, accessed March 17, 2022, https://www

.ewtn.com/catholicism/library/relativism-the-central-problem-for
-faith-today-2470.

33. Joseph Ratzinger, *Without Roots: The West, Relativism, Christianity, Islam* (New York: Basic Books, 2006), 128.

34. Ratzinger, *Salt of the Earth*, 181–213.

35. See Francis A. Sullivan, "Guideposts from the Catholic Tradition," *America* 173, no. 19 (1995): 6; also his "Recent Theological Observations on Magisterial Documents and Public Dissent," *Theological Studies* 58 (1997): 509–15.

36. Avery Dulles found the example of Anglican orders debatable; see "Commentary on Profession of Faith's Concluding Paragraphs," sidebar in *Origins* 28, no. 8 (1998): 117.

37. CDF, "Considerations Regarding Proposals to Give Legal Recognition to Unions between Homosexual Persons," July 31, 2003, no. 8.

38. CDF, "Concerning the Criteria for the Discernment of Vocations with regard to Persons with Homosexual Tendencies in View of Their Admission to Holy Orders," November 4, 2005.

39. Jacques Dupuis, *Towards a Christian Theology of Religious Pluralism* (Maryknoll, NY: Orbis Books, 1997).

40. CDF, *Dominus Iesus, Origins* 30, no. 14 (2000): 209–19.

41. Cited by Thomas C. Fox, *Pentecost in Asia: A New Way of Being Church* (Maryknoll, NY: Orbis Books, 2002), 192; see also Stephen J. Pope and Charles Hefling, eds., *Sic et non: Encountering Dominus Iesus* (Maryknoll, NY: Orbis Books, 2002).

42. "Commitment of Ecumenism Called Irrevocable," *Origins* 30, no. 16 (2000): 256.

43. Reported by Catholic News Service; cited in *The Tidings* (November 24, 2000): 2.

44. Ratzinger responded to the criticism occasioned by *Dominus Iesus* in his book *Truth and Tolerance: Christian Belief and World Religions* (San Francisco: Ignatius Press, 2004).

45. Joseph Ratzinger with Vittorio Messori, *The Ratzinger Report: An Exclusive Interview on the State of the Church* (San Francisco: Ignatius Press, 1985).

46. Gibson, *Rule of Benedict*, 79.

47. Cardinal Joseph Ratzinger, homily, *Pro Eligendo Romano Pontifice*, April 18, 2005, https://www.vatican.va/gpII/documents/homily-pro-eligendo-pontifice_20050418_en.html.

48. Thomas Massaro, "Don't Forget Justice," *America* 194, no. 9 (2006): 19.

49. N. T. Wright, "And What of This World," *The Tablet* (December 8, 2007): 10.

50. See Thomas P. Rausch, *Faith, Hope, and Charity: Benedict XVI on the Theological Virtues* (New York: Paulist Press, 2015).

51. Francis X. Clooney, "Dialogue Not Monologue: Benedict XVI and Religious Pluralism," *Commonweal* 132, no. 18 (October 21, 2005): 15–16.

52. When Benedict visited Vienna in September 2007, he made a stop at its Judenplatz to pay his respects to the victims of Nazism. On the plane, he had told reporters that he was going there to demonstrate "our sadness, our repentance and also our friendship for our Jewish brothers" (Catholic News Service, September 7, 2007).

53. James V. Schall, *The Regensburg Lecture* (South Bend, IN: St. Augustine's Press, 2007), 125.

54. John L. Allen Jr., *The Rise of Benedict XVI* (New York: Doubleday, 2005).

55. Clooney, "Dialogue Not Monologue," 14.

56. Clooney, "Dialogue Not Monologue," 14.

57. Christmas Address of His Holiness Benedict XVI to the Roman Curia, December 22, 2006.

58. George Weigel, *God's Choice: Pope Benedict and the Future of the Catholic Church* (New York: HarperCollins, 2005), 217.

59. Joseph Ratzinger/Pope Benedict XVI, *Jesus of Nazareth: From the Baptism in the Jordan to the Transfiguration* (New York: Doubleday, 2007), xxiii–xxiv.

Chapter 2

1. Joseph Ratzinger, *Milestones: Memoirs 1927–1977* (San Francisco: Ignatius Press, 1998), 44.

2. Avery Dulles, *The Reshaping of Catholicism* (San Francisco: Harper & Row, 1988), 191.

3. "Pope Gives Advice to Roman Seminarians," *ZENIT* (February 19, 2007).

4. Joseph Ratzinger, *Salt of the Earth: The Church at the End of the Millennium; An Interview with Peter Seewald* (San Francisco: Ignatius Press, 1997), 41.

5. Joseph Ratzinger, *Principles of Catholic Theology: Building Stones for a Fundamental Theology* (San Francisco: Ignatius Press, 1987), 347.

6. Ratzinger, *Principles of Catholic Theology*, 360.

7. Ratzinger, *Principles of Catholic Theology*, 361.

8. Ratzinger, *Principles of Catholic Theology*, 359–62.

9. Walter Kasper, "Das Wesen des Christlichen. B," *Theologische Revue* 65, no. 3 (1969): 182–88; Ratzinger's response, "Glaube, Geschichte und Philosophie: Zum Echo auf *Einführung in das Christentum*," is in *Hochland* 61 (1969): 533–43; Kasper responded in "Theorie und Praxis innerhalb einer *theologia crucis*: Antwort auf Joseph Ratzingers Glaube, Geschichte und Philosophie. Zum Echo auf *Einführung in das Christentum*," in *Hochland* 62 (1970): 152–57; and finally, Ratzinger's "Schlusswort," 157–59, in the same journal.

10. Kasper, "Das Wesen des Christlichen," 185–86; for a close review of the controversy, see Jim Corkery, "Joseph Ratzinger's Theological Ideas: 4. *Quaestiones Disputatae*–1," *Doctrine and Life* 56, no. 10 (2006): 12–18.

11. Walter Kasper, "On the Church: A Friendly Reply to Cardinal Ratzinger," *America* 184, no. 4 (April 23, 2001): 13.

12. Jim Corkery, "Joseph Ratzinger's Theological Ideas: 2. The Facial Features of a Theological Corpus," *Doctrine and Life* 56, no. 4 (2006): 6.

13. Ratzinger, *Principles of Catholic Theology*, 60; in the remainder of this section, page references to this work are given in parentheses in the text.

14. Joseph Ratzinger, *Called to Communion: Understanding the Church Today* (San Francisco: Ignatius Press, 1996), 142.

15. Michael Fahey, "Joseph Ratzinger as Ecclesiologist," in *Neo-conservatism: Social and Religious Phenomenon*, Concilium 141, ed. Gregory Baum (New York: Seabury, 1981), 80; see Ratzinger, *The Order of Priesthood* (Huntington, IN: Our Sunday Visitor, 1978), 131, 134.

16. Joseph Ratzinger, "Glaube, Geschichte und Philosophie: Zum Echo auf *Einführung in das Christentum*," *Hochland* 61 (1969): 543; cited by Aidan Nichols, *The Thought of Pope Benedict XVI: An*

Introduction to the Theology of Joseph Ratzinger, new ed. (New York: Burns and Oates, 2007), 17.

17. Joseph Ratzinger, *Volk und Haus Gottes in Augustins Lehre von der Kirche* (Munich: Zink, 1954).

18. This sense of voluntarism is very different from that which sees the divine freedom as meaning that God is not bound by the rational order. In his Regensburg address, Ratzinger sees this tradition as beginning with Duns Scotus ("The Regensburg Academic Lecture," *Origins* 36, no. 16 [2006]: 250).

19. Ratzinger, *Principles of Catholic Theology*, 350.

20. Ratzinger, *Principles of Catholic Theology*, 362.

21. Jim Corkery, "Joseph Ratzinger's Theological Ideas: 3. On Being Human," *Doctrine and Life* 56 (2006): 21.

22. Joseph Ratzinger/Pope Benedict XVI, *Jesus of Nazareth: From the Baptism in the Jordan to the Transfiguration* (New York: Doubleday, 2007), 92.

23. Thomas Aquinas, *Summa Theologiae*, I.84.5; trans. Fathers of the English Province.

24. Joseph A. Komonchak, "Vatican II and the Encounter between Catholicism and Liberalism," in *Catholicism and Liberalism: Contributions to American Public Philosophy*, ed. R. Bruce Douglass and David Hollenbach (New York: Cambridge University Press, 1994), 88.

25. Ratzinger, *Principles of Catholic Theology*, 344–46.

26. Joseph Ratzinger with Vittorio Messori, *The Ratzinger Report: An Exclusive Interview on the State of the Church* (San Francisco: Ignatius Press, 1985), 79.

27. Joseph Ratzinger, *Theological Highlights of Vatican II* (New York: Paulist Press, 1966), 154.

28. Ratzinger, *Theological Highlights of Vatican II*, 155–58.

29. See Ratzinger, *Principles of Catholic Theology*, 380.

30. Ratzinger, *Principles of Catholic Theology*, 380. Karl Rahner also worked on *GS*; he too found its undertone "too euphoric in its evaluation of humanity and the human condition," insisting that all human endeavors often wind up in blind alleys, including those of the church, which he refers to as a "Church of sinners" (*Theological Investigations*, vol. 22 [New York: Crossroad, 1991], 158).

31. Joseph A. Komonchak, "The Church in Crisis: Pope Benedict's Theological Vision," *Commonweal* 132, no. 11 (2005): 13; see

also Ratzinger in Herbert Vorgrimler, *Commentary on the Documents of Vatican II*, vol. 5 (New York: Herder & Herder, 1969), 119–40.

32. Ratzinger, *Principles of Catholic Theology*, 381–82.

33. Ratzinger, *Principles of Catholic Theology*, 167; he is quoting Rahner's *Grundkurs des Glaubens* (Freiburg: Herder, 1976), 225–26.

34. Ratzinger, *Principles of Catholic Theology*, 166. Consider, e.g., how these two different approaches might deal with the question of homosexuality.

35. Corkery, "Joseph Ratzinger's Theological Ideas: 2. The Facial Features of a Theological Corpus," 8–9.

36. Corkery, "Joseph's Ratzinger's Theological Ideas: 3. On Being Human," 16.

37. Brandon Peterson, "Critical Voices: The Reaction of Rahner and Ratzinger to Schema XIII (Gaudium et Spes)," *Modern Theology* 31, no. 1 (January 2015): 20–26.

38. Joseph Ratzinger, *Die Geschichtstheologie des heiligen Bonaventura* (Munich: Schnell und Steiner, 1959); Eng.: Joseph Ratzinger, *The Theology of History in St. Bonaventure* (Chicago: Franciscan Herald Press, 1971).

39. Ratzinger, *Milestones*, 104.

40. I am dependent here on Nichols's analysis in his *Thought of Pope Benedict XVI*, 38–44.

41. Ratzinger, *Theology of History*, 39.

42. Nichols, *Thought of Pope Benedict XVI*, 38.

43. Nichols, *Thought of Pope Benedict XVI*, 64–65.

44. Ratzinger, *Theology of History*, 13–14.

45. Ratzinger, *Theology of History*, 67.

46. Ratzinger, *Theology of History*, 160.

47. Komonchak, "Church in Crisis," 13.

48. Ratzinger, *Theology of History*, 71.

49. For example, David Gibson's book is entitled *The Rule of Benedict: Pope Benedict XVI and His Battle with the Modern World* (San Francisco: HarperSanFrancisco, 2006).

50. Ratzinger, *Milestones*, 42.

51. Fahey, "Joseph Ratzinger as Ecclesiologist and Pastor," 76; Corkery says that Ratzinger's writings exhibit a remarkable consistency over a half century ("Joseph Ratzinger's Theological Ideas: 2. The Facial Features of a Theological Corpus," 3).

52. Komonchak, "Church in Crisis," 12.

53. Ratzinger, *Principles of Catholic Theology*, 134.

54. Anthony Grafton, "Reading Ratzinger: Benedict XVI, the Theologian," *The New Yorker* (July 25, 2005): 49.

55. Joseph Ratzinger, *Truth and Tolerance: Christian Belief and World Religions* (San Francisco: Ignatius Press, 2004), 252. See also Ratzinger, *Values in a Time of Upheaval* (San Francisco: Ignatius Press, 2006), 65–66.

56. See Nichols, *Thought of Benedict XVI*, 167–70.

57. Nichols, *Thought of Benedict XVI*, 170.

58. Some, like Luke Timothy Johnson, will argue that many have found that same-sex unions can be holy and good; see "Homosexuality and the Church: Scripture and Experience," *Commonweal* 134, no. 12 (2007): 15.

59. Komonchak, "Church in Crisis," 13.

60. See Aylward Shorter, *Evangelization and Culture* (London: Geoffrey Chapman, 1994); Peter C. Phan, *In Our Own Tongues: Perspectives from Asia on Mission and Inculturation* (Maryknoll, NY: Orbis Books, 2003).

61. Ratzinger, *Theological Highlights of Vatican II*, 174.

62. See "Cardinal Ratzinger Urges Asian Bishops to Adopt Term 'Inter-culturality,'" UCAN Archives AS7025.0705 (March 9, 1993); see also Ratzinger, *Truth and Tolerance*, 64.

63. Francis Schüssler Fiorenza, "From Theologian to Pope: A Personal View Back, Past the Public Portrayals," *Harvard Divinity Bulletin* 33, no. 2 (2005): 62.

64. Ratzinger with Messori, *Ratzinger Report*, 193.

65. Benedict XVI, "Regensburg Academic Lecture," 250; cf. John Paul II, *Fides et Ratio* (1998), no. 16.

66. Benedict XVI, "Regensburg Academic Lecture," 251.

67. Benedict XVI, "Regensburg Academic Lecture," 250.

68. Ratzinger, *Truth and Tolerance*, 79.

69. James Fredericks, "The Catholic Church and the Other Religious Paths: Rejecting Nothing That Is True and Holy," *Theological Studies* 64 (2003): 232; see *DI* 7.

70. Ratzinger, *Milestones*, 129.

71. Ratzinger, *Truth and Tolerance*, 252.

72. Francis X. Clooney, "Dialogue Not Monologue: Benedict XVI and Religious Pluralism," *Commonweal* 132, no. 18 (October 21, 2005): 14.

73. Ratzinger, *Truth and Tolerance*, 105; this was reiterated in the CDF document "Doctrinal Note on Some Aspects of Evangelization" (December 14, 2007), begun under Ratzinger's prefecture.
74. Ratzinger, *Truth and Tolerance*, 89.

Chapter 3

1. Joseph Ratzinger, "The Transmission of Divine Revelation," in *Commentary on the Documents of Vatican II*, ed. Herbert Vorgrimler, vol. 3 (New York: Herder & Herder, 1969), 192.
2. Joseph Ratzinger, *Church, Ecumenism and Politics* (New York: Crossroad, 1988), 95.
3. Ratzinger, *Church, Ecumenism and Politics*, 182.
4. Joseph Ratzinger, *Milestones: Memoirs 1927–1977* (San Francisco: Ignatius Press, 1998), 52–53.
5. Ratzinger, *Milestones*, 109.
6. Joseph Ratzinger, *Principles of Catholic Theology: Building Stones for a Fundamental Theology* (San Francisco: Ignatius Press, 1987), 321.
7. Ratzinger, *Milestones*, 127; see also 108–9.
8. Ratzinger, *Principles of Catholic Theology*, 168.
9. Joseph Ratzinger, *The Theology of History in St. Bonaventure* (Chicago: Franciscan Herald Press, 1989), 67.
10. John L. Allen Jr., *Cardinal Ratzinger: The Vatican's Enforcer of the Faith* (New York: Continuum, 2000), 38; Guardini also had a great influence on Flannery O'Connor and Thomas Merton.
11. See Ratzinger's review, "Guardini on Christ in Our Century," *Crisis* 14 (June 1996): 14.
12. See Robert A. Krieg, *Romano Guardini: A Precursor of Vatican II* (Notre Dame, IN: University of Notre Dame Press, 1997), 152–59.
13. Ratzinger, "The Transmission of Divine Revelation," 193.
14. See Joseph Ratzinger, "Biblical Interpretation in Crisis: On the Question of the Foundations and Approach of Exegesis Today," in *Biblical Interpretation in Crisis: The Ratzinger Conference on Bible and Church*, ed. Richard John Neuhaus (Grand Rapids: Eerdmans, 1989), 1–23; numbers in parentheses in the text refer to pages

in the Neuhaus edition; the lecture is also available online. Neuhaus was later received into the Catholic Church and ordained a priest in 1991.

15. Ratzinger refers here to a dissertation by Rainer Blank entitled "Analysis and Criticism of the Form-Critical Works of Martin Dibelius and Rudolph Bultmann" ("Biblical Interpretation," 8); for the dissertation, see *Theologische Dissertationen* monograph series 16 (Basel: F. Reinhardt, 1981).

16. See Romano Guardini, *Das Christusbild der paulinischen und johanneischen Schriften* (Wurzburg: Werkbund-Verlag, 1961), 14.

17. Raymond E. Brown, "The Contribution of Historical Biblical Criticism to Ecumenical Church Discussion," in Neuhaus, *Biblical Interpretation in Crisis*, 44.

18. Joseph Ratzinger, *God and the World: A Conversation with Peter Seewald* (San Francisco: Ignatius Press, 2002), 449.

19. See Joseph Ratzinger, *Called to Communion: Understanding the Church Today* (San Francisco: Ignatius Press, 1996), 14–19.

20. Joseph Ratzinger/Benedict XVI, *Jesus of Nazareth: From the Baptism in the Jordan to the Transfiguration* (New York: Doubleday, 2007), xv; cf. *DV* 12; also, the Pontifical Biblical Commission, "The Interpretation of the Bible in the Church, I, Methods and Approaches for Interpretation," *Origins* 23, no. 29 (1994): 500–502.

21. See Ratzinger/Benedict, *Jesus of Nazareth*, xv–xvi.

22. Ratzinger/Benedict, *Jesus of Nazareth*, xviii.

23. Ratzinger/Benedict, *Jesus of Nazareth*, 234. I am grateful to John R. Donahue, SJ, for bringing this to my attention.

24. Ratzinger, *Called to Communion*, 58.

25. Ratzinger, *Jesus of Nazareth*, 229.

26. Ratzinger, *Called to Communion*, 24–29.

27. See Ratzinger, *Principles of Catholic Theology*, 273–77.

28. Benedict XVI, General Audience, March 7, 2007.

29. Joseph Ratzinger, *Many Religions—One Covenant* (San Francisco: Ignatius Press, 1999); see also *The Spirit of the Liturgy* (San Francisco: Ignatius Press, 2000), 49, 67.

30. Ratzinger, *Milestones*, 53.

31. Origen, *Homily* 6.4: *PG* 12:855.

32. Ratzinger, *Principles of Catholic Theology*, 279.

33. Augustine, *Quaest. In Heptateuchum* 2.73; *PL* 34:625.

34. Sandra M. Schneiders, *The Revelatory Text: Interpreting the New Testament as Sacred Scripture* (Collegeville, MN: Liturgical Press, 1999).

35. Brevard S. Childs, *Biblical Theology in Crisis* (Philadelphia: Westminster, 1970), 110.

36. Gerhard Ebeling, *Word and Faith* (Philadelphia: Fortress Press, 1963), esp. 79–97 ("The Meaning of 'Biblical Theology'").

37. James A. Sanders, *Canon and Community: A Guide to Canonical Criticism* (Philadelphia: Fortress Press, 1984), xvi.

38. Childs, *Biblical Theology in Crisis*, 102.

39. See Schneiders, *Revelatory Text*, 25.

40. See *The Five Gospels: The Search for the Authentic Words of Jesus*, a new translation and commentary by Robert W. Funk, Roy W. Hoover, and the Jesus Seminar (New York: Macmillan, 1993).

41. John Dominic Crossan, *The Historical Jesus: The Life of a Mediterranean Jewish Peasant* (San Francisco: HarperSanFrancisco, 1991) and *Jesus: A Revolutionary Biography* (San Francisco: HarperSanFrancisco, 1994); Burton L. Mack, *A Myth of Innocence: Mark and Christian Origins* (Philadelphia: Fortress Press, 1988), 79; see also his *The Lost Gospel: The Book of Q and Christian Origins* (San Francisco: HarperSanFrancisco, 1993).

42. Mack, *Myth of Innocence*, 371.

43. Hans Küng, *On Being a Christian* (Garden City, NY: Doubleday, 1976), 439–42.

44. Roger Haight, *Jesus Symbol of God* (Maryknoll, NY: Orbis Books, 1999), 176–77.

45. Elisabeth Schüssler Fiorenza, *Jesus: Miriam's Child, Sophia's Prophet; Critical Issues in Feminist Christology* (New York: Continuum, 1994), 96.

46. Schüssler Fiorenza, *Jesus*, 46–47.

47. Schüssler Fiorenza, *Jesus*, 48.

48. Ernst Käsemann, "Paul and Early Catholicism," in his *New Testament Questions of Today* (London: SCM Press, 1969), 236–51; also *Essays on New Testament Themes* (London: SCM Press, 1964), 63–134.

49. James D. G. Dunn, *Unity and Diversity in the New Testament: An Inquiry into the Character of Earliest Christianity*, 2nd ed. (London: SCM Press, 1990; first published, 1977), 369.

50. Leonardo Boff, *Church, Charism and Power: Liberation Theology and the Institutional Church* (New York: Crossroad, 1985), 110–15.

51. Joseph Ratzinger, "Assessment and Future Prospects," in *Looking Again at the Question of the Liturgy with Cardinal Ratzinger: Proceedings of the July 2001 Fontgombault Liturgical Conference*, ed. Alcuin Reid (Farnborough: Saint Michael's Abbey Press, 2003), 148.

52. Joseph Ratzinger, "The Theology of the Liturgy," in Reid, *Looking Again at the Question of the Liturgy with Cardinal Ratzinger*, 21–22.

53. Ratzinger, "Biblical Interpretation in Crisis," 23.

54. Brown, "Contribution of Historical Biblical Criticism," 40.

55. Ratzinger/Benedict, *Jesus of Nazareth*, xviii.

56. "The Interpretation of the Bible in the Church," III; *Origins*, 513.

57. "The Interpretation of the Bible in the Church," IV.A; *Origins*, 519–23.

58. The Interpretation of the Bible in the Church," Conclusion; *Origins*, 524.

59. Joseph Ratzinger, in the Pontifical Biblical Commission, "The Jewish People and Their Sacred Scriptures in the Christian Bible, Introduction," https://www.vatican.va/roman _curia/congregations/cfaith/pcb_documents/rc_con_cfaith_doc _20020212_popolo-ebraico_en.html.

60. Ratzinger, *Principles of Catholic Theology*, 276.

61. Ratzinger, *God and the World*, 366; see also Eldon Jay Epp, *Junia: The First Woman Apostle* (Minneapolis: Fortress Press, 2005).

62. Ratzinger, *Called to Communion*, 125.

63. Christopher Ruddy, "No Restorationist: Ratzinger's Theological Journey," *Commonweal* 132, no. 11 (June 3, 2005): 17.

64. Ratzinger/Benedict, *Jesus of Nazareth*, xvii.

Chapter 4

1. Joseph Ratzinger, *Called to Communion: Understanding the Church Today* (San Francisco: Ignatius Press, 1996), 15.

2. See "Does He Have Legitimate Concerns?" on pages 76–79 of this book.

3. Joseph Ratzinger, *Introduction to Christianity* (San Francisco: Ignatius Press, 2004), 197.

4. Joseph Ratzinger/Pope Benedict XVI, *Jesus of Nazareth: From the Baptism in the Jordan to the Transfiguration* (New York: Doubleday, 2007), xxiii; in this section, page references to this book are given in parentheses in the text.

5. See Pontifical Biblical Commission, "Instruction on the Historical Truth of the Gospels"; for a translation and commentary, see Joseph A. Fitzmyer, *Theological Studies* 25 (1964): 386–408.

6. See John P. Meier, *A Marginal Jew: Rethinking the Historical Jesus*, vol. 1, *The Roots of the Problem and the Person*, Anchor Bible Reference Library (New York: Doubleday, 1991), 168–77; also Edward Schillebeeckx, *Jesus: An Experiment in Christology* (New York: Seabury, 1979), 88–100.

7. In a review of *Jesus of Nazareth*, Jack Miles observes that "Ratzinger's thinking tracks positively with his *Introduction to Christianity*" ("Between Theology and Exegesis," *Commonweal* 134, no. 13 (2007): 23.

8. Joseph Ratzinger, *Truth and Tolerance: Christian Belief and World Religions* (San Francisco: Ignatius Press, 2004), 134.

9. Ratzinger/Benedict, *Jesus of Nazareth*, 4–6, at 6.

10. Robert Mickens and Philip Crispin, "Cardinal Martini Queries Aspects of Pope Benedict's Book," Church in the World, *The Tablet*, June 2, 2007, 29.

11. See John P. Meier, *A Marginal Jew: Rethinking the Historical Jesus*, vol. 2, *Mentor, Message, and Miracles*, Anchor Bible Reference Library (New York: Doubleday, 1994), 129.

12. See Jacob Neusner, *A Rabbi Talks with Jesus* (New York: Doubleday, 1993), 76–81.

13. Neusner, *A Rabbi Talks with Jesus*, 68–69.

14. Neusner, *A Rabbi Talks with Jesus*, 53.

15. On the fuller sense, see Raymond E. Brown and Sandra M. Schneiders, "Hermeneutics," in *The New Jerome Biblical Commentary*, ed. Raymond E. Brown, Joseph A. Fitzmyer, and Roland E. Murphy (Englewood Cliffs, NJ: Prentice Hall, 1990), 1157.

16. Walter Kasper, *Jesus the Christ* (New York: Paulist Press, 1977), 110.

17. Marinus de Jonge, *Christology in Context: The Earliest Christian Response to Jesus* (Philadelphia: Westminster, 1988), 95.

18. Gerald O'Collins, "He Who Is," *America* 196, no. 20 (2007): 23.
19. Miles, "Between Theology and Exegesis," 21.
20. Richard B. Hays, "Benedict and the Biblical Jesus," *First Things* 175 (August–September 2007): 51.
21. O'Collins, "He Who Is," 23.
22. Aidan Nichols, *The Thought of Pope Benedict XVI: An Introduction to the Theology of Joseph Ratzinger*, new ed. (New York: Burns and Oates, 2007), 118.
23. Joseph Ratzinger, *Church, Ecumenism and Politics* (New York: Crossroad, 1988), 206.
24. D. Vincent Twomey, "The Mind of Benedict XVI," *Claremont Review of Books* 5, no. 4 (Fall 2005): 70; Twomey provides a good overview of Ratzinger's political philosophy.
25. Ben Witherington III, *The Jesus Quest: The Third Search for the Jew of Nazareth* (Downers Grove, IL: InterVarsity, 1995), 27.
26. Hays, "Benedict and the Biblical Jesus," 51.
27. Harvey Cox, *The Silencing of Leonardo Boff: The Vatican and the Future of World Christianity* (Oak Park, IL: Meyer-Stone Books, 1988), 41.
28. Ratzinger, *Truth and Tolerance*, 119–26.

Chapter 5

1. Joseph Ratzinger, *Volk und Haus Gottes in Augustins Lehre von der Kirche* (Munich: Karl Zink, 1954).
2. Christopher Ruddy, *The Local Church: Tillard and the Future of Catholic Ecclesiology* (New York: Crossroad, 2006), 100.
3. Joseph Ratzinger with Vittorio Messori, *The Ratzinger Report: An Exclusive Interview on the State of the Church* (San Francisco: Ignatius Press, 1985), 49.
4. Joseph Ratzinger, *Das neue Volk Gottes: Entwürfe zur Ekklesiologie* (Düsseldorf: Patmos, 1969); in this section on Ratzinger's early ecclesiology, I am dependent on Aidan Nichols, *The Thought of Pope Benedict XVI: An Introduction to the Theology of Joseph Ratzinger*, new ed. (New York: Burns and Oates, 2007), 94–109.
5. See Ruddy, *Local Church*, 9–30.

6. Ratzinger, *Das neue Volk Gottes*, 285; cited by Nichols, *Thought of Pope Benedict XVI*, 107.

7. Joseph Ratzinger, *Church, Ecumenism and Politics* (New York: Crossroad, 1988), 3–62; *Called to Communion: Understanding the Church Today* (San Francisco: Ignatius Press, 1996); *Principles of Catholic Theology: Building Stones for a Fundamental Theology* (San Francisco: Ignatius Press, 1987), 239–84.

8. Ratzinger, *Called to Communion*, 23.

9. Ratzinger, *Called to Communion*, 24.

10. Ratzinger, *Called to Communion*, 27.

11. Ratzinger, *Called to Communion*, 31.

12. Ratzinger, *Called to Communion*, 37.

13. Nichols, *Thought of Pope Benedict XVI*, 31.

14. Ratzinger, *Principles of Catholic Theology*, 53.

15. Ratzinger, *Church, Ecumenism and Politics*, 8.

16. Ratzinger, *Called to Communion*, 39.

17. Ratzinger, *Principles of Catholic Theology*, 273.

18. Ratzinger, *Principles of Catholic Theology*, 239; see also 245–47.

19. Ratzinger, *Principles of Catholic Theology*, 234.

20. Ratzinger, *Church, Ecumenism and Politics*, 11–13.

21. Nichols, *The Thought of Benedict XVI*, 178–79; see Ratzinger, *Church, Ecumenism and Politics*, 52–57.

22. Ratzinger, *Called to Communion*, 47–72, at 72.

23. Nichols, *Thought of Pope Benedict XVI*, 99.

24. Ratzinger, *Called to Communion*, 52–58.

25. Ratzinger, *Called to Communion*, 68.

26. Ratzinger, *Called to Communion*, 76.

27. Ratzinger, *Principles of Catholic Theology*, 254.

28. Joseph Ratzinger, "Eucharist, Communion and Solidarity" (June 2, 2002), no. 2; https://www.vatican.va/roman_curia/congregations/cfaith/documents/rc_con_cfaith_doc_20020602_ratzinger-eucharistic-congress_en.html.

29. Joseph Ratzinger, *Salt of the Earth: The Church at the End of the Millennium; An Interview with Peter Seewald* (San Francisco: Ignatius Press, 1997), 188–89.

30. Ratzinger, *Church, Ecumenism and Politics*, 14–28.

31. See Killian McDonnell, "The Ratzinger/Kasper Debate: The Universal Church and the Local Churches," *Theological Studies* 63, no. 2 (2002): 238; Ratzinger's article was published in *Frankfurter*

Allgemeine Zeitung (December 22, 2000): 46; see also Joseph Ratzinger, *Pilgrim Fellowship of Faith: The Church as Communion*, ed. Stephan Otto Horn and Vinzenz Pfnür (San Francisco: Ignatius Press, 2005), 145.

32. Philip A. Franco, "The Communion Ecclesiology of Joseph Ratzinger," in *Vatican II: Forty Years Later*, ed. William Madges (Maryknoll, NY: Orbis Books, 2006), 15.

33. Dennis Doyle, *Communion Ecclesiology: Vision and Versions* (Maryknoll, NY: Orbis Books, 2000), 113.

34. Ratzinger, *Church, Ecumenism and Politics*, 75.

35. See McDonnell, "Ratzinger/Kasper Debate," 237; see also Joseph Ratzinger, "The Local Church and the Universal Church: A Response to Walter Kasper," *America* 185 (November 19, 2001): 10.

36. McDonnell, "Ratzinger/Kasper Debate," 230.

37. Hermann J. Pottmeyer, *Towards a Papacy in Communion: Perspectives from Vatican Councils I and II* (New York: Crossroad, 1998), 116.

38. Ruddy, *Local Church*, 52.

39. Richard R. Gaillardetz, "Episcopal Leadership and the Church in the United States" (unpublished essay).

40. McDonnell, "Ratzinger/Kasper Debate," 231.

41. John L. Allen Jr., *Cardinal Ratzinger: The Vatican's Enforcer of the Faith* (New York: Continuum, 2000), 307.

42. Ratzinger, *Principles of Catholic Theology*, 24; he is referring to the church's struggle with Gnosticism.

43. Ratzinger, *Pilgrim Fellowship of Faith*, 190.

44. Ratzinger, *Principles of Catholic Theology*, 260–61.

45. Ratzinger, *Principles of Catholic Theology*, 245.

46. Ratzinger, *Principles of Catholic Theology*, 246.

47. Ratzinger, *Called to Communion*, 97–99.

48. Ratzinger, *Principles of Catholic Theology*, 246.

49. Ratzinger, *Principles of Catholic Theology*, 288–91.

50. Ratzinger, *Church, Ecumenism and Politics*, 9.

51. Ratzinger, *Principles of Catholic Theology*, 293.

52. Ratzinger, *Principles of Catholic Theology*, 294. The argument on the community's right to the Eucharist surfaced again in 2007 when four Dutch Dominicans published *Kerk en Ambt* (*Church and Ministry*), arguing that in the absence of ordained priests, lay men and women should be allowed to celebrate the Eucharist; see

Andre Lascaris, "To Serve and to Celebrate," *The Tablet*, September 22, 2007, 8–9.

53. Ratzinger, *Principles of Catholic Theology*, 252.

54. Ratzinger, *Pilgrim Fellowship of Faith*, 258.

55. See CDF, "Letter to the Bishops of the Catholic Church on Some Aspects of the Church Understood as Communion" (May 28, 1992), no. 17, a letter published under Ratzinger's prefecture.

56. Joseph Ratzinger, *Theological Highlights of Vatican II* (New York: Paulist Press, 1966), 69–73.

57. Ratzinger, *Church, Ecumenism and Politics*, "Part II: Ecumenical Problems."

58. Ratzinger, *Church, Ecumenism and Politics*, 120.

59. Nichols, *Thought of Pope Benedict XVI*, 191–93.

60. Heinrich Fries and Karl Rahner, *Unity of the Churches: An Actual Possibility* (New York: Paulist Press, 1985).

61. Ratzinger, *Church, Ecumenism and Politics*, 120.

62. Ratzinger, *Church, Ecumenism and Politics*, 141.

63. Ratzinger, *Church, Ecumenism and Politics*, 199.

64. Ratzinger, *Church, Ecumenism and Politics*, 223.

65. Ratzinger, *Church, Ecumenism and Politics*, 236; see CDF, "Declaration in Defense of Catholic Doctrine against Certain Errors of the Present Day."

66. See "Briefwechsel von Landesbischof Johannes Hanselmann und Joseph Kardinal Ratzinger über das Communion-Schreiben der Römischen Glaubenskongregation," *Una Sancta* 48 (1993): 348; see also Ratzinger, *Pilgrim Fellowship of Faith*, 248.

67. See "Commentary on Profession of Faith's Concluding Paragraphs," *Origins* 28, no. 8 (1998): 119; Avery Dulles found this Anglican example debatable; see "Commentary," sidebar, 117.

68. Michael Root, "Bishops, Ministry, and the Unity of the Church in Ecumenical Dialogue: Deadlock, Breakthrough, or Both," *Proceedings of the Sixty-Second Annual Convention of the Catholic Theological Society of America* 62 (2007): 33; Root suggests that such a category is already present in Vatican II's use of *defectus* (*UR* 22), understood as defect and not as absence or lack.

69. Ratzinger, *Principles of Catholic Theology*, 293.

70. Ratzinger, *Church, Ecumenism and Politics*, 132; in regard to Protestant celebrations of the Lord's Supper, he says, "We know that the people can also meet the Lord here, but we cannot allow

the fact to be obscured that the question of apostolic succession and of priesthood—as of the Catholic faith and teaching in its entirety—marks a boundary here." (Joseph Ratzinger, *God and the World: A Conversation with Peter Seewald* [San Francisco: Ignatius Press, 2002], 412).

71. Lutheran–Catholic Dialogue, "Joint Declarations on the Doctrine of Justification," *Origins* 28, no. 8 (1998).

72. Interestingly, he criticized the Fries-Rahner proposal in their *Unity of the Churches* for its being confined to the German-speaking world, explicitly excluding the Free churches; see Ratzinger, *Church, Ecumenism and Politics*, 131.

73. Joseph Ratzinger, *Without Roots: The West, Relativism, Christianity, Islam* (New York: Basic Books, 2006), 112–13.

74. See Ratzinger, *Pilgrim Fellowship of Faith*, 38–50.

75. Ratzinger, *Pilgrim Fellowship of Faith*, 54.

76. CDF, "Responses to Some Questions regarding Certain Aspects on the Doctrine of the Church" (July 10, 2007), Fifth Question; *Origins* 37, no. 9 (2007): 134–36; see also *DI* 17; Walter Kasper commented, "An attentive reading of the text shows that the document does not say that Protestant churches are not churches, but that they are not churches in the proper sense, that is, they are not churches in the sense in which the Catholic Church defines Church" (ZENIT [July 12, 2007]). According to Cardinal Karl Lehmann, president of the German Bishops' Conference, "It is not appropriate to repeat and republish reminders and admonitions on binding church teaching, which are moreover frequently incomplete or abbreviated, with a period of just a few years—even if they are necessary" (*The Tablet*, October 6, 2007, 29).

77. CDF, "Letter to the Bishops of the Catholic Church on Some Aspects of the Church Understood as Communion," no. 9, *Origins* 22 (1992): 108–12.

78. *Missa Pro Ecclesia*, First Message of His Holiness Benedict XVI at the End of the Eucharistic Concelebration with the Members of the College of Cardinals (April 20, 2005), no. 5.

79. Walter Kasper, "The Current Ecumenical Transition," *Origins* 36, no. 26 (2006): 407.

80. Walter Kasper observes that the Reformers' "understanding of the church is grounded not on the eucharist but primarily on the Word of God as *creatura verbi*" ("Decree on Ecumenism: Read

Anew after Forty Years," *PCPCU Information Service* 118 [2005/I–II]: 36).

81. WCC, "Called to Be One Church," adopted at the Ninth WCC Assembly, Porto Alegre, Brazil, February 14–23, 2006, no. 6.

82. Simon Caldwell, "Vatican Official to Anglicans: Women Bishops Would Destroy Unity," Catholic News Service, June 7, 2006; see also Brian Farrell, "The Dialogues and the Dialogue: A Summary of the Official Ecumenical Dialogues of the PCPCU from 2004 to Today," *PCPCU Information Service* 123 (2006/III–IV): 108.

Chapter 6

1. Joseph Ratzinger, *Milestones: Memoirs 1927–1977* (San Francisco: Ignatius Press, 1998), 18–19.

2. Ratzinger, *Milestones*, 20.

3. See Eamon Duffy, "Benedict XVI and the Spirit of the Liturgy," *Doctrine and Life* 55, no. 10 (2005): 35–36.

4. See John L. Allen Jr., *Cardinal Ratzinger: The Vatican's Enforcer of the Faith* (New York: Continuum, 2000), 73.

5. Ratzinger, *Milestones*, 57.

6. Ratzinger, *Milestones*, 146–49, at 148.

7. Joseph Ratzinger, *God and the World: A Conversation with Peter Seewald* (San Francisco: Ignatius Press, 2002), 416.

8. See Joseph Ratzinger, *The Feast of Faith* (San Francisco: Ignatius Press, 1986), 18–25.

9. Ratzinger, *Feast of Faith*, 37.

10. Ratzinger, *Feast of Faith*, 144.

11. Ratzinger, *Feast of Faith*, 41.

12. Ratzinger, *Feast of Faith*, 44.

13. Joseph Ratzinger, *God Is Near Us: The Eucharist, the Heart of Life*, ed. Stephan Otto Horn and Vinzenz Pfnür (San Francisco: Ignatius Press, 2003), 57–60.

14. Eamon Duffy, "Benedict XVI and the Eucharist," *New Blackfriars* 88, no. 1014 (2007): 206.

15. Ratzinger, *Feast of Faith*, 42–49.

16. Joseph Ratzinger, *Pilgrim Fellowship of Faith: The Church as Communion*, ed. Stephan Otto Horn and Vinzenz Pfnür (San Francisco: Ignatius Press, 2005), 94–95.

17. Joseph Ratzinger, *The Spirit of the Liturgy* (San Francisco: Ignatius Press, 2000).

18. Ratzinger, *Spirit of the Liturgy*, 37.

19. Ratzinger, *Spirit of the Liturgy*, 43.

20. Ratzinger, *Spirit of the Liturgy*, 45–46, at 46; in *Feast of Faith*, he characterizes *logike latreia* as "worship characterized by logos," to contrast earlier animal sacrifices with the sacrifice of a humbled heart, noting that the Roman Canon uses the expression *oblatio rationabilis*, a sacrifice expressed with words (37).

21. Ratzinger, *Spirit of the Liturgy*, 49; cf. 67.

22. Ratzinger, *Spirit of the Liturgy*, 171–74; in an earlier collection of essays on the liturgy, he speaks of the people of God in the liturgy as "active co-celebrants" (*A New Song for the Lord: Faith in Christ and Liturgy Today* [New York: Crossroad, 1996], 171).

23. Ratzinger, *Feast of Faith*, 37.

24. Ratzinger, *Spirit of the Liturgy*, 80; see also *Feast of Faith*, 139–45.

25. Ratzinger, *New Song for the Lord*, 148.

26. Ratzinger, *Feast of Faith*, 144.

27. Ratzinger, *Spirit of the Liturgy*, 83.

28. Ratzinger, *Feast of Faith*, 77.

29. John F. Baldovin, "In Form and Expression," *America* 184, no. 15 (2001): 29–30.

30. Ratzinger, *Spirit of the Liturgy*, 50; see also *Feast of Faith*, 36–39.

31. Ratzinger, *Feast of Faith*, 65.

32. Ratzinger, *Spirit of the Liturgy*, 78.

33. Ratzinger, *Spirit of the Liturgy*, 143; *Feast of Faith*, 117–21; Ratzinger's views on liturgy and church music are collected in *New Song for the Lord*.

34. Ratzinger, *New Song for the Lord*, 195.

35. "Some Questions regarding Collaboration of Non-ordained Faithful in the Sacred Ministry of Priests," August 15, 1997; *Origins* 29, no. 13 (1997): 403.

36. Benedict XVI, "Apostolic Letter *Summorum Pontificum*," July 7, 2007, *Origins* 37, no. 9 (2007): 129–32.

37. Duffy, "Benedict XVI and the Spirit of the Liturgy," 49.

38. Benedict XVI, "*Motu Proprio* on the Tridentine Mass" and "Letter Accompanying *Motu Proprio* on the Tridentine Mass," *Origins* 37, no. 9 (2007): 129–34.

39. Benedict XVI, "Letter Accompanying *Motu Proprio*," 133.

40. Joseph Ratzinger, *Called to Communion: Understanding the Church Today* (San Francisco: Ignatius Press, 1996), 75.

41. Ratzinger, *Spirit of the Liturgy*, 23.

42. Ratzinger, *New Song for the Lord*, 91.

43. Bruce T. Morrill, "What Difference Does It Make for Me as a Liturgist to Be a Jesuit—or Vice Versa?" in *Jesuit Postmodern: Scholarship, Vocation, and Identity in the 21st Century*, ed. Francis X. Clooney (Lanham, MD: Lexington Books, 2006), 70.

44. See Rita Ferrone, "A Step Backward," *Commonweal* 134, no. 14 (August 17, 2007): 15.

45. Ratzinger, *Feast of Faith*, 73.

Chapter 7

1. See Jared Wicks, "Six Texts by Prof. Joseph Ratzinger as *Peritus* before and during Vatican Council II," *Gregorianum* 89, no. 2 (2008).

2. John L. Allen Jr., "2007's Neglected Story: Benedict XVI and 'Affirmative Orthodoxy,'" *National Catholic Reporter*, January 3, 2008.

3. Allen, "2007's Neglected Story."

4. For example, Francis Schüssler Fiorenza, "From Theologian to Pope," *Harvard Divinity Bulletin* 33, no. 2 (Fall 2005): 58; Joseph A. Komonchak refers to the "deeper continuity" in his basic theological approach and vision, "The Church in Crisis: Pope Benedict's Theological Vision," *Commonweal* 132, no. 11 (2005): 11.

5. See Thomas P. Rausch, "Introduction," in Joseph Ratzinger, *Theological Highlights of Vatican II* (New York: Paulist Press, 2009), 1–16.

6. Ratzinger, *Theological Highlights*, 246–47.

7. Ratzinger, *Theological Highlights*, 58–59.

8. Ratzinger, *Theological Highlights*, 91–93, at 93.

9. John L. Allen Jr., *The Rise of Benedict XVI* (New York: Doubleday, 2005), 150.

10. John L. Allen Jr., *Cardinal Ratzinger: The Vatican's Enforcer of the Faith* (New York: Continuum, 2001), 67.

11. Robert Mickens, "Benedict's Papacy: The Way It's Shaping Up," *The Tablet*, September 16, 2011, https://www.thetablet.co.uk/article/161726.

12. See William V. D'Antonio, James D. Davidson, Dean R. Hoge, and Mary L. Gautier, *American Catholics Today: New Realities of Their Faith and Their Church* (Lanham, MD: Rowman and Littlefield, 2007).

13. David Tracy, *Blessed Rage for Order* (New York: Seabury Press, 1975), 43–45.

14. Roger Haight, "The American Jesuit Theologian," in *Jesuit Postmodern: Scholarship, Vocation, and Identity in the 21st Century*, ed. Francis X. Clooney (Lanham, MD: Lexington Books, 2006), 98.

15. Joseph Ratzinger, *A New Song for the Lord* (New York: Crossroad, 1996), 91.

16. Joseph Ratzinger, *Pilgrim Fellowship of Faith: The Church as Communion*, ed. Stephan Otto Horn and Vinzenz Pfnür (San Francisco: Ignatius Press, 2005), 180.

17. Richard R. Gaillardetz, ed., *When the Magisterium Intervenes: The Magisterium and Theologians in Today's Church* (Collegeville, MN: Liturgical Press, 2012), vii.

18. Charles E. Curran traces these developing tensions in his *The Catholic Theological Society of America: A Story of Seventy-Five Years* (New York: Paulist Press, 2021), 70–87, 143–50.

19. See Bradford E. Hinze, "A Decade of Disciplining Theologians," in Gaillardetz, *When the Magisterium Intervenes*, 12–19; for a more complete list see 3–39.

20. Joseph Ratzinger/Pope Benedict XVI, *Jesus of Nazareth: From the Baptism in the Jordan to the Transfiguration* (New York: Doubleday, 2007), xxii.

21. Joseph Ratzinger, *Principles of Catholic Theology: Building Stones for a Fundamental Theology* (San Francisco: Ignatius Press, 1987), 53.

22. See Ludwig Hertling, *Communio: Church and Papacy in Early Christianity* (Chicago: Loyola University Press, 1972).

23. Ratzinger, *Principles of Catholic Theology*, 254.

24. Ratzinger, *Principles of Catholic Theology*, 260–61.

25. Roger Haight, *Christian Community in History*, 2 vols. (New York: Continuum, 2004, 2005).

26. Charles M. Murphy, "Collegiality: An Essay toward Better Understanding," *Theological Studies* 46 (1985): 41.

27. See Richard R. Gaillardetz, *The Church in the Making* (New York: Paulist Press, 2006), 128–29.

28. Joseph Ratzinger and Vittori Messori, *The Ratzinger Report: An Exclusive Interview on the State of the Church* (San Francisco: Ignatius Press, 1985), 59. In *Evangelii Gaudium* 32, Pope Francis wrote that "a juridical status of episcopal conferences which would see them as subjects of specific attributions, including genuine doctrinal authority, has not yet been sufficiently elaborated."

29. Michael Fahey, "The Synod of America: Reflections of a Nonparticipant," *Theological Studies* 59 (1998): 498.

30. Massimo Faggioli, *Vatican II and the Battle for Meaning* (New York: Paulist Press, 2012), 103–4.

31. Massimo Faggioli, "*Sacrosanctum Concilium* and the Meaning of Vatican II," *Theological Studies* 7 (2010): 444.

32. Tom Roberts, "Battle Lines in the Liturgy Wars," *National Catholic Reporter*, March 1, 2010.

33. Rita Ferrone, "A Living Catholic Tradition: Pope Francis Unifies the Roman Rite," *Commonweal* 148, no. 8 (September 2021), https://www.commonwealmagazine.org/living-catholic-tradition; Massimo Faggioli sees these traditionalist movements as examples of a new integralism, "looking forward to the nineteenth century," in his "A Church within the Church: Behind the New Integralism Is the Old Intransigentism," *Commonweal* (January 8, 2019).

34. See Peter A. Kwasniewski, ed., *From Benedict's Peace to Francis's War: Catholics Respond to the Motu Proprio "Traditionis Custodes" on the Latin Mass* (New York: Angelico Press, 2021).

35. See Miroslav Volf, *After Our Likeness: The Church as the Image of the Trinity* (Grand Rapids: Eerdmans, 1998), 133–34; Veli-Matti Kärkkäinen, *An Introduction to Ecclesiology: Ecumenical, Historical and Global Perspectives* (Downers Grove, IL: InterVarsity, 2002), 70–72.

36. John Beal, "It Shall Not Be So Among You!" in *Governance, Accountability, and the Future of the Catholic Church*, ed. Francis Oakley and Bruce Russett (New York: Continuum, 2004), 97.

37. USCCB Committee on Doctrine, "Statement on Book by Father Peter Phan," *Origins* 37, no. 28 (2007): 445–50.

38. Aidan Nichols, *The Thought of Pope Benedict XVI: An Introduction to the Theology of Joseph Ratzinger*, new ed. (New York: Burns and Oates, 2007), 224.

39. Joseph Ratzinger, *Truth and Tolerance: Christian Belief and World Religions* (San Francisco: Ignatius Press, 2004), 57.

40. Joseph Ratzinger, *Many Religions—One Covenant: Israel, the Church and the World* (San Francisco: Ignatius Press, 1999), 109–13.

41. Thomas R. Rourke, *The Social and Political Thought of Benedict XVI* (New York: Rowman and Littlefield, 2011), 119.

42. Joseph Ratzinger, "Crisis of Law," *Zenit Daily Dispatch*, November 10, 1999.

43. Eric Vögelin, *The New Science of Politics* (Chicago: University of Chicago Press, 1995), 120; Vincent Twomey in his *Pope Benedict XVI: The Conscience of Our Age* (San Francisco: Ignatius Press, 2007), 52n22, notes a direct influence of Vögelin's thought on Ratzinger.

44. Ratzinger, *Principles of Catholic Theology*, 156.

45. See "Vatican Goes on Defense in Response to Media Reports," *America*, April 12, 2010.

46. Joseph Ratzinger, *Called to Communion: Understanding the Church Today* (San Francisco: Ignatius Press, 1991), 140–41.

47. Joseph A. Komonchak, "The Church in Crisis: Pope Benedict's Theological Vision," *Commonweal* (June 3, 2005): 13.

48. Dennis M. Doyle, *Communion Ecclesiology: Vision and Versions* (Maryknoll, NY: Orbis Books, 2000), 113.

49. See Bernard J. F. Lonergan, "The Transition from a Classicist World View to Historical Mindedness," in *A Second Collection*, ed. William F. J. Ryan and Bernard J. Tyrrell (London: Darton, Longman and Todd, 1974), 1–9.

50. "Declaration in Defense of the Catholic Doctrine on the Church against Certain Errors of the Present Day," *Origins* 3 (1973): 97–100.

51. Ratzinger and Messori, *The Ratzinger Report*, 35.

52. Benedict XVI, "Address of His Holiness Benedict XVI to the Roman Curia," December 22, 2005; see "Interpreting Vatican II," *Origins* 35, no. 32 (2006): 536.

53. James Corkery, *Joseph Ratzinger's Theological Ideas: Wise Cautions and Legitimate Hopes* (Mahwah, NJ: Paulist Press, 2009), 135.

54. Benedict XVI, "Interpreting Vatican II," 538.

55. "Introduction," Decree on Religious Freedom, *The Documents of Vatican II*, ed. Walter M. Abbott (New York: America Press, 1966), 673.

56. John Courtney Murray, "Appendix III: The Declaration on Religious Freedom," in *Declaration on Religious Freedom of Vatican Council II*, ed. Thomas F. Stransky (New York: Paulist Press, 1966), 143.

57. See J. Robert Dionne's careful analysis in *The Papacy and the Church: A Study of Praxis and Reception in Ecumenical Perspective* (New York: Philosophical Library, 1987), 193. Dionne argues that Vatican II, in affirming that the right to religious freedom is based on the dignity of the human person, "reversed the positions of Pius IX and his successors, with the possible exception of John XXIII."

58. Ratzinger, *Pilgrim Fellowship of Faith*, 256–58; GE 2002.

59. Richard R. Gaillardetz, "Between Reform and Rupture: The Council according to Benedict XVI," *Commonweal* 134, no. 17 (2007): 21; see also Thomas P. Rausch, "Does Doctrine Change?," *America*, November 30, 2015.

60. Joseph Ratzinger, *Without Roots: The West, Relativism, Christianity, Islam* (New York: Basic Books, 2006), 128; see Allen, *Cardinal Ratzinger*, ch. 5, "Culture Warrior."

61. See John P. Langan, "See the Person: Understanding Pope Francis' Statement on Homosexuality," *America*, February 25, 2014.

Epilogue

1. Joseph Ratzinger, *Einführung in das Christentum* (Munich: Kösel, 1968).

2. James Corkery, *Joseph Ratzinger's Theological Ideas: Wise Cautions and Legitimate Hopes* (New York: Paulist Press, 2009), 109; see also Lieven Boeve, "Europe in Crisis: A Question of Belief or Unbelief? Perspectives from the Vatican," *Modern Theology* 23, no. 3 (2007): 205–27.

3. Joseph Ratzinger, *Values in a Time of Upheaval* (New York: Crossroad, 2006), 137.

4. See Thomas P. Rausch, *Global Catholicism: Profiles and Polarities* (Maryknoll, NY: Orbis Books, 2021).

5. Philip Pullella, "Pope Says in Book He Would Resign if Incapacitated," *Reuters*, November 22, 2010.

6. Stephan Faris, "The Vatican Scandals: What Did the Pope's Butler Know," *Time*, May 29, 2012.

7. "Pope Benedict XVI Announces His Resignation at End of Month," Vatican Radio, February 11, 2013.

8. Nicole Winfield, "Two Popes—One Retired, One Reigning—Cause a Furor," AP, January 14, 2020; see also Massimo Faggioli, "The Fiction behind the Idea of the 'Pope Emeritus,'" *La Croix International*, August 20, 2019.

9. Vincent J. Miller, "The Humanity of the Papacy," *America* 208, no. 7 (2013): 15.

10. John O'Malley, *Tradition and Transition: Historical Perspectives on Vatican II* (Wilmington: Glazier, 1989), 17.

11. Cited by Robert P. Imbelli, "Benedict and Vatican II: A Response to Massimo Faggioli," *Commonweal* (March 11, 2020).

12. Pope Benedict XVI, "Meeting with the Members of the General Assembly of the United Nations," April 18, 2008.

13. Pope Benedict XVI, "Meeting with the Bishops of the United States," April 16, 2008; see *Origins* 37, no. 46 (2008): 737.

14. Cited by Drew Christiansen in "Reading Benedict: Reviewing the Pope's Love for the Word," *America*, February 28, 2013.

SELECTED BIBLIOGRAPHY

Works by Joseph Ratzinger/ Pope Benedict XVI

"Address of His Holiness Benedict XVI to the Roman Curia." December 22, 2005.

A New Song for the Lord: Faith in Christ and Liturgy Today. New York: Crossroad, 1996. Ger. *Ein Neues Leid für Den Herrn: Christusglaube und Liturgie in der Gegenwart.* Freiburg im Breisgau: Herder, 1995.

"Assessment and Future Prospects." In *Looking Again at the Question of the Liturgy with Cardinal Ratzinger: Proceedings of the July 2001 Fontgombault Liturgical Conference,* edited by Alcuin Reid, 145–53. Farnborough: Saint Michael's Abbey Press, 2003.

"Biblical Interpretation in Crisis: On the Question of the Foundations and Approach of Exegesis Today." In *Biblical Interpretation in Crisis: The Ratzinger Conference on Bible and Church,* edited by Richard John Neuhaus. Grand Rapids: Eerdmans, 1989.

Called to Communion: Understanding the Church Today. San Francisco: Ignatius Press, 1996. Ger. *Zur Gemeinschaft gerufen: Kirche heute verstehen.* 2nd ed. Freiburg im Breisgau: Herder, 1991.

Church, Ecumenism and Politics. New York: Crossroad, 1988. Ger. *Kirche, Ökumene, und Politik.* Einsiedeln: Johannes, 1987.

"Crisis of Law." *Zenit Daily Dispatch,* November 10, 1999.

Deus Caritas Est. Origins 35, no. 33 (2006): 541–57.

"Eucharist, Communion, and Solidarity." June 2, 2002. https://www .vatican.va/roman_curia/congregations/cfaith/documents/ rc_con_cfaith_doc_20020602_ratzinger-eucharistic-congress _en.html.

The Feast of Faith: Approaches to a Theology of the Liturgy. San Francisco: Ignatius Press, 1986. Ger. *Das Fest des Glaubens*. Einsiedeln: Johannes, 1981.

God and the World: A Conversation with Peter Seewald. San Francisco: Ignatius Press, 2002. Ger. *Gott und die Welt: Glauben und Leben in unserer Zeit; Ein Gespräch mit Peter Seewald*. Stuttgart: Deutsche Verlags-Anstalt, 2000.

God Is Near Us: The Eucharist, the Heart of Life. Edited by Stephan Otto Horn and Vinzenz Pfnür. San Francisco: Ignatius Press, 2003.

Introduction to Christianity. San Francisco: Ignatius Press, 1990, 2004. Ger. *Einführung in das Christentum*. Munich: Kösel-Verlag, 1968.

Jesus of Nazareth: From the Baptism in the Jordan to the Transfiguration. New York: Doubleday, 2007.

Jesus of Nazareth: Holy Week; From the Entrance into Jerusalem to the Resurrection. San Francisco: Ignatius Press, 2011.

Jesus of Nazareth: The Infancy Narratives. New York: Image, 2012.

Many Religions—One Covenant: Israel, the Church, and the World. San Francisco: Ignatius Press, 1999. Ger. *Die Vielfalt der Religionen und der Eine Bund*. Hagen: Verlag Urfeld, 1998.

"Meeting with the Bishops of the United States." April 16, 2008.

"Meeting with the Members of the General Assembly of the United Nations." April 18, 2018.

Milestones: Memoirs 1927–1977. San Francisco: Ignatius Press, 1998. Ger. *Aus meinem Leben: Erinnerungen (1927–1977)*. Stuttgart: Deutsche Verlags-Anstalt, 1998.

Das neue Volk Gottes: Entwürfe zur Ekklesiologie. Düsseldorf: Patmos, 1969.

Pilgrim Fellowship of Faith: The Church as Communion. Edited by Stephan Otto Horn and Vinzenz Pfnür. San Francisco: Ignatius Press, 2005. Ger. *Weg Gemeinschaft des Glaubens: Kirche als Communio*. Augsburg: Sankt Ulrich Verlag, 2002.

Principles of Catholic Theology: Building Stones for a Fundamental Theology. San Francisco: Ignatius Press, 1987. Ger. *Theologische Prinzipienlehre*. Munich: Erich Wewel Verlag, 1982.

The Ratzinger Report: An Exclusive Interview on the State of the Church, with Vittorio Messori. San Francisco: Ignatius Press, 1985.

"The Regensburg Academic Lecture." *Origins* 36, no. 16 (2006): 248–52.

Sacramentum Caritatis: Post-Synodal Apostolic Exhortation on the Eucharist. https://www.vatican.va/content/benedict-xvi/en/apost_exhortations/documents/hf_ben-xvi_exh_20070222_sacramentum-caritatis.html.

Salt of the Earth: The Church at the End of the Millennium; An Interview with Peter Seewald. San Francisco: Ignatius Press, 1997.

Spe Salvi. https://www.vatican.va/content/benedict-xvi/en/encyclicals/documents/hf_ben-xvi_enc_20071130_spe-salvi.html.

The Spirit of the Liturgy. San Francisco: Ignatius Press, 2000. Ger. *Der Geist der Liturgie: Eine Einführung.* Freiburg: Herder, 2000.

Summorum Pontificum. Motu Proprio on the Tridentine Mass and "Letter Accompanying *Motu Proprio.*" *Origins* 37, no. 9 (2007): 129–34.

Theological Highlights of Vatican II. New York: Paulist Press, 1966.

The Theology of History in St. Bonaventure. Chicago: Franciscan Herald Press, 1971. Ger. *Die Geschichtstheologie des heiligen Bonaventura.* Munich: Schnell und Steiner, 1959.

"The Theology of the Liturgy." In *Looking Again at the Question of the Liturgy with Cardinal Ratzinger,* edited by Alcuin Reid, 18–31. Farnborough: Saint Michael's Abbey Press, 2003.

Truth and Tolerance: Christian Belief and World Religions. San Francisco: Ignatius Press, 2004. Ger. *Glaube–Wahrheit–Toleranz: Das Christentum und die Weltreligionen.* Freiburg im Breisgau: Herder, 2003.

Values in a Time of Upheaval. New York: Crossroad, 2006.

Without Roots: The West, Relativism, Christianity, Islam. New York: Basic Books, 2006.

Works Consulted

Abbott, Walter M., ed. *The Documents of Vatican II.* New York: America Press, 1966.

Allen, John L., Jr. "2007's Neglected Story: Benedict XVI and 'Affirmative Orthodoxy.'" *National Catholic Reporter,* January 3, 2008.

―――. *Cardinal Ratzinger: The Vatican's Enforcer of the Faith.* New York: Continuum, 2000.

―――. *The Rise of Benedict XVI.* New York: Doubleday, 2005.

Aquinas, Thomas. *Summa Theologiae.* Translated by the Fathers of the English Province.

Beal, John. "It Shall Not Be So among You." In *Governance, Accountability, and the Future of the Catholic Church,* edited by Francis Oakley and Bruce Russett. New York: Continuum, 2004.

Boeve, Lieven. "Europe in Crisis: A Question of Belief or Unbelief? Perspectives from the Vatican." *Modern Theology* 23, no. 3 (2007): 205–27.

Boff, Leonardo. *Church, Charism and Power: Liberation Theology and the Institutional Church.* New York: Crossroad, 1985.

Brown, Raymond E. "The Contribution of Historical Biblical Criticism to Ecumenical Church Discussion." In *Biblical Interpretation in Crisis: The Ratzinger Conference on Bible and Church,* edited by Richard John Neuhaus. Grand Rapids: Eerdmans, 1989.

Brown, Raymond E., and Sandra M. Schneiders. "Hermeneutics." In *The New Jerome Biblical Commentary,* edited by Raymond E. Brown, Joseph A. Fitzmyer, and Roland E. Murphy. Englewood Cliffs, NJ: Prentice Hall, 1990.

Childs, Brevard S. *Biblical Theology in Crisis.* Philadelphia: Westminster Press, 1970.

Clooney, Francis X. "Dialogue Not Monologue: Benedict XVI and Religious Pluralism." *Commonweal* 132, no. 18 (October 21, 2005): 12–17.

Congregation for the Doctrine of the Faith. "Concerning the Criteria for Discernment of Vocations with regard to Persons with Homosexual Tendencies in View of Their Admission to Holy Orders." November 4, 2005.

―――. "Considerations Regarding Proposals to Give Legal Recognition to Unions Between Homosexual Persons." July 31, 2003.

Corkery, Jim. "Joseph Ratzinger's Theological Ideas: 1. Origins: A Theologian Emerges." *Doctrine and Life* 56, no. 2 (2006): 6–14.

―――. "Joseph Ratzinger's Theological Ideas: 2. The Facial Features of a Theological Corpus." *Doctrine and Life* 56, no. 4 (2006): 2–12.

————. "Joseph Ratzinger's Theological Ideas: 3. On Being Human." *Doctrine and Life* 56, no. 7 (2006): 7–24.

————. "Joseph Ratzinger's Theological Ideas: 4. *Quaestiones Disputatae–1.*" *Doctrine and Life* 56, no. 10 (2006): 12–24.

————. *Joseph Ratzinger's Theological Ideas: Wise Cautions and Legitimate Hopes.* Mahwah, NJ: Paulist Press, 2009.

Cox, Harvey. *The Silencing of Leonardo Boff: The Vatican and the Future of World Christianity.* Oak Park, IL: Meyer-Stone Books, 1988.

Crossan, John Dominic. *The Historical Jesus: The Life of a Mediterranean Jewish Peasant.* San Francisco: HarperSanFrancisco, 1991.

————. *Jesus: A Revolutionary Biography.* San Francisco: HarperSanFrancisco, 1994.

Curran, Charles. *The Catholic Society of America: A Story of Seventy-Five Years.* Mahwah, NJ: Paulist Press, 2021.

D'Antonio, William V., James D. Davidson, Dean R. Hoge, and Mary L. Gautier. *American Catholics Today: New Realities of Their Faith and Their Church.* Lanham, MD: Rowman and Littlefield, 2007.

de Jonge, Marinus. *Christology in Context: The Earliest Christian Response to Jesus.* Philadelphia: Westminster, 1988.

"Declaration in Defense of the Catholic Doctrine on the Church against Certain Errors of the Present Day." *Origins* 3 (1973): 97–100.

Dionne, J. Robert. *The Papacy and the Church: A Study of Praxis and Reception in Ecumenical Perspective.* New York: Philosophical Library, 1987.

Doyle, Dennis M. "Communion and the Common Good: Joseph Ratzinger and the Brothers Himes." In *Communion Ecclesiology: Vision and Versions,* 103–18. Maryknoll, NY: Orbis Books, 2000.

Duffy, Eamon. "Benedict XVI and the Eucharist." *New Blackfriars* 88, no. 1014 (2007): 195–212.

————. "Benedict XVI and the Spirit of the Liturgy." *Doctrine and Life* 55, no. 10 (2005): 30–50.

Dulles, Avery. *The Reshaping of Catholicism.* San Francisco: Harper & Row, 1988.

Dunn, James D. G. *Unity and Diversity in the New Testament: An Inquiry into the Character of Earliest Christianity.* 2nd ed. London: SCM Press, 1990; first published, 1977.

Ebeling, Gerhard. *Word and Faith*. Philadelphia: Fortress Press, 1963.

Epp, Eldon Jay. *Junia: The First Woman Apostle*. Minneapolis: Fortress Press, 2005.

Faggioli, Massimo. "A Church within the Church: Behind the New Integralism Is the Old Intransigentism." *Commonweal* (January 8, 2019).

————. "*Sacrosanctum Concilium* and the Meaning of Vatican II." *Theological Studies* 7 (2012): 444.

————. *Vatican II and the Battle for Meaning*. New York: Paulist Press, 2012.

Fahey, Michael. "Joseph Ratzinger as Ecclesiologist." In *Neoconservatism: Social and Religious Phenomenon*. Concilium 141. Edited by Gregory Baum. New York: Seabury, 1981.

————. "The Synod of America: Reflections of a Nonparticipant." *Theological Studies* 59 (1998): 498.

Faris, Stephan. "The Vatican Scandals: What Did the Pope's Butler Know." *Time*, May 29, 2012.

Ferrone, Rita. "Living Catholic Tradition." *Commonweal* (July 23, 2021).

Fitzmyer, Joseph A. "Instruction on the Historical Truth of the Gospels." *Theological Studies* 25 (1964): 386–408.

Franco, Philip A. "The Communion Ecclesiology of Joseph Ratzinger: Implications for the Church of the Future." In *Vatican II Forty Years Later*, edited by William Madges, 3–25. Maryknoll, NY: Orbis Books, 2006.

Fredericks, James. "The Catholic Church and the Other Religious Paths: Rejecting Nothing That Is True and Holy." *Theological Studies* 64 (2003): 232.

Funk, Robert W., Roy W. Hoover, and the Jesus Seminar. *The Five Gospels: The Search for the Authentic Words of Jesus*. New York: Macmillan, 1993.

Gaillardetz, Richard R. "Between Reform and Rupture: The Council according to Benedict XVI." *Commonweal* 134, no. 17 (October 12, 2007): 16–21.

————. *The Church in the Making*. Mahwah, NJ: Paulist Press, 2006.

————, ed. *When the Magisterium Intervenes: The Magisterium and Theologians in Today's Church*. Collegeville, MN: Liturgical Press, 2012.

Gibson, David. *The Rule of Benedict: Pope Benedict XVI and His Battle with the Modern World*. San Francisco: HarperSanFrancisco, 2006.

Grafton, Anthony. "Reading Ratzinger: Benedict XVI, the Theologian." *The New Yorker* (July 25, 2005): 42–49.

Haight, Roger. "The American Jesuit Theologian." In *Jesuit Postmodern: Scholarship, Vocation, and Identity in the 21st Century*, edited by Francis X. Clooney. Lanham, MD: Lexington, 2006.

———. *Christian Community in History*. 2 vols. New York: Continuum, 2004, 2006.

———. *Jesus Symbol of God*. Maryknoll, NY: Orbis Books, 1999.

Hays, Richard B. "Benedict and the Biblical Jesus." *First Things* 175 (August–September 2007): 51.

Hertling, Ludwig. *Communio: Church and Papacy in Early Christianity*. Chicago: Loyola University Press, 1972.

Hinze, Bradford E. "A Decade of Disciplining Theologians." In *When the Magisterium Intervenes: The Magisterium and Theologians in Today's Church*, edited by Richard R. Gaillardetz. Collegeville, MN: Liturgical Press, 2012.

Imbelli, Robert P. "Benedict and Vatican II: A Response to Massimo Faggioli." *Commonweal* 147, no. 3 (2020).

Johnson, Luke Timothy. "Homosexuality and the Church: Scripture and Experience." *Commonweal* 134, no. 12 (2007): 15.

Käsemann, Ernst. *Essays on New Testament Themes*. London: SCM Press, 1964.

———. "Paul and Early Catholicism." In *New Testament Questions of Today*. London: SCM Press, 1969.

Kasper Walter. *Jesus the Christ*. New York: Paulist Press, 1977.

———. "On the Church: A Friendly Reply to Cardinal Ratzinger." *America* 184, no. 4 (2001): 13.

Kerr, Fergus. "Joseph Ratzinger." In *Twentieth-Century Catholic Theologians*, 183–202. Malden, MA: Blackwell, 2007.

Krieg, Robert A. *Romano Guardini: A Precursor of Vatican II*. Notre Dame, IN: University of Notre Dame Press, 1997.

Komonchak, Joseph A. "The Church in Crisis: Pope Benedict's Theological Vision." *Commonweal* 132, no. 11 (2005): 23–30.

———. "Vatican II and the Encounter between Catholicism and Liberalism." In *Catholicism and Liberalism: Contributions to American Public Philosophy*, edited by R. Bruce Douglass and

David Hollenbach. New York: Cambridge University Press, 1994.

Küng, Hans, *On Being a Christian*. Garden City, NY: Doubleday, 1976.

Kwasniewski, Peter A., ed. *From Benedict's Peace to Francis's War: Catholics Respond to the Motu Propio "Traditionis Custodes" on the Latin Mass*. New York: Angelico Press, 2021.

Langan, John P. "See the Person: Understanding Pope Francis' Statement on Homosexuality." *America*, February 25, 2014.

Lonergan, Bernard J. F. "The Transition from a Classicist World View to Historical Mindedness." In *A Second Collection*, edited by William F. J. Ryan and Bernard J. Tyrrell. London: Darton, Longman and Todd, 1974.

Mack, Burton L. *The Lost Gospel: The Book of Q and Christian Origins*. San Francisco: HarperSanFrancisco, 1993.

———. *A Myth of Innocence: Mark and Christian Origins*. Philadelphia: Fortress Press, 1988.

Meier, John P. *A Marginal Jew: Rethinking the Historical Jesus*. Vol. 1: *The Roots of the Problem and the Person*. Anchor Bible Reference Library. New York: Doubleday, 1991.

———. *A Marginal Jew: Rethinking the Historical Jesus*. Vol. 2: *Mentor, Message, and Miracles*. Anchor Bible Reference Library. New York: Doubleday, 1994.

Mickens, Robert. "Benedict's Papacy: The Way It's Shaping Up." *The Tablet*, September 2011.

Mickens, Robert, and Philip Crispin. "Martini Queries Aspects of Pope's Book." *The Tablet*, June 2, 2007.

Miles, Jack. "Between Theology and Exegesis." *Commonweal* 134, no. 13 (2007): 21–23.

Miller, Vincent J. "The Humanity of the Papacy." *America* 208, no. 7 (2013): 15.

Murphy, Charles M. "Collegiality: An Essay toward Better Understanding." *Theological Studies* 46 (1985): 41.

Murray, John Courtney. "Appendix III: The Declaration on Religious Freedom." In *Declaration on Religious Freedom of Vatican Council II*, edited by Thomas F. Stransky. New York: Paulist Press, 1967.

———. "Religious Freedom." In *The Documents of Vatican II*, edited by Walter M. Abbott. New York: Guild Press, 1966.

Neuhaus, Richard John, ed. *Biblical Interpretation in Crisis: The Ratzinger Conference on Bible and Church.* Grand Rapids: Eerdmans, 1989.

Neusner, Jacob. *A Rabbi Talks with Jesus.* New York: Doubleday, 1993.

Nichols, Aidan. *The Thought of Pope Benedict XVI: An Introduction to the Theology of Joseph Ratzinger.* New ed. New York: Burns and Oates, 2007.

O'Collins, Gerald. "He Who Is." *America* 196, no. 20 (2007): 23.

Phan, Peter C. *In Our Own Tongues: Perspectives from Asia on Mission and Inculturation.* Maryknoll, NY: Orbis Books, 2003.

Pontifical Biblical Commission. "Instruction on the Historical Truth of the Gospels." 1964.

———. "The Interpretation of the Bible in the Church." 1994.

———. "The Jewish People and Their Sacred Scriptures in the Christian Bible." 2002.

Puella, Philip. "Pope Says in Book He Would Resign if Incapacitated." *Reuters.* November 22, 2010.

Rausch, Thomas P. "Does Doctrine Change?" *America*, November 30, 2015.

———. *Faith, Hope, and Charity: Benedict XVI on the Theological Virtues.* Mahwah, NJ: Paulist Press, 2015.

———. *Global Catholicism: Profiles and Polarities.* Maryknoll, NY: Orbis Books, 2021.

Reid, Alcuin, ed. *Looking Again at the Question of the Liturgy with Cardinal Ratzinger: Proceedings of the July 2001 Fontgombault Liturgical Conference.* Farnborough: Saint Michael's Abbey Press, 2003.

Roberts, Tom. "Battle Lines in the Liturgy Wars." *National Catholic Reporter*, March 1, 2010.

Rourke, Thomas R. *The Social and Political Thought of Benedict XVI.* New York: Lexington Books, 2011.

Rowland, Tracey. "A Christian Humanist Pope." *America* 208 (2013).

Ruddy, Christopher. *The Local Church: Tillard and the Future of Catholic Ecclesiology.* New York: Crossroad, 2006.

———. "No Restorationist: Ratzinger's Theological Journey." *Commonweal* 132, no. 11 (2005): 15–18.

Sanders, James A. *Canon and Community: A Guide to Canonical Criticism.* Philadelphia. Fortress Press, 1984.

Schall, James V. *The Regensburg Lecture*. South Bend, IN: St. Augustine's Press, 2007.

Schillebeeckx, Edward. *Jesus: An Experiment in Christology*. New York: Seabury, 1979.

Schneiders, Sandra M. *The Revelatory Text: Interpreting the New Testament as Sacred Scripture*. Collegeville, MN: Liturgical Press, 1999.

Schüssler Fiorenza, Elisabeth. *Jesus: Miriam's Child, Sophia's Prophet; Critical Issues in Feminist Christology*. New York: Continuum, 1994.

Schüssler Fiorenza, Francis. "From Theologian to Pope: A Personal View Back, Past the Public Portrayals." *Harvard Divinity Bulletin* 33, no. 2 (2005): 58–62.

Shorter, Aylward. *Evangelization and Culture*. London: Geoffrey Chapman, 1994.

Tracy, David. *A Blessed Rage for Order*. New York: Seabury, 1975.

Twomey, D. Vincent. "The Mind of Benedict XVI." *Claremont Review of Books* 5, no. 4 (Fall 2005): 66–70.

———. *Pope Benedict XVI: The Conscience of Our Age*. San Francisco: Ignatius Press, 2007.

USCCB Committee on Doctrine. "Statement on Book by Father Peter Phan." *Origins* 37, no. 28 (2007): 445–50.

"Vatican Goes on Defense in Response to Media Reports." *America*, April 12, 2010.

Vatican Radio. "Pope Benedict Announces His Resignation at End of Month." February 11, 2013.

Veil-Matti Kärkkäinen. *An Introduction to Ecclesiology: Ecumenical, Historical and Global Perspectives*. Downers Grove, IL: InterVarsity, 2002.

Vögelin, Eric. *The New Science of Politics*. Chicago: University of Chicago Press, 1995.

Volf, Miroslav. *After Our Likeness: The Church as the Image of the Trinity*. Grand Rapids: Eerdmans, 1998.

Vorgrimler, Herbert. *Commentary on the Documents of Vatican II*. Vol. 5. New York: Herder & Herder, 1969.

Weigel, George. *God's Choice: Pope Benedict XVI and the Future of the Catholic Church*. New York: HarperCollins, 2005.

Wicks, Jared. "Six Texts by Professor Joseph Ratzinger as *Peritus* before and during Vatican Council II." *Gregorianum* 8, no. 2 (2008).

Winfield, Nicole. "Two Popes—One Retiring, One Reigning—Cause a Furor." AP, January 14, 2020.

Witherington, Ben, III. *The Jesus Quest: The Third Search for the Jew of Nazareth.* Downers Grove, IL: InterVarsity, 1995.

Wright, N. T. "And What of This World." *The Tablet*, December 8, 2007.

INDEX

Rahner, Karl, 1, 8, 14, 17, 21,
50, 55, 61, 67, 115, 141,
172n30
Rationalism, 70
Ratzinger, Georg, 10, 13, 19
Ratzinger, Joseph. *See* Benedict
XVI, Pope
Ratzinger, Joseph (father),
10, 12
Ratzinger, Maria (mother), 10
Ratzinger, Maria (sister), 10
Ratzinger Report, The (Benedict),
29–30
Reason, 56, 59, 71–72
Redemptoris Missio (John Paul
II), 60
Reese, Tom, 4, 27, 163
Reform, 45, 140–41, 142,
147, 150
Regensburg, 19, 35–36, 59
Reiser, Konrad, 119
Relativism, 24–25, 31, 36,
109, 147
Renewal, church, 17–18
Resignation of Benedict,
162–63
Resistance to Nazis, 12
Responsum ad Dubium
(Benedict), 25
Ressourcement, 19, 55, 61
Revelation, 52, 62, 66–67
Rilke, Rainier Maria, 68
Robinson, John A. T., 8
Roman Rite. See *Missale
Romanum*
Root, Michael, 117
Ruddy, Christopher, 82, 111
Ruether, Rosemary Radford,
78–79

Rule of Benedict, The
(Gibson), 4–5

Sacramentum Caritatis
(Benedict), 131–34
Sacred Congregation for the
Doctrine of the Faith (CDF):
Benedict, 1, 8, 19, 20–31,
144; Boff, 22–23; canon
of issues, 25; ecumenism,
119–20; Gutiérrez, 23;
homosexuality, 26–27;
John Paul II, 20; pluralism,
religious, 27–29; relativism,
24–25; sexual abuse,
155–56; theologians, 27,
144; women, 25–26
Sacrifice, 125, 126–27, 133,
136–37
Salvation history, 52–53
Sanders, James, 77
Sarah, Robert, 150
Schall, James, 36
Schillebeeckx, Edward, 8, 55,
141
Schlink, Edmund, 114
Schmaus, Michael, 16
Scholl, Hans, 12
Scholl, Sophie, 12
Scripture: Benedict, 64, 74–76,
81–82; Bonaventure,
66–68; Brown, 72–73;
canon, 76–77; and
Christ, 74, 77–78, 80;
and Christianity, 82–83;
and church, 73, 79–80, 82;
continuity, 87; crisis,
76–77; exegesis, 71–73, 78;
fuller sense (*sensus plenior*),